A TRAILS BOOKS GUIDE

# KANSAS
# OUTDOOR
# TREASURES

**A guide to over 60 natural destinations**

*Julie M. Cirlincuina* (signature)

JULIE M. CIRLINCUINA

**TRAILS BOOKS**
Madison, Wisconsin

Library of Congress Control Number: 2008922926
ISBN: 978-1-934553-11-4


Editor: Melissa L. Faliveno
Book design and maps: Rebecca Finkel
Photography: all photos by Julie M. Cirlincuina,
except where noted.
Cover Photo: Rusty Dodson


Printed in the United States of America.
13  12  11  10  09  08        6  5  4  3  2  1


TRAILS BOOKS
a division of Big Earth Publishing
923 Williamson Street • Madison, WI 53703
(800) 258-5830 • www.trailsbooks.com

## MANY THANKS

Thanks to my husband, family, and many hiking friends
from the Kansas City Outdoor Club who accompanied me
on explorations and research. A heartfelt thank you
to the hardworking volunteers who design and maintain Kansas trails.
Their dedication makes it possible for us all
to enjoy nature along with the fantastic,
varied geography of this greatly under-appreciated state.

# Contents

| Cheyenne | Rawlins | Decatur | Norton | Phillips | Smith |
| Sherman | Thomas | Sheridan | Graham | Rooks | Osborne |

## Western

| Wallace | Logan | Gove | Trego | Ellis | Russell |
| Greeley | Wichita | Scott | Lane | Ness | Rush | Barton |

| Hamilton | Kearney | Finney | Hodgeman | Pawness | | Stafford |
| | | | | Edwards | |

| Staton | Grent | Haskell | Gray | Ford | Kiowa | Pratt |
| Morton | Stevens | Seward | Meade | Clark | Comanche | Barber |

# Introduction

THIS BOOK IS DEDICATED TO ordinary people who daydream of moments outdoors, have a love for wildlife, and ponder what they will find on the next trail. I am an

- - - - - Scenic Byway
———— Santa Fe Trail
· · · · · · · Oregon Trail

avid hiker who also enjoys bird watching, biking, and kayaking—I'm not a geologist or trained naturalist. Thus the text offers the perspective of an explorer and observer much like you.

Growing up on the Missouri/Kansas state line in Kansas City, I was quite familiar with Missouri's natural attractions. I had hiked nearly half of

our country's national parks, but still had no idea what geological wonders and scenic vistas awaited me in my home state of Kansas. Most Kansans, in fact, aren't familiar with the 11 geological regions of the state and most have heard only of the Flint Hills Region. But for those who treasure uncrowded or undiscovered places, Kansas is a gold mine.

Hunters and anglers have always known about Kansas's wildlife and wide-open spaces, but its natural areas remain greatly unknown to naturalists, hikers, cyclists, and wildlife watchers. These activities are not regulated and do not require permits, so they provide little income to the state. They do, however, help drive the economies of small towns and gateway communities nearby. Visitors benefit from a friendly, inexpensive, and uncrowded experience and the thrill that comes from seeing places that few people know about. So do your homework, select a natural area that appeals to you, and take a road trip. I hope you enjoy exploring the outdoor treasures of Kansas as much as I have.

## WHEN TO PLAN YOUR TRIP

Summer is generally the season to avoid. Temperatures soar over 90 degrees in July and August with humidity over 60 percent (less humidity in the western third of the state). Despite these uncomfortable conditions, crowds persist, on weekends especially—just one more reason to avoid summer when possible. To avoid ticks, mosquitoes, poison ivy, and uncomfortable weather, the best time to visit is September through May. Late April to mid-June is the ideal time to see wildflowers when the temperatures are tolerable. The chances for rainfall are usually highest in May and June. From mid-January to mid-February, temperatures can be brutal for camping, but winter is often mild, with large snowfalls occurring infrequently. September to November offers perfect temperatures and stunning color changes, especially where hardwood trees are prevalent. March and April present pastel colors of new growth without an understory or canopy to block panoramic views.

## PARK ENTITIES AND FEES EXPLAINED

Often more than one governing agency presides over a natural area. A federal office, such as the Army Corps of Engineers, may begin a project for flood-control measures. After the reservoir is completed, one or more sections of land surrounding the body of water may be developed with facilities. Some of these park areas may be governed by the state (Kansas Department of Wildlife and Parks, KDWP), while other areas are managed by local municipalities or counties.

All areas governed by KDWP are state parks and admission requires a daily vehicle pass or permit for a nominal fee. Because office hours are limited, self-pay stations are always available. Camping fees are typically additional to entry fees. Reservation fees are also assessed, but most parks retain some sites that cannot be reserved. Recently, popular or prime camping sites have come at a higher cost. Camping is always limited to 14 days in a state park. Hunting and fishing always require a state permit and may require local permits as well—and penalties for violations are stiff.

Entrance to federal areas is usually free, but activities in federal areas (boating, camping, swimming, etc.) require usage fees. State laws commonly govern hunting and fishing, even on federal properties. To avoid trouble, be sure you understand the governing agency, park boundaries, and fees.

## WORDS OF CAUTION

Some might assume that hunting is not allowed at state parks or federal areas and certainly not in areas with maintained trails. In Kansas, however, some trails pass through wildlife areas that are cultivated specifically to manage wildlife for hunting. Hunting is not allowed within developed park boundaries, but is often allowed in adjacent areas where trails sometimes extend. Hunting dates and regulations change according to hunting pressure and success rates for certain species. It would be wise to wear bright colors at all times, but hikers can check park Web sites or call the area office when in doubt. Park maps also indicate areas where hunting is allowed and where it is prohibited. In most cases, signs are clearly posted; pay attention and adhere to all postings and regulations.

KDWP offers a wealth of information at regional offices and on its Web site, www.kdwp.state.ks.us. Because local offices are open only Monday through Friday (most offices extend hours in summer), it's advisable to find information and obtain permits in advance if your trip is over a weekend.

By May and sometimes even in April, ticks and mosquitoes can be the greatest nuisance until a hard frost or through October. Disease-carrying insects are worse in wooded areas, especially near water. They will also be found (or will find you) in prairies, but not quite as heavily. Ticks and mosquitoes are worse in the eastern half of the state, which is more densely wooded. A high percentage of DEET is required to repel them. A clothing treatment called permethrin works fairly well as a tick repellent, but must be used in advance. (Follow the directions on the can.)

Poison ivy is also a problem, with an ever-increasing growing season. It prefers shade, streams, and waterways and frequently grows trailside. The best way to prevent a miserable reaction is to wear long pants instead of shorts. Wash your hands immediately after removing your boots and pants.

Finally, weather is often very difficult to predict in the Midwest. Be prepared for windy conditions, and storms that may produce hail. Ridges and open plains are not places to be when lightning moves in. As in any state, flash floods occur along rivers and streams and even intermittent creeks. Many roads in central and western Kansas are dirt or sand; they may dry quickly, but don't venture out during wet weather or be caught on them when a storm rolls in. Pay attention to forecasts as much as possible and plan for varying conditions.

## ABOUT SELECTION AND CRITERIA

It was sometimes difficult to determine what should or should not make the list of Outdoor Treasures. Because this is a guide to natural areas, I chose to eliminate destinations consisting only of paved trails in urban or suburban areas to allow room for areas that offer opportunities for more than one activity. Sometimes small areas are so scenic or geologically unique that I could not exclude them. Sometimes large areas lack scenic beauty but offer much in the way of activities. Also, seasonal changes often play a big part in scenery. Because beauty is so subjective, I typically did not base selections solely upon aesthetics. Finally, all the natural areas highlighted are open to the public.

If you want to keep current on Kansas trails and parks, visit www.trailsofkansas.com to sign up to receive updates, changes, and additions made to Kansas parks, natural areas, and trail systems. The Web site also offers seasonal itineraries, color photos of scenic areas, and a list of outfitters that enable an outdoor experience in Kansas.

## GEOLOGICAL REGIONS

Although Kansas has been stereotyped as flat, the terrain actually varies greatly, thanks to the geological structures. Understanding the geological history will enhance the journey as you explore new places. Although there are several variations on this theme, three major geological factors are primarily responsible for shaping the Kansas landscape: glacial activity, the forming of the Rocky Mountains to our west, and the fact that Kansas was long ago covered by the sea. The state is divided into 11 geological regions, sometimes called physiographic provinces:

- High Plains
- Smoky Hills
- Glaciated
- Ozark Plateau
- Arkansas River Lowlands
- Wellington-McPherson Lowlands
- Cherokee Lowlands
- Chautauqua Hills
- Red Hills (or Gypsum Hills)
- Flint Hills
- Osage Cuestas

Thanks to the geologists of the Kansas Geological Survey for providing an abundance of public information in an easy-to-understand Web site called GeoKansas, www.kgs.ku.edu/Extension/home.html.

# WESTERN
# KANSAS

Limestone bluffs on the south side of Cedar Bluff Reservoir.

| | | |
|---|---|---|
| 2 Cheyenne | Rawlins | Decatur | 10 Norton |

Sherman | Thomas | Sheridan | Graham

Wallace | Logan | Gove 9 | Trego 8

1 | Greeley | Wichita | Scott | Lane | Ness

Kearney | Finney | Hodgeman

Hamilton | 4

Staton | Grent | Haskell | Gray | Ford

Morton 3 | Stevens | Seward | Meade 5 | Clark 6 | 7

- - - - - Scenic Byway
───────── Santa Fe Trail

# WESTERN KANSAS

## Geology of the High Plains Region

KANSAS'S LARGEST GEOLOGICAL REGION, the High Plains, occupies the western third of the state. Low rainfall, abundant sunshine, and heavy south winds make for a semi-arid climate. The conditions are right for slow-growing plants such as shortgrass, yucca, and sagebrush. Pockets of mixed grass and tallgrass occur in more moist areas and become increasingly prominent as you travel east through Kansas. These vast flatlands are interrupted or varied only when rivers and streams carve away at their surface.

You may be surprised to hear that the Rocky Mountains are greatly responsible for the topography found here. Snowmelt and streams flowing eastward from the mountains began to unload sediments, sand, gravel, silt, and rock over the western half of Kansas. Although it may appear flat, over millions of years, a gradual slope of sediment formed to bury evidence of the shallow seas that previously covered Kansas. Today, the unconsolidated deposits of sand and gravel that lie below the surface are called the Ogallala Formation. This formation results in an underground aquifer—a major source of water for Native Americans, early settlers, and today's landowners. Springs at Big Basin and Lake Scott provide visual examples of this aquifer. Another example exists in the Cimarron National Grassland, where the Cimarron River actually travels underground.

In the northwest corner of the state, the Arikaree River has cut a path through the High Plains exposing loess, very fine silt deposited by high winds. The result is deep canyons with near vertical faces and terrain that comes as a surprise even to Kansans.

# Lake Scott State Park
## and Monument Rocks National Natural Landmark

LAKE SCOTT APPEARS in a desertlike environment like a mirage. Enveloped by Ladder Creek Canyon, the blue, spring-fed lake is surrounded by buttes and mesas that are dotted with yucca and cactus. Within the canyon walls surrounding the lake, sediment has hardened to form porous sandstone mortar beds that can be seen where Ladder Creek exposes them.

Monument Rocks is one of the most picturesque places in Kansas.

Previous caretakers of this arid landscape are remembered at Lake Scott State Park. History indicates that the Taos Indians, who fled Spanish rule, established a village named El Cuartelejo along Ladder Creek in the 1600s. Homesteader Herbert Steele uncovered the ancient settlement in the 1890s. The reconstructed foundation of a seven-room pueblo can be seen at the State Park as well as a granite monolith erected to commemorate the Steele family, who envisioned their property as a public park. The state purchased the Steele homestead in 1928, but the original four-room house, built of sandstone, still stands as a museum. Visitors can learn more about El Cuartelejo, the northernmost pueblo in America, at a museum in Scott City only 15 miles south of the lake. The ruins were given the status of National Historic Landmark in 1964 and restoration of the pueblo's foundation began in 1970.

**WILDLIFE**—Turkeys, mule deer, white-tailed deer, bobcats, and beavers are commonly seen near the lake and creek. Turkey vultures soar over the shoreline and canyons. Watchful drivers may spot pronghorn antelope out on the high plains. Western kingbirds, orchard orioles, yellow-breasted chats, and swallows can be spotted from the hiking trail. Lizards racing across the path will be seen only by the person in the lead. Red-winged blackbirds, killdeers, and Canada geese can be spotted near the lake. Butterflies frequent the trail along with a profusion of wildflowers: milkweed, purple poppy mallow, Indian blanket flower, prince's plume, coreopsis, and yucca.

**HIKING**—A quarter-mile nature trail encircles Big Springs. Near the southern information station, follow signs to the multipurpose trail west of the park road. A short nature trail branches off to the right; take this path to watch for wildlife near the pond, but be wary of poison ivy any time you're in wooded areas near water.

Scenic views from the trail surrounding Lake Scott.

A 7-mile, multipurpose trail circles the lake and park road with terrain that varies from mowed grass to sand and dirt. The west side of the loop offers the most scenic views, often traveling below a ridge with outcrops of the Ogallala Formation. The path is rugged, with frequent elevation changes. Side trails scramble up the craggy bluffs for bird's-eye views of the canyon and lake below. Some of these side trails can be lengthy, but offer the best views and surprising vistas, so take time to explore them to get the most from your hike. You'll find boulders strewn about the path below the bluffs with tufts of yucca and prairie sage growing from them. You just may forget you're in Kansas, as you can scarcely take a photo without a yucca plant in the foreground.

The east side of the lake is less scenic as the trail passes through campgrounds and hugs the lake and the park road rather closely. Nevertheless, views of the buttes from across the lake and the picturesque marina are worthwhile. Some of the largest poison ivy plants in Kansas can also be found on the east side, so you may be forced to walk back on the park road if you're highly allergic or squeamish about contact. There is little shade on the trail, so wear a hat and sunscreen and bring more water and salty snacks than you think you'll need. Fortunately, there are many opportunities to detour for restrooms, picnics, and water (although water will be scarce in the off-season). The park map is very handy in this regard, marking restrooms and developed areas. Know that you may be sharing the trail with cyclists and horses, which have the right-of-way, but more often than not you'll have the trail to yourself.

**BIKING**—Mountain bikers may ride the 7-mile, multipurpose trail. (See Hiking.) Road bikers may circle the lake on the park roads, a circuit that is also around 7 miles, but should be aware that a section on the northeast side changes to gravel. State Highway 95 makes a steep and scenic ascent from south to north, so if you prefer a downhill ride, reverse this. Highway 95 and U.S. Highway 83 also form a loop of about 12 miles. Add the park road circling the lake for an 18- to 20-mile ride.

**HORSEBACK RIDING**—A horse camp with watering facilities and hitching posts can be found at Timber Canyon Campground, just west of the dam. Horses must remain on the multipurpose trail. Some sections of the trail prohibit horses, but they are allowed on all the developed park roads.

**FISHING AND HUNTING**—Fishing is a popular pastime here, as the lake is equipped with fishing piers, a handicapped fishing dock, boat ramps (for fishing only), and a stocked trout pond. According to the *Kansas Fishing Forecast 2007,* an annual report compiled by the Kansas Department of Wildlife and Parks (KDWP), bluegill and redear are rated excellent; channel cat are rated good. Walleye, crappie, and largemouth bass are rated fair. Public hunting is allowed in the wildlife area west of the park. Note that landowner permission is required to hunt on nearby private land. Hunting guides and outfitters are available in the outlying areas.

**PADDLING**—Canoe and paddleboat rentals are available by the hour in season at the marina. Paddle the lake from the Elm Grove Campground to the dam for about 3 miles of calm, peaceful water. How often do you get the opportunity to paddle an oasis surrounded by towering rock bluff?

**CAMPING AND FACILITIES**—Horse camping, primitive camping, and utility camping are permitted without reservation. Picnic areas, group shelters, modern shower houses, and vault toilets are provided. A swimming beach and playground are located near the marina, where a concessionaire rents canoes and paddleboats and stocks camping and fishing supplies.

**TRAFFIC**—Traffic is typically light, heaviest in June.

**LOCATION AND DIRECTIONS**—In Scott County, take I-70 to Exit 76 at Oakley. Follow U.S. Highway 40 west to U.S. Highway 83. Travel south on Highway 83 and turn west onto State Highway 95 to enter the park.

**ENTRY**—State park entrance fees apply. Official office hours are from 8:00 A.M. to 4:00 P.M., Monday-Friday, but hours may vary according to staff and training needs. It's best to phone ahead and collect any information you need in advance of your trip.

**ON THE WEB**—www.kdwp.state.ks.us, search "Lake Scott."

**CONTACT**—Lake Scott State Park office, (620) 872-2061; 520 West Scott Lake Drive, Scott City, KS 67871.

**NEARBY**—**MONUMENT ROCKS** is recognized by the National Park service as a National Natural Landmark. Made of Niobrara chalk, the formations sculpted by the Smoky Hill River are some of the strongest evidence we have of the vast sea that covered the state 80 million years ago. The chalk is a soft form of limestone, which is perfect for enveloping and preserving fossils. As you make the drive across flat farmland toward this destination, it's almost unimaginable that there could be anything hidden on the open plains. But suddenly, there it is—a freestanding wall carved in the shape of a city skyline. Park your car and explore the small area on foot, but don't forget your camera—the monument is one of the most photogenic sites in Kansas. Remember: the monument is on private property, but visitors are allowed access; the land and its owner deserve our respect.

**DIRECTIONS**—From Lake Scott, take U.S. Highway 83 north and cross the Smoky Hill River. About 2.5 miles north of the river, a large sign directs you to turn east. Take this road for 4 miles until it ends at a "T," where you'll be directed south. The monument appears 2 miles later. There is no entry fee.

# Arikaree Breaks

IN CONTRAST TO THE PLAINS AND FLATLANDS that generally characterize Kansas, the upper-west corner of Kansas hides a stretch of canyons and badlands 36 miles long and nearly 3 miles wide. A combination of wind-deposited sand, silt, and clay (called loess soil) composes the upper layer, which can be up to 100 feet thick. Under the loess layer is the Ogallala Formation, sands and gravel cemented with calcium carbonate. The base is made of Pierre Shale from the Cretaceous Period. The Republican and Arikaree rivers have aggressively cut through these layers, slicing dramatic gullies and ravines.

The newest layers of loess likely traveled from the Nebraska Sand Hills or arrived via the Platte River system. While there is some uncertainty about where the loess soil comes from and how old the deposits are, one thing is certain—you've never seen anything like this in Kansas.

This is an arid environment of rough terrain and few trees. The landscape of shortgrass prairie is riddled with soapweed, yucca, and prickly pear cactus. Sixteen species of rare plants and two species of sage thrive here. Although grasses and plants are abundant, water is difficult to come by; wells are often drilled many miles away and water is piped into the area. A few public roads traverse the area, but this is private property; please respect landowners by remaining on the roads. Although the roads are maintained, they should be avoided in wet weather.

**WILDLIFE**—Some of the more unusual species residing here include black-tailed prairie dogs, mule deer, kangaroo rats, burrowing owls, and porcupines. Look for enterprising predators that stand watch over the prairie-dog communities. Coyotes may be easy to spot when they're on the move, especially at dusk.

**AUTO TOUR**—Well-placed, red markers direct visitors through a 45- to 50-mile loop along country roads. The tour begins in Saint Francis at the Republican River Bridge, just 1 mile north of the Cheyenne County courthouse at Benton Street and Main Street. The bridge marks a 1-mile riverside trail where you can stretch your legs and enjoy this place that few people see. On the tour is a cemetery established in 1889 for Civil War veterans, as well as views of four spring-fed streams that once drew settlers to the area. As the name suggests, Plum Creek is lined with wild plums; Hackberry Creek was once the site of Native American encampments; Spring Creek drew early homesteaders. If you visit Horsethief Cave (in dry weather only), you'll discover that it has caved in over the years. According to legend, in the late 1800s horses were kept in back of the two-chamber cave while thieves used the front chamber as living quarters. Jaw-dropping views of Hay Canyon appear at lookout point (marker 11), near the Nebraska border. Just past the marker, parking is provided. Although there are no designated hiking trails, the dirt roads may suit you for a hike among the canyons. Please respect landowners and remain on the designated roads.

The auto tour map indicates a turnoff for Devil's Gap, which offers another outstanding view of the breaks (dry weather only). The dirt road becomes narrow and steep, but the views match the adventure. You can find the auto tour posted at www.stfranciskansas.com.

**HIKING**—For best views of the canyons, walk the most scenic part of the auto tour from marker 9 north to marker 13. Hikers should be in good physical condition and carry plenty of water. If you are unsure of your abilities, drive to marker 13 so you can preview the terrain you'll be hiking.

In Saint Francis at the Republican River Bridge, an easy 1-mile riverside trail lets walkers enjoy a peaceful backcountry stream that was partially responsible for carving the canyons in the area.

**FISHING AND HUNTING**—Hunters can hire numerous outfitters in the area to search the prairie grasses for pheasant, quail, and deer. The Prairie Castle Guest House bed-and-breakfast (Kuhrt Ranch) offers unique lodging and guided hunting trips. See www.adventurehunting.com.

**CAMPING AND FACILITIES**—No restrooms are available along the drive, so make a stop in Saint Francis before you begin.

**LOCATION AND DIRECTIONS**—In Cheyenne County. Take I-70 to Goodland and travel north on State Highway 27 for 30 miles, then west on U.S. Highway 36. The tour begins in Saint Francis at the Republican River Bridge, 1 mile north of the Cheyenne County courthouse at Benton Street and Main Street.

**ENTRY**—There are no fees. Do not attempt to travel the roads after dark or when they are wet. Travel slowly and remain on the public roads.

**ON THE WEB**—www.stfranciskansas.com.

**CONTACT**—Saint Francis Area Chamber of Commerce, (785) 332-2961; P.O. Box 793, Saint Francis, KS 67756.

# Cimarron National Grassland

CACTUS, SAGEBRUSH, and sandy, semi-arid terrain may trick visitors into thinking they're anywhere but Kansas. Artesian springs and oil wells may further evoke visions of Texas or New Mexico. Three ecosystems provide diverse scenery and a challenge for park management: shortgrass prairie, sand-sage prairie, and wooded riparian habitat each attract unique wildlife and require different management strategies. In addition, staff is responsible for preserving the history of the park's ever-changing inhabitants. And this corner of Kansas has much history to remember.

Prehistoric inhabitants included camels, horses, and giant turtles. Later, Indian tribes moved about the High Plains, so did huge herds of bison. As settlers arrived, so did the Santa Fe Trail. Wagon wheel ruts are still visible today. Later, a cattle ranch flourished until a flood claimed it in 1914. After the Great Depression and Dust Bowl, frustrated landowners sold their dysfunctional farmland to the government. Today, the USDA Forest Service, with the help of numerous organizations and laborers, has transformed the desolate land back into thriving prairie grassland.

Cimarron National Grassland is the largest tract of public land in Kansas, protecting the longest publicly owned stretch of the Santa Fe Trail. At an elevation of 3,540 feet, the third highest point in the state, **POINT OF ROCKS** is a park landmark that was used as a lookout by both Native Americans and settlers. From the lookout on a clear day, visitors can see into Colorado and Oklahoma.

A few words of caution may improve your trip and pique your sense of adventure. Few roads are paved, many are gravel, and some are dirt. If weather looks threatening, return to the gravel roads. Begin with a full tank of gas; carry emergency equipment and the park map. Be prepared for thunderstorms and hailstorms, which are common. Pack appropriately for arid environments: long pants, leather boots, a hat, sunglasses, sunscreen, a first-aid kit, and a compass are a must. Always carry water, on your person and in your car. Finally, portions of the grassland are open range, so you may encounter livestock on the roads. Use caution when you top hills, slow down for cattle guards and gates, and make sure you close any gates you open. Be careful when crossing barbed-wire fences, as some may be electrified.

**WILDLIFE**—Herds of elk and pronghorn graze the grasslands. Ask the district office for the location of herds. Look for white-tailed and mule deer, porcupine, and prairie dog towns. Several species of toads and frogs, box turtles, lizards, and western rattlesnakes enjoy the riparian habitat here. Birds not usually associated with Kansas are sometimes identified here, including the Steller's jay, scrub jay, roadrunner, mountain chickadee, curve-billed thrasher, and western tanager. Watch for the illusive bobwhite, scaled quail, and lesser prairie chicken. Prairie chicken booming grounds, also known as *leks*, can be publicly viewed through blinds. Here you can watch a fascinating display as male prairie chickens extravagantly compete for the attention of females during the breeding season. **NOTE:** *Visitors are cautioned to stay away from prairie dog towns and to keep pets away as well. Fleas carry bubonic* *plague and have infected the colonies here. Bug spray is effective in warding off fleas.*

**HIKING AND BACKPACKING**—THE COMPANION TO THE SANTA FE TRAIL is 19 miles long, rated easy to moderate, and is handicapped accessible. The lengthy trail is open to backpackers, cyclists, and equestrians as well as day hikers. Two trailheads, Conestoga and Murphy, provide gravel parking lots and restrooms, but bring your own water. The clearly marked, grassy trail closely follows the original Santa Fe route. Wagon wheel ruts can be observed from the trail. As sagebrush and cactus are prevalent, you may wish to wear long pants for hiking or biking. The trail crosses open, flat, and rolling prairie, slowly climbing to Point of Rocks for great views. Some mini canyons that formed by erosion can be seen from the trail. A profusion of wildflowers will compete with amazing vistas for your attention. Sandy areas may slow your pace but will give you time to appreciate the solitude and quiet beauty found on vast prairies and grasslands.

The 10.5-mile **TURKEY TRAIL** begins at the Cottonwood Picnic Grounds, but you can shorten the trail by beginning at the Cimarron Recreation Area. Restrooms can be found at either location. The shady, wooded trail passes two fishing ponds and offers great opportunities for bird-watching. Easy to moderate, this relatively flat but sandy trail follows a primitive road that winds along the Cimarron River corridor. Sometimes the river disappears as it travels underground until flooding occurs.

**MIDDLE SPRING** is an Outdoor Wildlife Learning Site (OWLS) with a nature trail located at the Cottonwood Picnic Grounds. This dependable, year-round artesian spring is also stop #9 on the auto tour. Restrooms and water are available.

**BIKING**—Companion to the Santa Fe Trail allows for mountain biking on a maintained, sandy, and grassy surface that is mostly level with gradual inclines. Turkey Trail is a primitive road that can be biked, but watch for other vehicles. Riding cross-country can prove hazardous due to cactus spines and is not recommended.

**HORSEBACK RIDING**—The Conestoga and Murphy trailheads on the Companion to the Santa Fe Trail provide gravel parking lots and can accommodate trailers. There are facilities for unloading, watering, tying, and mounting/dismounting, and restrooms. Livestock is not allowed in the Cimarron Recreation Area or the Cottonwood Picnic Grounds.

**FISHING AND HUNTING**—10 fishing ponds make the park a great destination for anglers. Mallard, Wilburton, and Point of Rocks ponds are designated for fishing within the Cimarron Recreation Area year-round. Trout are stocked in the winter and channel catfish are stocked during the summer. Only Point of Rocks has facilities available at the pond. KDWP licensing, rules, and limitations apply even though this is a national park unit. Hunting for quail, pheasant, turkey, lesser prairie chicken, dove, and white-tailed and mule deer is permitted. Some elk are also available.

**AUTO TOUR**—A 50-mile historic and scenic auto tour leads you to 17 points of interest, such as windmills, grazing areas, fishing ponds, riparian habitat, grave sites, Santa Fe Trail ruts, oil wells, artesian springs, scenic overlooks, and monuments. A brochure is available online or by request.

**CAMPING AND FACILITIES**—Established campsites are provided within the recreation area for a nightly fee on a first-come, first-served basis. 14 sites are available, with tables, water, grills, and restrooms on-site. There are no hookups and no fires allowed (charcoal and gas stoves only). Dispersed primitive camping is free and allowed anywhere except the Recreation Area or established picnic grounds and Point of Rocks. Picnic areas with restrooms and water are located at Cimarron River, Cimarron Recreation Area, and Middle Spring/Cottonwood.

**LOCATION AND DIRECTIONS**—The district office is located in Elkhart in Morton County on U.S. Highway 56. Travel 7 miles north of Elkhart on State Highway 27 and turn east on FS 700. Continue east 4 miles to the Cimarron Recreation Area.

**ENTRY**—There are no entrance fees. As office hours are 8:00 A.M. to 5:00 P.M. (excluding lunch hour), Monday-Friday, it is wise to write in advance for materials and a park map. Send your request and $6 (check made out to USDA Forest Service) to 242 Highway 56 East, P.O. Box 300, Elkhart, KS 67950.

**ON THE WEB**—www.fs.fed.us/r2/psicc/cim.

**CONTACT**—USDA Forest Service office in Elkhart, (620) 697-4621; 242 Highway 56 East, P.O. Box 300, Elkhart, KS 67950.

# Sandsage Bison Range and Wildlife Area

Located in the High Plains Region, Sandsage is where the oldest publicly owned herd of bison roams. Underfoot is the Sandsage Prairie Ecosystem, a unique plant community composed of grasses such as sand bluestem, giant sandsage, and sand lovegrass. While bison are the main attraction for visitors here, this rare ecosystem is also worth discovering. Sandsage prairie occurs where sandy soils dominate and it is considered a harsh environment, with low moisture and unpredictable rainfall. Storms from the Pacific lose moisture as they climb over the Rockies and dry out as they reach the Great Plains. The semi-arid conditions are right for slow-growing or limited-growth plants such as shortgrass, yucca, and sagebrush.

In addition to the interesting ecology, Sandsage Bison Range has an interesting past. Prior to state ownership, the land was federally owned as the Kansas National Forest, a trial project in 1905 to determine what species of trees would survive in the Great Plains. Over 800,000 seedlings were planted, but the project was considered a failure. Subsequently, in 1916 Woodrow Wilson granted over 3,000 acres to Kansas for use as a game preserve. Today, just a small smattering of trees still survives in the middle pasture on the bison range. In 1924 bison were reintroduced on the range. The herd size is maintained between 80 and 100 bison. Because bison are unpredictable and potentially dangerous, visitors are not allowed in pastures where bison graze; however, notices are posted to indicate which pastures are open to the public.

**WILDLIFE**—The unique habitat of the sandsage prairie supports lesser prairie chickens, scaled quail, pheasant, spotted ground squirrels, kangaroo rats, black-tailed jack rabbits, black-tailed prairie dogs, and mule deer. Visit in May or early June for an explosive display of wildflowers.

**FISHING AND HUNTING**—A sand pit in the north portion of the range allows limited fishing opportunities. When water levels are sufficient, channel cat and rainbow trout are stocked on a seasonal basis. Hunting is somewhat restricted and allowed by posted notice only. Bobwhite and scaled quail, doves, deer, pheasant, and rabbits are plentiful. Coyotes are also present.

**GUIDED TOURS**—Volunteers for Friends of Sandsage Bison Range conduct tours that can last from 30 minutes to two hours. With advance notice you can customize your tour. Seven-passenger Chevrolet Suburbans are used for smaller groups and an open-air trailer is used for large groups. The Friends will try to accommodate you sunrise through sundown seven days a week; however, they are dependent upon availability of their volunteers, so make arrangements in advance. Donations, memberships, and bison adoptions are their only means of support. Tours may be canceled in case of extreme weather conditions.

**CAMPING AND FACILITIES**—Camping is not allowed. The only facilities are parking lots and a vault toilet. A state park office is on the premise.

**LOCATION AND DIRECTIONS**—In Finney County. Take U.S. Highway 83 south from Garden City.

**ENTRY**—Self-guided tours are not available. Bison are fenced within a high-voltage, short-duration electric fence. Visitors should not come into contact with either the fence or the bison.

**ON THE WEB**—www.fosbr.com or www.kdwp.state.ks.us, search "bison range." Park maps can be located via the "Docs" button on the Web site.

**CONTACT**—KDWP office in Garden City, (620) 276-8886; 785 South Highway 83, Garden City, KS 67846. Friends of Sandsage Bison Range, (620) 276-9400, for guided tours.

**NEARBY**—Less than a mile from the refuge in Garden City is the **LEE RICHARDSON ZOO,** where visitors can see more than 350 fascinating creatures from all over the world. Of particular interest to bird-watchers, a nesting house for finch and Mississippi kite and a pond that attracts migrating fowl. There is a small fee per vehicle but it's free for pedestrians. Open seven days a week from 8:00 A.M. to 7:30 P.M. (daylight savings time) and 8:00 A.M. to 4:30 P.M. during CST. Closed major holidays; (620) 276-1250.

# Meade State Park

T HIS SMALL FISHING LAKE represents the only designated state park in the southwest quadrant of Kansas. The site once offered a unique illustration of the underground aquifer found in the west—an artesian well, which is a natural spring formed when water under pressure is forced to the surface. Windmills and solar wells dot the landscape west of Meade Lake and Fish Hatchery, but the artesian well is now capped off. Most of the surrounding area is flat, except where creeks and streams have carved away the Ogallala Formation, creating canyons. As in most of western Kansas, wildflowers flourish in the sandy soils here in May and June.

A new visitor center is currently under construction, scheduled to open in the spring of 2008. A swim beach adds to the enjoyment of camping under shade trees near the water's edge.

**WILDLIFE**—Trees lining the lake provide cover for red-headed woodpeckers, orioles (summer only), western kingbirds, bluebirds, and robins. Watch for lark buntings and black-billed magpies. Both are black and white, but their markings are opposite: the lark bunting is mostly black, with a white patch on its wing, while the black-billed magpie has a white torso with black wings, tail, and head. The cattail marsh is the perfect habitat for red-winged blackbirds as well as both tree and barn swallows. Also keep your eyes open for wildflowers and deer along the hiking trail.

**HIKING**—A three-quarter-mile linear trail passes through shortgrass prairie and runs along the length of a cattail marsh where many birds take cover. You can hike a circuit trail by linking the park roads, campgrounds, and hiking trail to complete a 2-mile loop around the lake. The trail is indicated on the state park map.

**FISHING AND HUNTING**—The lake is small and shallow (about 12 feet deep), but several species are present for fishing. White crappie is considered excellent; largemouth bass are fair. Anglers may also chase bluegill and channel cat. There is one boat ramp available and boats must be operated at no-wake speeds. The small, 360-acre wildlife area supports some waterfowl, quail, turkeys, mule and white-tailed deer, and cottontail rabbits. Note that deer may be hunted only with bows or muzzle-loading firearms. Meade is currently the smallest state park in terms of land size.

**CAMPING AND FACILITIES**—Shaded campsites surround the lake, only a few of which may be reserved. There are plenty of primitive sites, some improved sites, shower houses, a sanitary dump station, a boat ramp, a courtesy dock, a swim beach, and shelters.

**TRAFFIC**—Below average, with the most visitors in May.

**LOCATION AND DIRECTIONS**—In Meade County. From Wichita, head west on U.S. Highway 400/54 to Meade and turn south on

State Highway 23. From Dodge City, head west on U.S. Highway 56 and turn south on Highway 23.

**ENTRY**—State park entrance fees apply. Open all year.

**ON THE WEB**—www.kdwp.state.ks.us, search "Meade."

**CONTACT**—KDWP office in Meade, (620) 873-2572; 13051 V Road, Meade, KS 67864.

# Big Basin Prairie Preserve

WITHIN THE RED HILLS AND HIGH PLAINS REGIONS, the Permian Period left in its wake thick deposits of gypsum and salt several hundred feet below the surface. These water-soluble chemicals dissolve or wash away over time, causing the overlying earth to collapse. This is very likely the

A sinkhole one mile wide and one hundred feet deep creates interesting terrain for hikers at Big Basin.

cause of Big Basin—a gigantic sinkhole 1 mile wide and 100 feet deep with nearly vertical walls. Nearby, the considerably smaller Little Basin is about 840 feet in diameter and 35 feet deep with an eternal spring: Saint Jacob's Well is a pool of water about 84 feet deep that has never been known to go dry.

The basins and springs served as dependable watering holes for cattle drives and early settlers heading for Dodge City. Today, a monument placed at the spring commemorates the importance to early settlers. In 1978, the preserve was added to the National Registry and designated as a National Natural Landmark. The preserve is managed by KDWP, whose primary objective is to sustain the site's unique ecological and geological elements. In an ecosystem that is predominantly mixed-grass prairie, wildflowers flourish in the dry and sunny terrain along with sumac, cedar, and sage. The occasional cactus or yucca plant can also be spotted. KDWP manages a herd of bison here, to keep the preserve grazed. Visitors should keep a respectful distance from these somewhat unpredictable animals.

**WILDLIFE**—Bison roam the preserve freely. Exercise caution and do not approach them, especially when their young are present. Collared lizards, Texas horned lizards, and six-lined racerunners may be spotted hiding under plants or sunning on rocks. Western meadowlarks and grasshopper sparrows may be common, but look for more species near the well. Pronghorn antelope wander the High Plains but are difficult to spot.

**HIKING/AUTO TOUR**—U.S. Highway 283 cuts through Big Basin, allowing visitors to drive into the giant sinkhole and climb out a mile later. A marker within the basin indicates the entrance to the preserve. A rather rugged gravel road leads around the rim of Big Basin, surrounded by scenic and expansive vistas of eroded canyons. Wildflowers dot the sandy soils and a windmill draws your attention from afar. The road forks at the rim of Little Basin: the left fork leads to a short but rugged path down to Saint Jacob's Well; the right fork leads to a monument and expansive views from across Little Basin. Visitors are encouraged to explore the preserve on foot; vehicles should never leave the road. As long as you're willing to make the climb out, you can hike down the rim into the crater. Or instead, you may choose to park at the fork in the gravel road and hike in either direction around the rim of Little Basin. Visitors are advised to determine the location of bison (which may even be on the road) before setting out on foot. The roundtrip route on gravel from the entrance at Highway 283 is about 4.5 miles. If you hike the gravel roads, be aware the route is not flat and may seem especially strenuous in heat or high wind.

**FISHING AND HUNTING**—There is no fishing or hunting allowed at the preserve. See Meade State Park and Clark State Fishing Lake. Both are nearby.

**CAMPING AND FACILITIES**—There are no facilities and no camping. See Meade State Park or Clark State Fishing Lake instead.

**LOCATION AND DIRECTIONS**—In Clark County. On U.S. Highway 283/160, 16 miles south of Minneola, a marker indicates the entrance to the preserve on the east side of the road.

**ENTRY**—No entrance fees. Open all year from sunup to sundown.

**ON THE WEB**—www.kdwp.state.ks.us, search "Big Basin."

**CONTACT**—KDWP in Dodge City, (620) 227-8609; 1001 West McArtor Road, Dodge City, KS 67801.

# Clark State Fishing Lake and Wildlife Area

NORTH OF BIG BASIN lies an oasis named Clark State Fishing Lake. Although rustic and largely undeveloped, this small fishing lake can be compared to Lake Scott as it also sits at the base of a canyon with nearly vertical walls. The lake surface is larger than Lake Scott, but the park surrounding it is slightly smaller in acreage. Upon entering the park, visitors are treated with a stunning view from the canyon rim. A parking pullout affords some of the best photos before you descend into the canyon to park facilities on the shoreline. Steep slopes are painted the muted hues of rust-colored prairie grasses, green sage, and cedar. Sandstone outcrops feature a blanket of black-eyed Susans at their base. Cottonwood, cedar, and pine make for fragrant, shaded picnic spots and hiding places for wildlife. Emerald-green reeds grow from the rocky banks and fishing piers on the shore of the clear blue lake.

**WILDLIFE**—White-tailed and mule deer, turkeys, quail, cottontail rabbits, and coyotes are prevalent. Beavers, raccoons, and bobcats can sometimes be spotted. Turkey vultures nest in the cliffs and bald eagles often migrate in fall and winter. Waterfowl visit during the spring and fall. Lizards and rattlesnakes may be seen as well.

Clark State Fishing Lake is a stunning oasis in southwest Kansas.

**HIKING**—A 2-mile gravel road extends from State Highway 94 above the north end of the lake. Hikers may park near the maintenance shed and walk the gravel road around the rim and then descend to lake level, where picnic tables and restrooms are located. Be aware that this hike requires a fairly steep climb to get back to your car. A 1-mile hiking trail also begins at the end of this gravel road, which crosses a bridge over the inlet and follows the creek. Unfortunately, poison ivy thrives here and the trail is not often maintained. Hikers may wander at will along the mesa overlooking the canyon, but in years of sufficient rainfall grasses will be knee-high. The gravel road leading south from the park office also makes for an easy, scenic walk that's great for photographers. It is advisable to wear bright colors when hiking off-road.

**BIKING/AUTO TOUR**—Highway 94, which leads to the park office on the east side of the lake, is paved; all other roads are gravel. You may ride or drive the gravel roads that circle the lake, but note that they do not form a full loop and you will have to return the same way you came. An auto tour will take 45 minutes to an hour. The undeveloped west side may require a four-wheel-drive vehicle. If you don't have four-wheel drive, check conditions with park staff before venturing these rocky roads.

**FISHING AND HUNTING**—Floating piers, boat ramps, and numerous fish attractors help anglers lure channel cat, crappie, bluegill, and carp. Walleye are stocked annually and are rated good. Largemouth and white bass are rated excellent. From the park office, two gravel roads extend north and south, providing access to fishing piers. No setlines, banklines, or trotlines are allowed.

Hunting is allowed with a license, but the wildlife area may be better suited for wildlife watching than hunting, as it covers only a small section of land.

**CAMPING AND FACILITIES**—Primitive camping is permitted anywhere, but areas designated as refuges (no hunting) are recommended. Boat ramps, fishing piers, primitive restrooms, one shelter, and picnic tables with fire rings or grills are the only amenities. Visitors must pack out their own trash. Boating is allowed for fishing purposes only.

**LOCATION AND DIRECTIONS**—In Clark County near the Oklahoma border. From Dodge City, take U.S. Highway 283 south, then U.S. Highway 54 east to Kingsdown, and then State Highway 94 south and then west to the lake. Follow the paved road to the park office.

**ENTRY**—There are no entrance fees. Open all year, but some roads are seasonal. Bring your own water and pack out your trash.

**ON THE WEB**—Download the park map at www.kdwp.state.ks.us, search "Clark."

**CONTACT**—KDWP in Dodge City, (620) 227-8609; 1001 West McArtor Road, Dodge City, KS 67801.

# Cedar Bluff Reservoir
## and the Smoky Valley Scenic Byway

CHARACTERISTICS of the Smoky Hills and the High Plains regions blend here. The landscape is at times composed of mixed-grass prairie, steep bluffs, and hills dotted with yucca and cactus. But views suddenly change to sandstone, limestone, and chalk outcrops that rise and fall away from endless, flat stretches—often without a man-made structure in sight.

Spanning the width of the Smoky Valley Scenic Byway, Cedar Bluff Reservoir is named for its cedar-topped limestone bluffs that glow in the sun. While water sports such as fishing, boating, windsurfing, and skiing have always been popular at the lake, hiking has recently been added to the list of activities that draw visitors. Thanks to a National Recreational Trails grant, two trails have been added to showcase the wildlife area, limestone and chalk outcrops, and wildflower displays. Primitive and improved cabins and campsites will no doubt boost this park's popularity, although it is off the beaten path in western Kansas.

Trails at Cedar Bluff State Park showcase limestone outcrops and mixed-grass prairie.

Drought has taken its toll on docks and boat ramps in the past, but after winters of heavy snowfall and spring rain, the park and its hiking trails are as lovely as any in Kansas. Prairie wildflowers and grasses are abundant and varied. Pick up a copy of Kansas Department of Transportation's wildflower chart to identify some of the area's numerous blooms. If you think you'd enjoy a wildflower tour, hire Wildflower Mary in nearby WaKeeney (contact information, on page 26).You'll learn to identify skullcap, milkweed, Indian blanket, echinacea, wavy-leaf thistle, upright coneflower, purple poppy mallow, narrow-leaf bluet, primrose, catclaw, spiderwort, prairie rose, prickly pear cactus, and yucca bloom. This just might be the wildflower capital of Kansas.

**WILDLIFE**—White-tailed and mule deer, wild turkeys, and pheasant love the prairie grasses and they can be spotted easily there. Bird-watching in the wildlife area is best during fall and spring migration. Canada geese, ducks, and pelicans are the most common visitors here, but food plots and a waterfowl refuge widen the opportunities. You'll recognize the black-tailed jackrabbits when you see them bound away. Raptors are numerous because of the supply of mice and rabbits. Vultures are common in the skies. Bald eagles have also nested on the reservoir in recent years. Baltimore orioles stand out in their showy orange and black. Black-billed magpies may be seen hunting insects in trees or pastures. Eastern kingbirds and killdeers are also fairly common.

**HIKING**—Although the park was without hiking trails until 2006, two paths are now available. The trails begin at the White Tail Campground, which is located at the west end of the Page Creek Area. The trailhead for the **THRESHING MACHINE NATURE TRAIL** is clearly marked on the south side of the road near a few parking spaces. A paved, three-quarter-mile loop begins with views of stark timber rising up from a teal blue cove. Wildflowers are plentiful early in the summer. Hiking counterclockwise, the paved trail loops back with a gentle climb for panoramic views of the lake. Enhancements such as benches and interpretive displays are forthcoming.

An additional 5 miles of trail branches off on your right at about a quarter-mile from the trailhead. The access point is not clearly marked as of yet and can easily be missed. This mowed extension soon turns to dirt and limestone as it passes under a bluff, then leads down to a wet-weather stream crossing. The extension will bring you to a loop that climbs to an overlook of the lake. Veer left for the most scenic views along the trail. Rock formations peak out from impressive green hills and buttes as you hike through prairie grasses, accompanied by the singing of birds. Deer hide in the brush

Save some time to admire the view from the scenic cedar bluffs.

and are easily spooked. Baltimore orioles create a spectacle with bright orange markings. Vultures and hawks soar overhead while colorful fishing boats and rafts float below you. Although you'll be surrounded by grass-covered, limestone canyons, don't expect to see the park's namesake bluffs—for that you'll need to take the scenic drive. Continue the loop until it returns you to the paved trail. There is not much shade, so start early and bring plenty of water and snacks. Sunscreen and insect repellent are a must. Wear long pants to avoid poison ivy and thorns. The new trails are not yet mapped and can be rugged and uneven in parts with short but steep climbs.

If you are interested in the Wildflower Nature Trail shown on the park map at the northern tip of the Bluffton area, save your time. According to park officials, this road no longer exists or is no longer maintained.

**BIKING**—Cyclists are allowed on both trails at the Page Creek Area. (See Hiking.) Mountain bikers may enjoy exploring the dirt or gravel roads traversing the park and wildlife areas. (See Auto Tours.) The scenic byway has a shoulder and offers high visibility as well as low-to-moderate traffic for road bikers.

**HORSEBACK RIDING**—Horses are allowed on the south side of the lake, just east of the information station. There are no designated trails for equestrians, but according to park officials you can ride the wildlife areas. Trail rides can be arranged with a special-use permit.

**FISHING AND HUNTING**—Stilling Basin, just below the Cedar Bluff Dam, is stocked with rainbow trout in the spring and fall. Cedar Bluff is predicted to be a trophy destination for white bass, which are prevalent in the area and often measure 16-18 inches in length. Catfish here are excellent; some channel cat weigh over 10 pounds and some flathead weigh over 20. Walleye are rated fair but improving. Wiper (a hybrid between the white bass and the striped bass) are good. Black bass are fair, typically weighing in at three or four pounds. Fish-cleaning stations, boat ramps, fishing piers, and docks are provided on the reservoir. Fish attractors have been marked with floating buoys throughout the lake.

Hunting pressure is high in western Kansas; Cedar Bluff is no exception. Check with rangers and officials before planning a hunt, as limitations are often used to optimize and manage wildlife populations. White-tailed deer were once pervasive, but numbers are declining. Pheasant, quail, and turkey populations fluctuate with environmental conditions. The land-based refuge is closed to all activity from September 10 to March 1. Waterfowl numbers are increasing as the lake rebounds from drought. Small game such as black-tailed jackrabbit and cottontail are plentiful. A portion of the Page Creek Area is designated as a handicapped-accessible hunting access area. Primitive camping in the wildlife area is limited, but improved camping is plentiful in the state park areas.

**AUTO TOUR**—A 60-mile paved route traces the **SMOKY VALLEY SCENIC BYWAY.** From I-70, exit at Ogallah (Exit 135). The byway heads south on State Highway 147, turns west on State Highway 4 at Brownell, goes north on U.S. Highway 283, and then ends at WaKeeney on I-70.

For a stunning view, drive to the top of the 100-foot-high, cedar-dotted limestone bluffs. Bring a picnic basket and a blanket to sit on. Wildflowers and birds add to your view, which translates into photographs more like the Mediterranean than Kansas. Enjoy the sight of pleasure boats and fishing boats as they pass below. Exercise caution as you scramble up the golden rock layers that overlook the teal lake; and stay away from the edges, which sometimes crumble before your eyes. There are no guardrails or fences to prevent a fall.

To find the bluffs from Highway 147, head south and cross over the reservoir dam to AA 474 (marked with a large gray shed). Turn on AA 474 for approximately 8 miles until you see a sign pointing north (right) to the Cedar Bluffs. From here, a very rutted gravel road winds through a canyon with steep climbs and sheered limestone exposures. You'll want a high-clearance vehicle for this drive and you'll find yourself hoping you don't meet any oncoming vehicles during the journey. You can shorten your tour of the byway by continuing on AA Road to U.S. Highway 283 or backtrack to Highway 147 and continue the route. (Note: Dirt roads should be avoided in wet weather.)

**OTHER**—Tour guide Wildflower Mary offers wildflower identification tours May through September on a 60-acre wildflower prairie restoration project. Mary has several routes to recommend in the WaKeeney area, depending on weather, roads, and whatever happens to be blooming at the time. Per person fees apply. Mary also owns the 1906 Cottage Garden Bed and Breakfast in WaKeeney. Visit www.visitourcottage.com.

Walking a field with Wildflower Mary on the Smoky Valley Scenic Byway.

**CAMPING AND FACILITIES**—Cedar Bluff State Park is divided into two areas: Bluffton on the north shore and Page Creek area on the south shore. The more developed and heavily used Bluffton area offers primitive and improved campsites with a sanitary dump station, two primitive and two modern cabins, boat ramps, fishing piers and docks, a swimming beach, group shelters, modern toilets and shower houses (during high season), picnic tables, grills, and fish-cleaning stations. A children's playground, a BMX track, volleyball and basketball courts, and horseshoe pits provide outdoor entertainment for the family. The more primitive and secluded Page Creek Area offers access to the trails, primitive sites, a large group camp and some sites with utilities, shelters, grills, boat ramps, fishing piers, modern facilities, and a playground.

A private cabin area is located north of Page Creek, just south of the dam on Highway 147. Located in the cabin area, Cedar Bluff Lodge is a luxury experience for the outdoor enthusiast with great service at reasonable rates. The owners may also accommodate your horse on a nearby ranch. See www.cedarblufflodge.com.

**TRAFFIC**—Below average, with May being the heaviest month.

**LOCATION AND DIRECTIONS**—Located in Trego County. Take I-70 to Exit 135 at Ogallah, turn south onto State Highway 147, and follow it 13 miles to find the state park entrance and park office on your right.

**ENTRY**—State park entrance fees apply. The park is open all year, but water hookups and showers are available only from mid-April to mid-October. Office hours are 8:00 A.M. to 4:30 P.M., Monday-Friday. During the high season, hours are extended to cover weekends. Some areas require special permits to access or to hunt. The refuge is closed to all activities November 1 through February 1. Be sure to consult the wildlife area map and speak with park officials during office hours for current status.

**ON THE WEB**—www.kdwp.state.ks.us, search "Cedar Bluff."

**CONTACT**—KDWP office in Ellis, (785) 726-3212: RR 2, Box 76A, Ellis, KS 67637.

**NEARBY**—The **STERNBERG MUSEUM OF NATURAL HISTORY** is located in Hays (see Central Kansas). Expect to spend one to two hours learning about the Cretaceous Period and the great inland sea that shaped much of the terrain in western Kansas. Fascinating ancient fossils recovered from chalk formations and local digs are on display, with a video that shows the process of excavation. Geological time lines are explained and numerous ancient and extinct species are on display. Walk among life-sized, robotic dinosaurs, too. Open Tuesday - Saturday, 10:00 A.M. to 6:00 P.M., and Sunday, 1:00 P.M. to 6:00 P.M. Closed Mondays. Admission fees apply. Located on the Fort Hays State University campus at 3000 Sternberg Drive, Hays, KS 67601; (877) 332-1165. Visit www.fhsu.edu/sternberg for more information.

# Castle Rock, City of Chalk

OUT IN THE MIDDLE OF VAST FARMLAND, dirt roads lead to a fantastic spectacle. This may be Kansas's best kept secret. While few have ever heard of Castle Rock, you may encounter more people here than on the trails at nearby parks. As you make the final approach, climbing to an overlook appropriately named "table rock bluff," the valley floor falls away and a mystic city carved from the chalk bluff appears below. In the distance, what looks like a lonely castle looms with a chalk moat surrounding it. These towering chalk outcrops are the result of the deeper seas from the Cretaceous Period. Chalk is a soft, porous form of limestone that results from the accumulation of tiny marine organisms, and is carved into monoliths such as

Castle Rock chalk formations create a skyline in a Kansas field.

Visitors can squeeze between narrow passageways made of chalk at Castle Rock.

these by wind and water. The colors you see are impurities in the chalk from iron oxide or other properties.

Discovered in 1865 by surveyors exploring the Butterfield Trail, the large buildinglike creations are connected by a road of chalk, making it easy for sight-seers to explore the "city of chalk." Park your car and explore on foot. Some passages lead through narrow hallways, others to aerial views of striped hoodoos. The prairie floor peaks between the buttes and spires. Pastel farms and ranchlands color the distant background.

The Sternbergs, a local family of fossil hunters, found many specimens from the Cretaceous seas preserved in the chalk and sandstone of the area. George Sternberg became the curator of the Natural History museum, later named to honor the family. You can see many fossils from the area on display at the Sternberg Museum of Natural History in Hays.

**LOCATION AND DIRECTIONS**—Located in Gove County. From I-70 take Exit 107 (Quinter) and follow Castle Rock Road south for 15 miles to County Road K. Turn east and proceed 4 miles to a small sign that directs you north to Castle Rock. Cross the cattle guard, proceed straight (ignoring the right branch), and climb the knob for the stunning overlook. Then, backtrack toward the cattle guard and make the turn that you previously ignored. This road will lower you to the valley floor. The drive will take you in a full circle and bring you back to the entrance.

Castle Rock is located on private property, so respect the land and the local people. There are no facilities or visitor centers and no entry fees. The city of Quinter, located 20 miles north of Castle Rock, offers parks, picnic areas, gas, food, and lodging. Contact the Quinter Chamber of Commerce at (785) 754-3538 for a brochure.

# Prairie Dog State Park
## and Keith Sebelius Reservoir

IN THE HIGH PLAINS REGION, only 12 miles from the Nebraska border, Prairie Dog State Park got its name not just for its barking residents, but also for a creek that feeds it. The park, nestled in Norton County, offers historic interpretation and preserves two vintage buildings: a rare one-room schoolhouse and a surviving, renovated adobe house. Prairie Dog State Park is just one large unit on the north side of Keith Sebelius Reservoir. It's easy to navigate and you'll quickly become oriented. All the campgrounds and park facilities are on the shoreline.

The park is comprised of flat plains interrupted by rolling hills of short-grass prairie, with a rock bluff on the south shore. The dry soil and arid conditions are perfect for June wildflowers. The park falls short on maintained trails, but hikers are welcome to set out on foot anywhere in the park. The Norton Wildlife Area, which borders the Keith Sebelius Lake, offers great fishing, hunting, boating, hiking, and camping. Ask about hunting boundaries and pick up a copy of the park map for more recreational details.

**WILDLIFE**—Norton County claims fame as the "pheasant capital of Kansas," but unfortunately pheasant have been declining in recent years. The eastern edge of the State Park is interrupted by a long cove where you can set out on foot to view wildlife; there is also a boat ramp you may use to put in a canoe or kayak for wildlife viewing. A prairie dog colony can be found just inside the park entrance south of the railroad tracks and you can even view them from the park office. The prairie dogs attract coyotes, badgers, hawks, and prairie falcons. Look for white-tailed and mule deer, turkeys, and greater prairie chickens. During the winter, you might see bald eagles. Fall and spring bring migrating ducks, geese, and the occasional osprey.

**HIKING**—A 1.4-mile loop trail begins south of the railroad tracks and prairie dog town. Turn east after crossing the tracks to locate the trailhead. The trail offers interpretive signage along the route and the park map indicates the trail route. A connector trail leads to the restroom at Meadowlark Campground.

**FISHING AND HUNTING**—Walleye, bluegill, blue catfish, and crappie are all present in Sebelius Reservoir. The reservoir once held the record for saugeye, which are rated good. Wiper is rated excellent and can be had throughout the season. Largemouth is rated fair, but can be tempted near the shoreline and submerged cover. Spotted bass, rated fair, hang out in the rock along the dam. Don't forget to try the stilling basin below the dam. Flathead and channel cat are rated good. There are three boat ramp lanes and one courtesy dock at the state park. Adjacent to the State Park, the Norton Wildlife Area has many parking pullouts along Prairie Dog Creek and an additional boat ramp on the southwest corner of the lake.

Hunting for small game is popular in this small space, especially on opening weekend in November, so plan hunts during the week. White-tailed and mule deer see heavy pressure during the firearms season. Turkey hunting can be good, but again pressure is high early in the season.

**PADDLING**—This is a popular activity within the lake coves and also on Prairie Dog Creek. To access the creek, you can use the boat ramp on the southwest corner of the lake on the east side of State Highway 383 or you can launch in the wildlife area and float a couple of miles to the lake.

**CAMPING AND FACILITIES**—Walk-in camping is allowed throughout the entire Norton Wildlife Area and there are designated primitive camps. Campers must pack out trash from the wildlife area. The state park offers both primitive and improved camping options with a group camp and two rental cabins. The park has plentiful undesignated primitive sites (somewhat rare for state parks), as well as some designated primitive sites. There are shelters and shower houses, sanitary dump stations, a fish-cleaning station, boat ramps, a courtesy dock, and a swimming beach at Prairie Dog Campground. An archery range can be found on the western edge of the state park near Branded Cedar Campground. A small marina with concessions is located on the east side of the park.

**TRAFFIC**—Below average, with spikes in May and July.

**LOCATION AND DIRECTIONS**—In Norton County. Exit I-70 at WaKeeney (Exit 128) and travel 60 miles north on U.S. Highway 283 to Norton. Travel west on U.S. Highway 36 to the park entrance, which will be on your left. State Highway 261 south leads you to the park office.

**ENTRY**—State park entrance fees apply. The park office is open from 8:00 A.M. to 4:30 P.M., Monday-Friday. Hours are extended on summer weekends. Running water is available only from April 15 to October 15.

**ON THE WEB**—www.kdwp.state.ks.us, search "Prairie Dog" and "Norton."

**CONTACT**—State Park office in Norton, (785) 877-2953; Box 431, Norton, KS 67654.

# Prairie Chicken Viewing 101

FROM NATURE LOVERS TO AVID BIRD-WATCHERS, many people are fascinated by the seldom-seen prairie chicken. The lesser prairie chicken is predominantly found in the sandsage prairies of the southwest corner of Kansas, while the greater prairie chicken is common in the pastureland and tallgrass prairies of central Kansas. While very similar in features, the lesser is slightly smaller with red-orange air sacs on its neck and the greater is the bigger of the two, characterized by yellow-orange air sacs.

Prairie chicken populations have declined with drought and were seriously threatened during the Dust Bowl. Although numbers have slowly begun to climb, the loss of sandsage prairie habitat continues to be a major factor in decline of the lesser prairie chicken. The mixture of grasses, yucca, and sagebrush here provides nesting and cover desired for breeding.

It is the breeding and mating rituals that intrigue viewers and bird-watchers everywhere. Because the birds return to the same leks, or breeding grounds, every year, viewing blinds have been established in several locations. The season is very brief: males return to the lek in March and peak activity occurs in April when the hens come to mate. The presence of the female is short-lived; after only two or three weeks, they leave to attend their nests. These breeding grounds are often found atop hills where vegetation is relatively sparse and visibility is good.

The males court the females after re-establishing their territory. The male will bow, display his wings, ruffle the feathers on his neck, and perform a dance of tiny steps and stomping. A gobbling sound comes from the air sacs on the neck, followed by a laughing cackle that can sometimes be heard a mile away. The best time to view the mating ritual is half an hour prior to sunrise or just before sunset. To minimize disturbance, it is suggested that viewers arrive an hour ahead and leave an hour after sunset.

Viewing blinds for prairie chicken leks can be found at Cimarron National Grassland and throughout private property in Kansas. The Nature Conservancy occasionally offers guided viewing tours at the Konza Prairie Biological Station in March.

# CENTRAL
# KANSAS

Sandstone concretions are a unique geological feature on display at Rock City.

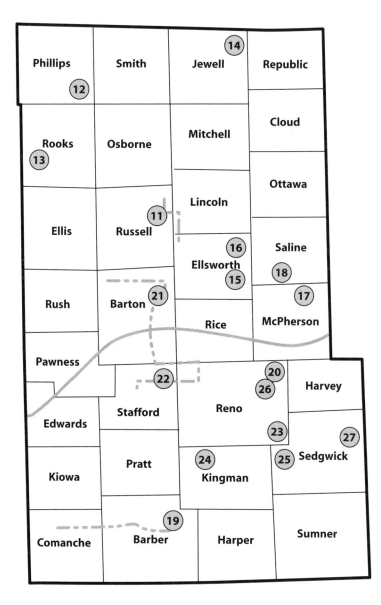

Scenic Byway
Santa Fe Trail

# Geology of the Smoky Hills Region

THIS REGION OF NORTH-CENTRAL KANSAS may have been named for the appearance of haze in its valleys, but it is truly defined by its geology, formed during the Cretaceous Period. Unlike the shallow seas of the Pennsylvanian and Permian periods, the seas of the Cretaceous Period were much deeper and larger, leaving more tumultuous deposits.

Three types of rock outcroppings make this area unique and defy Kansas stereotypes. First, Dakota sandstone is the result of beach sands and sediments carried by rivers to Cretaceous Period seas. This weather-resistant sandstone leaves behind smooth, slick-rock caps that protect the sediments beneath; canyons and valleys are the result. Besides the Dakota sandstone, two types of limestone are characteristic of the Smoky Hills Region. Greenhorn limestone is made of chalky limestone beds alternating with layers of thick shale. The top layers of greenhorn closest to the surface have been nicknamed *fence-post limestone* because innovative settlers used the stone to create fence posts in response to a shortage of wood on the prairie. The third sediment or rock outcropping that characterizes the Smoky Hills Region is Niobrara chalk. Deposited in the deepest basins, chalk is also a type of limestone, a byproduct of marine life. It is a softer, less-resistant form that erodes more erratically, leaving behind wildly distinctive spindles and spires. These soft sediments were the perfect packaging materials to encase fossils of the ancient seas. Geology buffs should make a point to stop at the Sternberg Museum on the northeast edge of Hays, Kansas (see page 27). The museum illustrates life during the Cretaceous Period and teaches about the sea that covered Kansas 80 million years ago. Visit www.fhsu.edu/sternberg for more information.

Although the Smoky Hills Region is not as well known as the Flint Hills, its scenery and natural landmarks are likely to be more captivating, thought-provoking, and certainly less traveled. Perhaps because much of its beauty is not visible from the interstate, it is often dismissed. A gold mine awaits those who love geology and roads less traveled.

# Wilson Reservoir and State Park
## and Post Rock Scenic Byway

UNIQUE FOR ITS RED ROCK FORMATIONS, sandstone hoodoos, and outcrops, a trio of sandcastles reaches from the Wilson Lake shoreline, simulating a village on a crescent-shaped beach. Sands from the Cretaceous Period were cemented with lime deposits to create the erosion-resistant yet picturesque features. Touted as "the clearest lake in Kansas," Wilson Lake's blue waters reflect the red formations and the sky, making it one of the most scenic places in Kansas. Cedar trees and yucca dot the rugged Smoky Hills with chasms eroding at their base. Greenhorn limestone fence posts created by early settlers still stand after a century. In late spring and summer, mixed-grass prairie and a profusion of wildflowers make this destination hard to beat.

Wilson Lake's Dakota sandstone formations create a skyline at Rocktown.

Annual festivals, grassroots art, scenic drives, museums, and architectural highlights round out the list of activities that will easily keep visitors busy for days.

**WILDLIFE**—Mule deer, foxes, coyotes, prairie chickens, and ring-necked pheasant love the mixed-grass prairie around the lake. Snakes, beavers, and muskrat thrive in the riparian habitat of the Saline River. Warm rocks attract collared lizards and ornate box turtles. Cliff swallows nest under bridges and killdeers are common in camp. Meadowlarks can be heard more easily than seen. Rare sightings of golden and bald eagles, sandhill cranes, cormorants, and ospreys may delight the lucky visitor. Pelicans drop by in spring and fall; their large white bodies are easily spotted floating on the blue lake.

**HIKING**—The **DAKOTA TRAIL** is 1 mile long and features native shrubs detailed in a coordinating trail brochure. Skunk bush, sandhill plum, soapweed, and cactus rest comfortably in western Kansas's sandy soils. Lichen-covered rocks and shelves are found along the trail, as are views of the Smoky Hills and Wilson Lake's defining Dakota sandstone, for which the trail is named. Slender ringneck snakes may cross your path, but are harmless. Limestone posts encase fossils of marine life. The path is steep, but well maintained with a crushed gravel surface and railroad ties. Restrooms are available at the trailhead, which is well marked in the Big Bluestem Campground at Hell Creek. A cutoff will allow you to shorten the hike to a half mile, but not before you climb a steep hill. Complete the mile for views of sunlit rocky shores and a scenic bridge that spans the reservoir. When the lake is low, you can see caves eroding in sandstone near the bridge.

**ROCK TOWN NATURAL AREA AND HIKING TRAIL**—Registered as a natural and scientific area by the Kansas Biological Survey and the Army Corps of Engineers, this 3-mile, mowed prairie loop is one of the most scenic trails in Kansas. Wildflowers are a bonus if you visit in late spring through early fall. Located in Lucas Park just west of the dam, the path ascends prairie hills and rocky terrain to overlook the lake and Rocktown Cove's crescent-shaped beach, marked by three colorful sandstone pillars. Depending on water levels, the weathered formations either peak out of the blue lake below or provide a spectacle for hikers to walk among. Either way, the sandstone pinnacles provide a picturesque setting at any time of day. Pack a picnic and take a seat in the natural stone amphitheater or rest on a driftwood log before returning. The trail is rated moderate for some steep slopes.

**BUR OAK NATIONAL RECREATION TRAIL** is an easy three-quarter-mile loop that includes interpretive stations behind the dam in Sylvan Park.

Descending the Dakota Trail at Wilson Lake State Park.

Interesting rock formations, outcrops, and plants such as cottonwood, soapberry, and bur oak are identified along the trail. While somewhat unremarkable in comparison with the Rocktown or Dakota Trails, the path offers easy access to great wildlife viewing. Beaver dams and oddly shaped muskrat dens are a few of the highlights to be seen where the path follows above the old river channel. Migrating waterfowl or resident ducks may scatter as you approach. Look for post-rock fence posts with embedded fossils near the trail.

**RED CEDAR TRAIL** is a three-quarter-mile, hard-surface trail at the entrance of the Otoe Area. The parking area provides access to the lakeshore and swim beach, while the trail enters a cedar-dotted area across the park road. Although labeled as accessible, the pavement is rough and uneven. The trail descends with views of private homes high over the valley and ends with a view of a bridge that spans the reservoir. Hike early or late in the day for a chance to see wildlife. Look for the harmless western ribbon snake with colorful, vertical stripes. Head back the way you came or take the road back to the trailhead.

**MOUNTAIN BIKING—SWITCHGRASS BIKE TRAIL** has grown to 12 outstanding miles of trail in Wilson State Park. Nicknamed "the Rollercoaster," the single track can be seen from the park road, hovering above ravines and hugging steep hillsides as it crosses the road several times for a wild and scenic ride. Panoramic vistas, sandstone cliffs, rock outcrops, and lake views are the payoff for this challenging ride on mowed grass, dirt, and rock. The official trailhead can be found at the Switchgrass Campground restroom and parking lot. Trails can also be accessed from a parking area at the west end of Hell Creek Bridge. Three color-coded loops have been marked as follows: Hell Creek Loop (marked in red) is 3.9 miles on the east side of the highway (use secondary access), Golden Belt Loop (also marked in red) rolls through the west side of the park for 6.4 miles, and Sandy Beach Loop (marked in green) is 1.7 miles. There are plans to expand the current trails and add a loop designed for beginners.

**TRAIL BUILDING**—The Kansas Trails Council recently adopted the Switchgrass Bike Trail. To volunteer for trail work, see www.kansas-trailscouncil.org.

**ROAD BIKING**—Shoulders are often absent, but traffic is light outside of summer months. Park roads and the Post Rock Scenic Byway present a scenic but challenging route with significant rolling hills. You'll find less traffic and better scenery on the east/west drive south of the lake. (Some roads are unpaved.) Don't expect any amenities along the route. Wind may pose as great a challenge as the terrain.

**FISHING AND HUNTING**—White and striped bass, walleye, and smallmouth bass are excellent at Wilson Lake. Largemouth bass, white perch, channel and flathead catfish, crappie, bluegill, and drum also dwell in the reservoir. A 13-pound walleye and a 43-pound striped bass have set records, and so have smallmouth bass. Success is often affected by changes in water level, weather, temperature, and habitat. Wilson Wildlife Area lies on the western end of the park, offering boat ramps and an archery range. The refuge (a small portion of the wildlife area) is closed to hunting.

**WATER SPORTS**—Because of Kansas's summer heat, swimming is popular at the four beaches. Windsurfing and sailing are good because of strong and frequent winds. The lake's clarity and submerged formations are good for scuba diving.

**AUTO TOUR**—The 18-mile Post Rock Scenic Byway skirts the park and crosses the Wilson Dam, highlighting a portion of the Smoky Hills and the natural beauty of the Saline River valley. From Wilson north to Lucas, drivers will enjoy panoramic views of rolling grassland, rock formations, Wilson Lake, historic post-rock fencing, prairie wildflowers, farmland, and pasture. Add another 16 miles of scenery that is even more spectacular by driving the east/west road south of the reservoir between State Highway 232 and Bunker Hill. Although part of this road is dirt, it is usually in good condition.

**PADDLING**—Begin a 15-mile float down the Saline River from a put-in on U.S. Highway 281 north of Russell, about a half mile north of Land Road (188th Street). This slow, scenic trip passes through sandstone bluffs. Alternatively, follow Bunker Hill/Luray Road north from I-70 (Exit 193) to a put-in near the Parks and Wildlife maintenance building for a 6-mile trip through the wildlife area. Take out at any of the boat ramps in the wildlife area or reservoir.

**CAMPING AND FACILITIES**—Five parks surround Wilson Lake. The Corps of Engineers operates Sylvan, Lucas, and Minooka while Wilson and Otoe compose the state park, operated by KDWP. All five parks offer camping with electrical hookups and trailer dump stations, restrooms, showers (in season), picnic grounds, water, and group shelters. A marina is located at Wilson State Park. Swimming beaches are available at all parks except Lucas; boat ramps are available at all but Sylvan. The park participates in the Rent-a-Camp program, which offers Coleman camping equipment (for details, read the KDWP brochure *What Is Rent-a-Camp?*, which can be found on their Web site). Four modern cabins are available for rent in the state park. More private cabins and rentals can be found nearby.

**TRAFFIC**—Average, spiking May through July, heaviest in July.

**LOCATION AND DIRECTIONS**—In Russell County. Take Exit 206 from I-70. Head north on State Highway 232 for 6 miles. Turn left at a sign indicating Minooka Park and the state park office. Cross the bridge over the lake and turn right to enter the state park. Follow signs to reach the park office.

**ENTRY**—Entry fees apply in Otoe Area and Wilson State Park. Office hours are 8:00 A.M. to 4:30 P.M., Monday-Friday. Hours are extended to weekends in summer months. Shower houses are closed off-season.

**ON THE WEB**—You will need both the KDWP State Park brochure and the COE brochure for trail maps. Visit www.kdwp.state.ks.us and search "Wilson." Also visit www.nwk.usace.army.mil/wi. See www.russell-lks.org for local museums and activities.

**CONTACT**—Corps of Engineers at Sylvan Grove, (785) 685-2551. KDWP state park office and wildlife area, (785) 658-2465; RR 1, Box 181, Sylvan Grove, KS 67481.

# Kirwin National Wildlife Refuge

THE FIRST National Wildlife Refuge in Kansas was designated in 1954 amidst the rolling Smoky Hills and vast High Plains. Kirwin lies in a transition zone between the tallgrass prairies and shortgrass plains, creating a mixed-grass refuge on the Central Flyway. As the reservoir is fed by two intermittent streams, (the North Fork of the Solomon River and Bow Creek), water levels fluctuate greatly. The U.S. Fish and Wildlife Service (USFWS) partners with state and local agencies, landowners, and farmers to maintain cropland, native mixed-grass prairie, riparian land, and wetland habitat. Cooperative farming provides food for migratory and endangered species while grazing cattle help maintain grasslands.

The USFWS manages three other refuges in Kansas: Quivira, which preserves wetland habitat; Marais des Cygnes (pronounced *mair-de-zeen*), which protects bottomland hardwood; and Flint Hills National Wildlife Refuge, which is flat, open, floodplain. Kirwin is a reservoir surrounded by diverse mixed-grass habitat with wooded riparian zones. Although each habitat is unique, you are likely to see some of the same species at all four. However, birders know that spring and fall bring a large increase in the number of waterfowl and shorebirds they are likely to see.

**WILDLIFE**—According to the USFWS, Kirwin provides a wintering habitat for bald eagles, ducks, and geese. In fact, 85,000 Canada geese arrive every November and December. Dabbling ducks such as mallard and northern pintail rest and feed. Diving ducks such as the redhead and lesser scaup also pass through during migration. A wetland area adjacent to the refuge headquarters enables convenient viewing. Shorebirds and even tree-dwelling neotropical migrants drop in. Kirwin is home to a rookery for great blue herons and double-crested cormorants. A wealth of resident animals may be spotted as you drive the roads that surround the reservoir, including entertaining black-tailed prairie dogs that have a colony labeled Dog Town. Grass dwellers such as greater prairie chickens, black-tailed jackrabbits, and mule deer may be seen bounding away, but horned larks and meadowlarks may not be quite as shy. The endangered least tern nests at the reservoir when water levels are low. You can't miss yellow-headed blackbirds when present. They travel in flocks and stand out among the cattails.

**HIKING**—Both Crappie Point and Dog Town host short trails with interpretive signage. Look for wild turkeys and white-tailed deer as you hike. Hiking is allowed anywhere in the refuge, but explorers should be aware of hunting areas and seasons and wear bright colors.

**BIKING**—Biking is allowed on any park roads open to vehicles. Park roads circle the reservoir for great views and wildlife-watching opportunities, but they can be a little confusing. Pick up a map before you set out. Roads that hug the lake are either gravel or dirt. The circuit is approximately 20 miles, depending on your route.

**FISHING AND HUNTING**—High water improves chances for crappie, walleye, and catfish. Fishing is also permitted in the North Fork of the Solomon River and in Bow Creek, which feed the reservoir. State fishing laws apply; signs and buoys will indicate any closures. A low-water boat ramp is positioned on the north end of the dam. Boat ramps can be found near Gray's Park on the north shore and just across the dam on the south shore. (No pleasure boating or skiing.) A fish-cleaning station is provided on the square in the city of Kirwin. Disposing of fish on the refuge is subject to fine for littering. Hunters are permitted waterfowl, mourning doves, upland game birds, snipes, coots, cottontail rabbits, fox squirrels, and deer. Deer hunting is limited to archery and requires a free permit. Not all hunting areas are open for all species and the park imposes a daily maximum of six shells. Only nontoxic shot may be used. Be sure to pick up or download information in advance.

**PADDLING**—A boat ramp at the south end of the dam allows you to put in and float southwest into the Bow Creek tributary, which is surrounded by a public hunting area. There is also a boat ramp on the north shore between Gray's Park and Cottonwood Grove, from which you can float westerly into the North Fork of the Solomon River. Hug the north shore, which is not a hunting area. Float as many as 4 miles, depending on water levels. The arm is only open to motorless boats from August 1 to October 31. Pleasure boating and skiing are not permitted anywhere in the reuge.

**AUTO TOUR**—Follow gravel roads along the south shore (South Refuge Road) and Bow Creek. Interpretive signs explain the role of the refuge, with information about the National Wildlife Refuge System. Crappie Point, Bluegill Point, and Prairie Dog Town are on the south shore drive. If you circle the entire reservoir, you're likely to rack up 20 miles. So plan on a minimum of one hour without stops. Obtain a park map online in advance.

**CAMPING AND FACILITIES**—Primitive camping is available in several designated areas, including Gray's Point, Cottonwood Grove, and Catfish Cove. Restrooms are located on both ends of the dam. There are no showers or utilities. Boat ramps are available. You must pack out your own trash.

**LOCATION AND DIRECTIONS**—In Phillips County. From I-70, turn north at Hays (Exit 159) onto U.S. Highway 183 and travel 60 miles to Glade. The entrance is located on State Highway 9, 6 miles east of Glade.

**TRAFFIC**—Light: the U.S. Fish and Wildlife Service reports annual visitation of 95,000.

**ENTRY**—There are no entrance or user fees, although state hunting and fishing licenses and regulations apply. A visitor center located at refuge headquarters highlights native wildlife and habitat from 7:30 A.M. to 4:00 P.M., Monday-Friday (except holidays).

**ON THE WEB**—Maps and more can be found at www.fws.gov/kirwin.

**CONTACT**—The USFWS office can be reached at (785) 543-6673; 702 E. Xavier Road Kirwin, KS 67644.

# Webster State Park

BORDERING THE SMOKY HILLS and the High Plains regions, Webster State Park is surrounded by gently rolling prairie strewn with wildflowers and it supports a cast of wildlife. Near the park entrance, a rest area is being converted to a wildlife-viewing center to educate visitors on the habitat of pheasant, which are currently declining in Kansas.

Fishing, boating, and skiing are the primary activities in the area, with excellent conditions for windsurfing, thanks to dependable Kansas wind. A two-room cabin that accommodates six people is located near a group camp loop and a swim beach on the north shore. The cabin has a waterfront view. In fact, unlike many parks, all development is right on the shoreline.

**WILDLIFE**—The area is home to white-tailed and mule deer, pheasant, quail, waterfowl, wild turkeys, and numerous songbirds.

**HIKING**—As illustrated on the state park map, a 1-mile loop is located near Old Marina Campground on the north shore. The trailhead is located west of the campground shower house; it begins in grassland and descends into an area that was flooded long ago. Watermarks on the trees amaze observant hikers. Rated easy, the path follows a bluff wooded with sumac and chokecherry trees. Watch for the park residents such as pheasant, quail, and deer. You might see geese or blue heron as the trail nears a sheltered cove on the lake.

**BIKING**—The park falls short on trails, but with immeasurable country roads that see little traffic, riders can set out for the entire day. Some suggestions are to ride U.S. Highway 24 west to the town of Nicodemus to see the National Historic Site. Alternatively, head east from the lake on back roads to Rooks State Fishing Lake. To return, head north to Stockton on Highway 183 and then go west on Highway 24 back to the lake. Stockton is a town of 1,500 people and thus has amenities, but know that much will be closed on Sundays. Park roads stay pretty close to the lake and offer nice views and plenty of places for a scenic picnic.

**HORSEBACK RIDING**—Horses are permitted only on established roads. There are no designated horse camps.

**FISHING AND HUNTING**—Bank and pier fishing are allowed at Rock Point, Marina Point, and Canada Campgrounds. Electric fish-cleaning stations, floating fishing docks, five boat ramp lanes, and three courtesy fishing docks serve anglers well to lure walleye, wiper, largemouth and white bass, crappie, and channel and flathead catfish. White bass and wiper are rated good.

A low-water boat ramp is available when conditions require it. Seasonal rainbow trout fisheries are maintained in the stilling basin below the dam and in the river directly above the reservoir. Trout are stocked in the stilling basin several times each year. Hunting is permitted in the wildlife area, which is home to white-tailed deer, quail, waterfowl, turkeys, and squirrels.

**CAMPING AND FACILITIES**—Six campgrounds all offer primitive camping. Point Rock, Lakeview, and Old Marina offer water and electricity for RVs. All campgrounds are open year-round except Marina Point. Old Marina is the most developed campground. Shower houses and restrooms, playgrounds, boat ramps, courtesy docks, picnic shelters, and a swimming beach round out the facilities. A sand volleyball court, a horseshoe pit, and a playground entertain groups and families.

**TRAFFIC**—Below average annually, but steady throughout summer months.

**LOCATION AND DIRECTIONS**—In Rooks County. Travel I-70 to Hays (Exit 159). Follow U.S. Highway 183 north for 37 miles. At Stockton, turn west on U.S. Highway 24 and go 8 miles. The park entrance will be on your left.

**ENTRY**—The park office is open 8:00 A.M. to 4:30 P.M., Monday–Friday. During high season (May 15 to Labor Day), hours are extended to 8:00 P.M. on Fridays and Saturdays. Campgrounds are open year-round, but access to water is available only from April 15 to October 15.

**ON THE WEB**—www.kdwp.state.ks.us, search "Webster."

**CONTACT**—In Stockton, phone KDWP at (785) 425-6775; or write 1210 Nine Road, Stockton, KS 67669-8834.

**NEARBY**—**NICODEMUS NATIONAL HISTORIC SITE** lies just west of Webster State Park on U.S. Highway 24. Visitors can tour the grounds of this unique all-black settlement that was formed in 1877 by former slaves; five of the original buildings remain. The township hall is used as a visitor center for exhibits, audio-visual programs, and a bookstore. Today the families of original settlers still carry on their ancestors' sense of accomplishment. Ranger-guided tours are available by appointment. Open daily from 8:30 A.M. to 5:00 P.M. except holidays, but it's best to phone ahead: (785) 839-4233; or write 304 Washington Avenue, Nicodemus, KS 67625. See www.nps. gov/nico. No entry fee.

# Lovewell State Park

WHAT IS IT that puts this small park on the map? It's truly a destination for people who want to get off the beaten path. If the whole point of camping is to leave civilization behind for a natural setting, then you're likely to find charm in this park, which offers over 300 primitive campsites, many on the shoreline of Lovewell Reservoir.

Oak-covered chalk hills and bluffs meet upland prairie. The south shore of the lake is bestowed with high bluffs that block Kansas winds, keeping the waters calm. Almost on the Nebraska border, Lovewell State Park began as a favorite escape for anglers. If your family isn't into fishing, they can enjoy the swimming beach, horseshoe pit, baseball field, and volleyball and basketball courts. A marina offers fishing supplies, groceries, and a grill. Plan your visit around some of the special events offered throughout the year, including a kid's fishing derby, a sand castle contest, an archery course, a campground cook-off, and fishing tournaments.

Located in the Smoky Hills Region, the park also offers sites of historic interest, such as a limestone schoolhouse that hosts church services on Sundays in summer months. An interpretive center at the entrance illustrates native species and provides a wildlife-habitat overlook.

**WILDLIFE**—Black-tailed prairie dogs bark from grasses north of the reservoir. Quail, ring-necked pheasant, and wild turkeys strut through the grasses. Look for cormorants, white pelicans, gulls, and herons in the open waters and coves.

**HIKING AND BIKING**—Short hiking or bike paths connect the amenities and park roads. Hikers can follow the shoreline along the reservoir, although there is no maintained trail. Bikers can ride the park roads.

**FISHING AND HUNTING**—The shielded south shore helps keep the lake calm despite the windy conditions in Kansas. Flathead catfish, walleye, and white crappie are rated fair, while white bass are rated good. A full-service marina, boat ramps, fishing piers, and cleaning stations help anglers enjoy northern Kansas.

**OTHER**—A seven-station, 14-target archery range is offered on the west side of the park near the Willow camp area.

**CAMPING AND FACILITIES**—Six camping cabins are available by reservation. Utility sites, primitive sites, and improved primitive sites are all available. All sites in Pioneer, Willow, and Walleye Point feature lake views. The park provides shower houses, vault toilets, boat ramps, a marina, a fish-cleaning station, picnic shelters, playgrounds, recreation fields, and a swimming beach.

**TRAFFIC**—Average, heaviest in July.

**LOCATION AND DIRECTIONS**—Located in Jewell County. From I-70 at Salina, take Exit 250 and head north on U.S. Highway 81 to Belleville. Turn west on U.S. Highway 36 and then north on State Highway 14. Follow the signs to Webber or Lovewell Reservoir.

**ENTRY**—State park entrance fees apply. Open all year. The park has freeze-proof water hydrants, but some facilities will be turned off during winter.

**ON THE WEB**—www.kdwp.state.ks.us, search "Lovewell."

**CONTACT**—KDWP office in Webber, (785) 753-4971; 2446 250 Road, Webber, KS 66970.

**NEARBY**—PAWNEE INDIAN VILLAGE STATE HISTORIC SITE is a significant archeological find. West of Lovewell State Park near the town of Republic, a large and thriving Pawnee village was built on a grassy knoll overlooking the Republican River. Visitors can see an excavated floor of the largest lodge, panoramic exhibits, and a Pawnee sacred bundle. During the tour, a Pawnee elder describes his culture and a video on Pawnee history helps to illustrate the lifestyle of this tribe. Walk in the footsteps of the Pawnee on the half-mile Kitkehahki nature trail, but don't forget to wear bug spray. Hours are Wednesday–Saturday, 10:00 A.M. to 5:00 P.M., and Sunday, 1:00 P.M. to 5:00 P.M. Admission fees apply. Call (785) 361-2255 or see www.kshs.org. The museum is 8 miles north of U.S. Highway 36 on State Highway 266, at 480 Pawnee Trail, Republic KS 66964.

# Kanopolis Lake and State Park

R ED SANDY TRAILS, pillars and hoodoos, sandstone caves, wind-eroded slickrock, and canyons are reminiscent of Arizona or Utah—but Kansas? Located in the Smoky Hills Region near Salina, Kanopolis State Park is only 30 miles south of I-70, but it offers a major change in scenery. You may feel as if you've been transported to the Wild West without the cost or the travel time. And the best part is that it feels remote; you won't find any national park crowds here.

Streams running through the park once watered bison and wild horses. Legends say Pawnee Indians hid stolen horses from the Cheyenne in Box Canyon. As you hike or ride the 25 miles of trails in one of Kansas's oldest state parks, you may find yourself borrowing that famous line from *The Wizard of Oz*: "I've a feeling we're not in Kansas anymore."

**WILDLIFE**—The lake at Kanopolis attracts hundreds of migrating visitors in the spring and again in the fall. Bald eagles soar in winter. Turkey vultures float in the summer air. Ring-necked pheasants may even be seen on the side of the road in the grasses. White-tailed deer, quail, and coyotes also love the grasses. Prairie dog colonies exist both on the trail and near the park road. Beaver prints are as common as footprints on the sandy paths. Gnawed stumps offer further evidence, but you'll find picture-perfect dams on the creeks crossing the Horsethief Trail. Located in an area behind the park office, a half-mile trail circles a cattail-lined pond in the Horsethief area, with photo blinds for wildlife viewing. Red-winged blackbirds call to each other while tree swallows swoop over the pond. Prairie grasses and wildflowers spatter the rolling hills throughout the park. In addition to purple poppy mallow, spiderwort, prairie wild rose, and butterfly milkweed, you'll also find western adornments such as yucca or soapweed.

**HIKING**—BUFFALO TRACK CANYON NATURE TRAIL is a self-guiding trail reserved for foot traffic, with coordinating markers found trailside. The sandy path dries quickly even after heavy rains. Pick up a trail brochure or download it from the KDWP Web site before you set out. Following the trail can be confusing, as there are several spur trails, so allow plenty of time to get sidetracked. The trail is worthy of any effort you put into it. The mapped route is three-quarters of a mile and can be done as an

Climbing sandstone outcrops at Kanopolis State Park.

out-and-back or as a connector to the Horsethief Trail. Take the middle trail of the three paths from trailhead C. You'll spot mini-caves eroded from Dakota sandstone in the upper reaches; you can even scramble up to some for a great lunch spot. Interesting wind-carved sculptures are left behind for admirers.

**MULTI-USE TRAIL SYSTEM.** A series of trails for hikers, bikers, and equestrians can keep you busy from sunrise to sunset. Hikers will not be able to complete the circuit in a day and camping is not allowed on the trail, so plan your route carefully. Pick up a color-coded trail map at the park office before setting out. Camping equestrians should use the Rockin' K Campground and trailhead A. Equestrians visiting for the day should use trailhead B. Hikers and cyclists begin at trailhead C. Restrooms and picnic tables are located at the trailheads. Hikers and bikers should dress accordingly for numerous water crossings. At times, the streams may be knee-deep. Note that the trail passes through areas where hunting is allowed.

**ROCKIN' K TRAIL** is an easy 2-mile linear path used to connect the Horsethief Campgrounds to the trail system.

**HORSETHIEF TRAIL** (5.5 miles) can be accessed from any of the three paths found at trailhead C. Lovely streams lined with red sand, caves, and colorful rock outcrops are found along the trail, which leads over rolling hills covered with prairie grasses to vistas high over the reservoir's marshy end. Watch for industrious beavers or listen for their conversation. Passing through a gate on the west end of the Horsethief Trail, continue right to view a red rock sandstone canyon that delights anyone privileged enough to see it. Turn left through the gate to access the Prairie Trail.

**PRAIRIE TRAIL** (6 miles) leads to vistas over the reservoir through a prairie dog town and then either loops back to Red Rock Canyon (not to be missed) or continues north to the Alum Creek Trail. Closed October 31 through February 1 for hunting season. The trail is easy to moderate in difficulty, with one water crossing.

**ALUM CREEK TRAIL** (8 miles) loops through vast prairie and pasture, canyons, and creeks to the Table Rock formations. There are two stream crossings on this trail of moderate difficulty. The trail is more secluded and a little tricky, with shortcuts marked in green. Be sure you have plenty of daylight before adding the Alum Creek Trail to your day hike. Closed October 31 to February 1 for hunting season.

**SPLIT BOULDER TRAIL** is located in the Horsethief Area and was designed for beginning mountain bikers. The trail is just under a mile in length and offers views of the lake and rocky outcrops. Concretions, geological features made of sedimentary rock and unique to the Smoky Hills Region, are on display.

**BIKING**—The multi-use trail is open to cyclists. Ideal for mountain bikers, the trail offers some deep sand with slickrock outcroppings and shelves. Moderate climbs, technical challenges, and stunning scenery may take your breath away. Begin at trailhead C. (See Multi-Use Trail System.) The Split Boulder Trail was designed with beginning cyclists in mind.

**HORSEBACK RIDING**—Camping with horses is allowed at the Rockin' K Campground, but reservations are recommended. With the exception of the nature trail, all trails are open to equestrians, who should begin at trailheads A or B. (See Multi-Use Trail System.) For individuals and small groups, Goverland Stage Stop offers quided trail rides and stagecoach rides, which will take you on short rides to Indian Cave or longer rides to Red Rock Canyon. They are located at the General Store in the Rockin' K Campground.

**FISHING AND HUNTING**—According to the park brochure, white bass fishing is good as soon as the ice thaws near Bluff Creek in April or during upriver spawning in March and April. Walleyes spawn along the face of the dam in early spring; later, they prefer under water ledges and drop-offs. Crappie fishing is best from March to May, but they can be caught year-round near the dam or Yankee Run Cove. Channel cats are best caught on summer nights at the upper end of the lake. Wipers provide a sport fishing challenge. Consider ice fishing for crappie, walleye, and white bass. Most of the 11,000-acre hunting area is at the upper end of the reservoir along the Smoky Hill River. Pheasant, quail, prairie chickens, rabbits, and white-tailed and mule deer are abundant. Coyotes, fox squirrels, mink, muskrat, beavers, raccoon, and opossums are also common. Portions of the waterfowl refuge and developed park areas are closed to hunting.

**PADDLING**—Canoeing is an option at Riverside Park near the dam outlet when water is high enough. Check with park rangers in advance when planning a canoe trip. There are no rentals available.

**OTHER**—You'll find an ATV area and motorcycle trail at Venango Park. The small park is under 30 acres and the trail runs approximately 1 mile.

**AUTO TOUR**—The Kanopolis Lake Legacy Tour is a self-guided auto tour that indicates 27 points of interest in the area surrounding the park. Most of the tour is on sand roads. Pick up a map at the park's information center, the first stop on the tour. Wagon-wheel trail ruts, a family cemetery, a petroglyph site, hills, and buttes and bluffs of the Dakota formation are some of the highlights on the auto tour. Even if you don't have the time or stamina to ride unpaved roads for 80 miles, the brochure itself offers an interesting collection of historic tidbits.

**CAMPING AND FACILITIES**—Four park areas offer all the usual amenities. Riverside and Venango are managed by the Corps of Engineers (COE). KDWP manages Langley Point and Horsethief. A marina at Langley Point offers boat slip rental, gas and oil, and a general store and snack bar in season. Two undeveloped access areas, Yankee Run and Boldt Bluff, are managed by the COE. Located on the west side of the lake, these areas can be reached only via an unpaved road where primitive camping and fishing are allowed. There are beaches at Langley Point and Venango. All developed areas have picnic tables, toilets, water supply, showers, primitive and improved camping, and sanitary dump stations. All areas but Riverside offer boat ramps.

**TRAFFIC**—Below average, heaviest in May.

**LOCATION AND DIRECTIONS**—In Ellsworth County, south-west of Salina. Take State Highway 140 west from Salina toward Carneiro and turn south on State Highway 141. To locate the trailheads, turn right at Venango and stay right at every juncture. To locate the information center, turn left from Highway 141 just after crossing the dam.

**ENTRY**—State park fees apply at Horsethief and Langley Point. Office hours may thwart your plans to pick up information, so request it ahead of time from your KDWP regional office or visit the Web site. Offices are open 8:00 A.M. to 4:30 P.M., Monday–Friday. The Prairie and Alum Creek trails are closed to horseback riding and mountain bikes from November 1 through January 31 as a safety precaution for hunting season. The Horse-thief Trail, Buffalo Track Canyon Nature Trail, and Rockin' K Trail remain open year-round, although portions may be closed if water crossings become hazardous.

**ON THE WEB**—www.kdwp.state.ks.us, search "Kanopolis." Equestrian outfitter, Goverland Stage Stop: www.goverlandstagestop.com.

**CONTACT**—Kanopolis State Park, (785) 546-2565; 200 Horsethief Road, Marquette, KS 67464. Corps of Engineers, (785) 546-2294. Goverland Stage Stop, (785) 826-0789, (785) 546-2565.

**NEARBY**—Children and adults will love **ROLLING HILLS WILDLIFE ADVENTURE,** the immaculate zoological park that showcases 80 unique and even rare species. While the park is small on acreage, it allows unusual close-up views and more interactivity than most large zoos with excellent landscaping. Often, zookeepers are nearby tending to the animals, ready to answer your questions. Imagine mountain lions that play with catnip four feet away from you. Curious giraffes tower overhead to see who is visiting. An enormous white tiger naps lazily on a tree trunk. Mountain goats pose on a boulder. Lions protect their pride with a thundering roar. Pick a cool day and most animals will be out in plain view. Visitors can ride a tram, but the park is small enough to hoof it in just a couple of hours.

Afterward, visit the museum for a truly unique experience. Walk through seven ecosystems around the world, including the Arctic, the Far East, and a rainforest. Animatronics and taxidermy are used in simulated habitats to create lifelike exhibits that showcase animals you've never seen or even heard of. Occasional traveling exhibits are a bonus. A restaurant and gift shop, restrooms, and vending machine are available. A huge picnic area is adjacent to the parking lot. Separate fees for the zoo and the museum apply; parking is free. Strollers, wheelchairs, and tram rides require extra fees. For further information, visit www.rollinghillswildlife.com or phone (785) 827-9488. Summer hours, 8:00 A.M. to 5:00 P.M.; winter hours, 9:00 A.M. to 5:00 P.M. daily Closed Christmas Eve and Day and New Year's Day. Located 6 miles west of Salina off I-70 (Exit 244), on Hedville Road. Watch for billboards and signs.

# Mushroom Rock State Park
## and Rock City National Natural Landmark

MUSHROOM ROCK STATE PARK, the smallest of the Kansas State Parks, will likely take you longer to reach than explore. This day-use park beckons visitors to follow a short path that leads to a geological phenomenon: rock formations resembling giant mushrooms that are larger than humans and appear to grow right out of the prairie. In reality, the "mushroom tops" are huge sandstone boulders composed of harder mineral or rock that is slower to erode than the softer rock beneath the boulders, which erodes more quickly, forming the pedestals. The historic Smoky Hill Wagon Trail once crossed this vicinity. It is said that Native Americans and settlers used the historic landmarks as a meeting place. Beautiful photos with long shadows can be taken early or late in the day. Be sure to explore both halves of the area, which has been split by the country road. There are no fees.

Towering sandstone concretions at Rock City National Natural Landmark.

**WILDLIFE**—Small mammals may be hiding in the grasses, while reptiles like to warm themselves on rocks and outcroppings. Look for colorful collared lizards and tread with care.

**CAMPING AND FACILITIES**—A parking lot, picnic tables, and a primitive toilet are your only facilities. Camping is not allowed.

**LOCATION AND DIRECTIONS**—In Ellsworth County. Take I-70 to Exit 238 and turn south on Brookville Road then west on State Highway 140 to Carneiro. Follow signs to the park.

**ENTRY**—No entrance fees. For day use only.

**ON THE WEB**—www.kdwp.state.ks.us, search "Mushroom."

**CONTACT**—For information on Mushroom Rock State Park, call Kanopolis State Park at (785) 546-2565; 200 Horsethief Road, Marquette, KS 67464.

**NEARBY**—Nicknamed **ROCK CITY,** a geological display north of Salina near Minneapolis, offers a field full of sandstone concretions. These phenomena are formed when sediments surround and encompass a nucleus to form spheres; the particles are cemented with minerals from a water source. Softer minerals then erode faster, leaving the concretions behind. If you use your imagination, they resemble giant rusted cannon balls that litter ancient battlefields. It's a bit difficult to think of Rock City as a natural area instead of a tourist attraction, but it's worth a mention; this National Natural Landmark illustrates a rare natural process and contains more specimens than Mushroom Rock State Park. Rock City is located in Ottawa County 3.6 miles south of Minneapolis, Kansas, off State Highway 106 on Ivy Road. Facilities include restrooms, water, a picnic area, and a gift shop. A small admission fee is charged from May through August. For information, call (785) 392-3068.

# Maxwell Wildlife Refuge
## and McPherson State Fishing Lake

O N THE EDGE of the Smoky Hills and McPherson Lowlands regions, Maxwell Wildlife Refuge offers visitors an opportunity to see herds of bison and elk, as well as native wildflowers and grasses, from the comfort of a narrated tram tour. Beginning in 1859 with only a small herd on their private homestead, the Maxwell family dreamed of creating a beautiful preserve with rolling hills, creeks, and springs where buffalo could roam freely. Nearly a century later, land was donated and bison were reintroduced to establish a wildlife refuge. Today, 200 head of bison and 50 elk roam on 2,800 acres of preserved land. Spring brings renewal and the emergence of young calves as birds migrate amid a sea of green hills. Summer adds fields of wildflowers to the equation. Male elk begin gathering their harems in the fall and provide quite a thrill to lucky visitors who hear their unmistakable bugle calls. Colors turn red, gold, and rust through October and into November. In winter, majestic elk in full antlers keep a higher profile for visitors while bison sport heavy winter coats.

At the visitor center you can reserve your place on a tram tour, review your prairie history, and of course shop for souvenirs or snacks in the gift shop. Climb to the top of an observation tower to spot wildlife; then continue down the road to McPherson State Fishing Lake to cast your line, take a hike, or enjoy a picnic on the prairie.

**WILDLIFE**—Herds of 200 bison and 50 elk wander at will. Over 100 species of birds have been sighted at the preserve.

**HIKING**—The **GYPSUM CREEK TRAIL** is a 1.5-mile (roundtrip), self-guiding nature trail. Although the preserve is predominantly prairie, the mowed trail passes through woods and climbs over sand hills for scenic views of the preserve, taunting you with the clear waters of Gypsum Creek at the end of the trail. You may see beaver dams on Gypsum Creek, but bison and elk will not share the trail. Beware of poison ivy. Follow Pueblo Road past the visitor center to the trailhead at the southwest corner of the lake. Brochures are available.

**FISHING AND HUNTING**—McPherson State Fishing Lake has a steep, rocky shoreline near the dam and shallow mud flats on the opposite end. The lake is stocked with channel cat, black bullhead, black crappie, redear sunfish, and bluegill. Largemouth bass are rated excellent. Anglers will find piers and a boat launch on the west side of the lake.

**TRAM TOURS**—Tram tours can be arranged for a per-person fee through the Friends of Maxwell, a private nonprofit foundation. Advance reservations are highly recommended. Regularly scheduled tours depart at 10:00 A.M. on Saturdays. Groups of 15 or more can schedule private tours any day of the week. Campfire meals can also be purchased. All proceeds fund the foundation, which provides labor and funding for tours, educational programs, and special events for visitors.

**CAMPING AND FACILITIES**—Primitive camping is allowed at McPherson State Fishing Lake. A few sites are available within the camp loop at the end of the gravel road. Primitive restrooms, fire rings, grills, and picnic tables are available at the lake. Fishing piers and a boat launch are located on the deeper west side of the lake. Boating is restricted to fishing purposes only. Visitors must pack out all garbage.

**LOCATION AND DIRECTIONS**—In McPherson County. Take I-135 to Exit 60. Go east on U.S. Highway 56, north on 27th Avenue, and west on Pueblo Road to the visitor center.

**ENTRY**—There is a per-person fee for tours, but no entrance fee. Hiking is not permitted within the refuge, as bison can be unpredictable and aggressive during breeding season.

**ON THE WEB**—For maps, see www.kdwp.state.ks.us, search "Maxwell"; Friends of Maxwell, www.cyberkraft.com/maxwell.

**CONTACT**—For KDWP, call (620) 628-4592; or write 2577 Pueblo Road, Canton, KS 67428. For tour reservations, call Friends of Maxwell, (620) 628-4455; or write 2565 Pueblo Road, Canton, KS 67428.

# Coronado Heights Park

JUST OUTSIDE LINDSBORG awaits one of the most scenic overlooks in Kansas; Coronado Heights is a 300-foot-high hill capped with weather-resistant Dakota sandstone. If it weren't for the sandstone cap, this hill would have eroded into the unending vista below. Between Coronado Heights and the Smoky Hills lies a valley dotted with red barns, farmhouses, and cedar trees. After a spring snowfall, the Smoky Hills resemble snow-capped mountains on the horizon.

As you approach Coronado from the dirt road below, a solitary hill looms with a medieval castle on its crest and a cemetery at its base. You have arrived when you see an enormous stone gate welcoming you to begin the climb. If you have plenty of energy, hike to the top on the foot trail that winds along the paved road. The rippled sands of what was once the ocean floor now appear to be converted into sandstone outcrops. Mixed-grass prairie, wild-flowers, and yucca plants grow alongside the red sandy trail. Colorful lichen attempt to return the castle and sandstone boulders to dust. If you drive to the top, be sure to walk the trail that skirts the outer edge of the hilltop.

The castle is a shelter and overlook platform completed by the Work Projects Administration (WPA) in 1932. A matching outhouse, a fire pit, and numerous picnic tables adorn the hilltop. Be sure to pack a lunch just to linger at the state's most beautiful picnic sites. Visitors will find a staircase inside the castle that leads to a fortress overlook, in case the 300-foot hill isn't high enough for quality photos. The Smoky Valley Historical Association (SVHA) obtained the land from Swedish pioneer farm families in 1919 and built the walking trail and auto road before handing over development to the WPA. Today, the SVHA still manages and maintains this beautiful park and overlook for the public.

How did the name come to be? In 1915, a professor from Lindsborg found Spanish armor chain mail at an excavation site nearby. The hill was subsequently named for the famous Spanish explorer, Francisco Vásquez de Coronado.

Pack a lunch for one of Kansas's most scenic picnic areas, Coronado Heights.

**HIKING**—A very steep, one-way, 1.5-mile foot trail winds up the hill along the paved road. Colorful lichen, sandstone outcrops, stone steps, wild-flowers, and plants add to the gorgeous panoramas.

**CAMPING AND FACILITIES**—Camping is not allowed. A primitive restroom, a fire pit and barbecue grills, picnic tables, a shelter, a lookout tower, and parking are provided.

**LOCATION AND DIRECTIONS**—In Saline County. From Lindsborg, follow State Highway 4 west. Take Coronado Avenue (County Road 450) 3 miles north to Winchester Road (Coronado Heights Road) and go 1 mile west. Look for the gate on your right.

**ENTRY**—No entrance fee. The gates are open from 8:00 A.M. to 11:00 P.M.

**ON THE WEB**—www.lindsborg.org.

**CONTACT**—Lindsborg Chamber of Commerce, (785) 227-3706.

Lichen-covered sandstone caps the hill named Coronado Heights.

## *Geology of the Red Hills Region*

ADJOINING THE OKLAHOMA BORDER, located mostly in Clark, Comanche, and Barber counties, the Red Hills Region converges with the High Plains Region for varied topography and scenery like that of an old Spaghetti Western. The deep red color results when iron in the soil is exposed to oxygen. Roughly 260 million years ago during the Permian Period, thousands of feet of red shale, siltstone, and sandstone, together with contrasting gypsum and dolomite, were deposited in the area. These Permian deposits have since been exposed by erosion, forming a series of sweeping flat-topped red hills and buttes that tower over the valleys.

Sinkholes are prevalent in the Red Hills Region, which were most likely formed by the solution of salt and gypsum beds lying hundreds of feet below the surface. As the salt and gypsum dissolved, large depressions were left in the surface. Big Basin and Little Basin are two examples of this phenomenon (see page 17–18).

# Gypsum Hills Scenic Byway

EXTENDING 41 MILES between Medicine Lodge and Coldwater, this paved scenic byway on U.S. Highway 160 just might become your favorite of the Kansas byways. The few who travel here are treated to views of red canyons and soil, flat mesas, soothing valleys, and blue watering holes. Red rock landmarks speckled with cedar and white gypsum outcrops provide the beautiful backdrop.

Stunning colors in summer months are nothing less than breathtaking, but vistas are so large that they're difficult to photograph. To round out the area's physical splendor, Barber State Fishing Lake lies just outside Medicine Lodge on the eastern end of the byway and Lake Coldwater awaits at the western end of the scenic journey.

For those who like a little dirt with their adventure, take an extra hour to drive a 20-mile extension on smooth dirt roads. Closer views of landmarks with names like Flowerpot Mound and Twin Peaks make the extra miles worthwhile.

**AUTO TOUR**—Begin your auto tour with a stop at Barber State Fishing Lake and Wildlife Area 1 mile north of Medicine Lodge on U.S. Highway 281. This state lake is the smaller of the area's two lakes but also seems more intimate and natural. The rural park is manicured and well-maintained with a trail worthy of hiking.

Just south of Medicine Lodge, stop to see the home of Prohibition activist Carry Nation. Or, perhaps a visit to the Stockade Museum will be of greater interest: here you can see an original cabin, stockade, and gypsum home from the frontier days in Medicine Lodge.

Heading west on U.S. Highway 160, you begin the 41-mile Gypsum Hills Scenic Byway. Be sure to pull out at the two designated overlooks for photos. If you're interested in the dirt route, you'll find the detour about 3 miles west of the intersection of Highway 281. Head south on Gypsum Hill Road (paved), west on Scenic Drive, and north on Lake City Road. The dirt loop is well-marked and truly showcases the best of Red Hills scenery, with the most stunning views from Gypsum Hill Road and Lake City Road. Continue west on Highway 160 to continue the scenic byway.

Just 1 mile southwest of the town of Coldwater, Lake Coldwater is significantly larger (250 acres) than Barber Lake (77 acres): the city park allows boating, swimming, and fishing and offers camping and picnic areas. A short nature trail can be walked at the south end of the park. A 4-mile road circles the spring-fed lake and doubles as a nice hike or bike trail.

**WILDLIFE**—This semi-arid environment supports inhabitants uncommon in Kansas. Because the Red Hills Region is composed of minerals that dissolve, the area is riddled with caves. You may see bats flitting and diving at sunset. Birds escaping the winters of the Rockies are attracted to the cedar tree berries. Look for armadillos, roadrunners, black-tailed prairie dogs, coyote, and bobcat tracks. It's a rarity when visitors happen upon the Texas horned lizard, a collared lizard, a western rattlesnake, or a tarantula.

**HIKING**—Hikers will find a nature trail at Lake Coldwater's south end. Barber State Fishing Lake offers the **RED CEDAR NATURE TRAIL,** which is 1.75 miles (one-way) of natural tread. Although it crosses the red dirt road many times, it is relatively easy to follow. The route is illustrated at the trailhead and the park map is available at the entrance. The trail crosses a grassy dike and traverses woodlands, thickets of sumac, and cedar tunnels, while the lake frequently sparkles through the foliage and glowing grasses. Wildflowers, dragonflies, and butterflies keep you company. Retrace your steps on the trail or walk the park road that crosses the dam to complete a 2.5-mile loop. Neither of the trails showcases the Gypsum Hills Region. To hike with views of the red buttes and mesas, find Lake City Road on Highway 160 and hike south on the unpaved road.

**BIKING**—Both the scenic byway and the dirt extension provide challenging yet scenic routes for the experienced cyclist. The traffic on both is light, but there are no shoulders. Parking pullouts can be found at mile markers 217 and 219. Ride early to avoid heat and traffic.

**FISHING AND HUNTING**—A minimal entrance fee is required at Lake Coldwater, where fishing is permitted with a license. Piers, docks, and boat ramps are provided. Barber State Fishing Lake has populations of large-mouth bass, channel catfish, walleye, crappie, bluegill, and carp. Channel cats are stocked annually. The northern 80 acres at Barber State Fishing Lake are open to public hunting for deer, turkey, quail, dove, waterfowl, and cottontail rabbit. Boat ramps and fishing docks are available.

**CAMPING AND FACILITIES**—Barber State Fishing Lake provides primitive camping and restrooms, boat ramps and courtesy docks, and a group shelter. Primitive and improved camping is allowed at Lake Coldwater, where shower houses and modern restrooms are also provided.

**LOCATION AND DIRECTIONS**—The scenic byway is in Barber and Comanche Counties between Medicine Lodge and Coldwater. From Wichita, head southwest on State Highway 42 for 44 miles to U.S. Highway 160. Continue west on Highway 160 for 31 miles to Medicine Lodge.

**ENTRY**—Parks are open year-round with limited facilities in the off-season.

**ON THE WEB**—www.ksbyways.org.

**CONTACT**—Lake Coldwater, (620) 582-2940; Stockade Museum, (620) 886-3553; Barber State Fishing Lake, (620) 672-0779.

**NEARBY**—One of four state nature centers in Kansas, the **PRATT EDUCATION CENTER** is quite extensive. Some of the many unique exhibits that make a stop worthwhile will teach visitors about raptors of Kansas, grassland regions of Kansas, tracks of Kansas mammals, and how wildlife survives Kansas winters. The Aquarium Room displays native fish species and features the history of the Pratt Fish Hatchery, also on site. An impressive 128 species of birds and their eggs are displayed in the Bird Room.

**DIRECTIONS**—From Medicine Lodge, head north on U.S. Highway 281 for about 30 miles, then east on U.S. Highway 54, and then south on SE 25th Avenue to 512 SE 25th Avenue. For more information, call KDWP in Pratt, (620) 672-5911. Hours are 8:00 A.M. to 4:30 P.M., Monday–Friday (except holidays). No entrance fee.

## Geology of the Arkansas River and Wellington-McPherson Lowlands Regions

THESE TWO SEPARATE BUT SIMILAR REGIONS in southwest and central Kansas can be described as an alluvial plain. Streams and rivers, particularly the Arkansas River, transport sediments from the Rocky Mountains down a great yet gradual slope across the High Plains, eventually reaching the Lowlands. At the foot of the Rockies, Denver sits 1 mile high—5,280 feet. Mount Sunflower, on the western edge of Kansas, is 4,039 feet high. Traveling east, the slope is reduced to an elevation of 2,000 feet at Hays. Continuing down slope, Hutchinson nears 1,500 feet, Wichita is at 1,300 feet, and Wellington, in the heart of the Lowlands, is only 1,200 feet above sea level. As the slope becomes more and more gradual, the rivers lose momentum and leave behind sand, silt, and gravel. Sandsage prairies, sand dunes, or sand hills are the result. The deposits also act as aquifers, absorbing and retaining water underground.

In addition to the great deposits of sandy soil, the Wellington-McPherson Lowlands sit upon a deep bed of salt. Salt was left behind after the evaporation of the Permian Period sea. Sand later buried the salt bed, which is sometimes as much as 400 feet deep. Quivira National Wildlife Refuge sits on this bed of salt, which has seeped to the surface and resulted in the formation of saltwater marshes, a rather unusual occurrence.

# Sand Hills State Park

HOW WERE SAND DUNES CREATED in the Lowlands Region? Rivers such as the Arkansas carried sediments from the Rocky Mountains across the High Plains and eventually unloaded the sediments on the lower-lying plains. Later, prevailing winds blew the finer sand grains out of the river valley into piles, forming a band of unstable dunes that shifted and changed shape until vegetation gained a solid foothold. Today, the dunes are considered inactive, anchored down by tallgrass prairie, brush, and woodland.

Sand Hills State Park offers the best illustration of these sand deposits, with dunes ranging from 10 to 40 feet high. These dunes support life: singing birds, tall waving grasses, yucca, and wildflowers delight the hiker or equestrian on 14 miles of sand-covered prairie trail. For half the year, the scenery is subdued and moody. Subtle, neutral colors like tan, gold, bronze, celery, and lavender tint your photos. On a sunny day, memories may transport you to the Outer Banks of North Carolina or a grassy seaside. Later in summer, wildflowers flourish in the sun and sandy soils, adding a louder splash of color to the canvas.

**WILDLIFE**—The primary habitat is tallgrass prairie, which can be maintained only with controlled burns. Waves of bluestem cover rolling dunes. Cottonwood and dogwood bushes compose the woodlands. Wildflowers and blooming shrubs abound spring through summer. Small ponds on the east side attract waterfowl and thirsty mammals. The pond trail offers hikers two wildlife observation blinds for spying on ducks, geese, songbirds, deer, or muskrat.

**HIKING**—There are no roads within the park, but four trailheads on the perimeter allow walk-in access. While the sandy trails dry quickly, expect some mud after rainy periods. The following three trails are designated for hiking only. They can be connected for a total of 3.5 miles:

**COTTONWOOD TRAIL** is a half-mile self-guided, interpretive trail on the north side of the park. It loops through a sandy, wooded area. Restrooms and brochures are available at the trailhead.

**PRAIRIE TRAIL** is a 1.9-mile sand-and-grass trail. It loops through woody thickets and brush, crossing prairie and dunes on mostly level terrain.

**DUNE TRAIL** is a 1-mile loop. It leads to the top of the highest dune and down to a low-lying area. Steps made from railroad ties help you climb for outstanding views of the trail below. If you have limited time, choose this trail for its length and scenery.

**MULTIPURPOSE TRAILS FOR HIKING AND HORSEBACK RIDING:**

**POND TRAIL** runs 1.5 miles. It begins in the northeast corner of the park and leads to marshlike ponds where visitors can take advantage of wildlife blinds along the trail. Canada geese, mallards, and American coots may squabble for privacy. A restroom and picnic tables are located at the ponds. It's not the most scenic of hikes, but it might be worth your while if special visitors drop in from the sky.

**ROLLING HILLS TRAIL** is the longest in the system. It measures 3.8 miles and boasts bountiful wildflowers during spring months.

**BLUESTEM SPUR TRAIL** connects with the Rolling Hills Trail to form a loop hike. The spur trail traverses bluestem grasses and rolls over sand hill vistas for 1.2 miles. Hikers and riders will find a restroom on the trail.

**TALLGRASS TRAIL** is a 2.2-mile loop that can be added to either the Pond Trail or the Rolling Hills Trail.

Hiking sand dunes and subdued scenery at Sand Hills State Park.

**WOODLAND TRAIL** is a 2.2-mile linear trail that extends along cottonwood trees and dogwood bushes before making a loop and returning the same way.

**HORSEBACK RIDING**—All but the Dune, Prairie, and Cottonwood Trails are designated for horses. (See Hiking for trail descriptions.) Riders must remain on horse trails. A horse camp is currently being built on 40 acres surrounding a large pond. (See Camping and Facilities.)

**FISHING AND HUNTING**—In the near future, the largest pond at a new campground will be stocked for fishing. Archery hunting is issued through a drawing and available only by special permit. Deer, turkeys, and upland game birds may be plentiful at times.

**CAMPING AND FACILITIES**—Improved camping for RVs and equestrians is currently being constructed just outside the park boundaries, south of 56th Street. The campground will circle a pond with pull-through sites and back-in sites. Half of the sites will provide horse pens and the pond will be stocked with fish. Parking lots, restrooms, picnic tables, and benches will be provided.

**TRAFFIC**—Below average, heaviest in May and June.

**LOCATION AND DIRECTIONS**—In Reno County. From Hutchinson, take State Highway 61 north to 56th Street. Turn right and cross the railroad tracks to locate the park. Trailhead parking will be on your left. To reach trailheads on the north side of the park, take Highway 61 to 69th Street and turn right to cross the railroad tracks. Parking will be on your right.

**ENTRY**—A per-person fee is payable at the trailhead. The park is designated for day-use only. Burning occurs to maintain the prairie, usually in April; trails will be closed and signs will be posted in advance. Call the office at Cheney State Park to verify the schedule. Dogs are welcome on a leash. Fires of any kind are prohibited, including cigarettes, camp stoves, and grills.

**ON THE WEB**—Trail maps are available at www.kdwp.state.ks.us, search "Sand Hills."

**CONTACT**—KDWP staff at Cheney State Park also maintains and operates Sand Hills State Park, (316) 542-3664; 16000 NE 50th St., Cheney, KS 67025.

# Cheyenne Bottoms Wildlife Area
## and Wetlands and Wildlife National Scenic Byway

IN THE UNITED STATES, about 300,000 acres of wetland are destroyed every year. Today, over half of North America's wetlands have been destroyed for farming, highways, and construction. Designated as a "Wetland of International Importance" under a worldwide treaty, Cheyenne Bottoms becomes more important every year as this type of habitat becomes increasingly scarce. The primary purpose of the refuge is to supply food, water, and resting places for waterfowl, shorebirds, and wading birds during the migration seasons. Wetlands are also important to mammals such as beavers, mink, and various rodents. Naturally, raptors and predators gather where birds and small mammals flourish. Reptiles and amphibians are also important sources of food as well as predators of insects. So, all types of wildlife thrive on wetland habitat. Cheyenne Bottoms holds the distinction of being the largest marsh in the interior of the United States.

The Bottoms are a natural occurrence that is managed by humans. Movements in the earth's crust caused an enormous sink about 100 million years ago. KDWP uses pumps, dams, gates, and canals to regulate the depth of water on the refuge. The type of plants that thrive in the refuge may also be controlled through drowning, burning, or planting in order to provide proper food or habitat. Cattails are a perfect example: while some creatures need cattails, others prefer open spaces. Flooding is used to control the spread of these plants.

An observation tower offers a bird's-eye view of the refuge, which is generally covered with shallow water. At times, Kansas's high winds make the enormous pools resemble the Great Lakes as white caps slap the banks. If you prefer to stay off your feet, the Cheyenne Bottoms can be toured in about an hour without even leaving your vehicle. The pools are surrounded by gravel roadways, so visitors are always within sight of water; this makes bird-watching extremely convenient. In fact, you are more likely to focus your binoculars on wildlife from within your vehicle than on foot, as the birds tend to scatter when approached. Flocks of American coot begin their run on the water before banking off. You may see white-tailed deer run the length of a dike to avoid you and the water. Flocks of yellow-headed blackbirds, an unusual site for most of us, are commonly seen here. At times segregated and at times intermingled, common and uncommon ducks float the pools and canals on either side of the roadway. A single egret or heron might be spotted in waterlogged grasses. Look for pelicans and cormorants on man-made floats or islands in the distance.

**WILDLIFE**—Mammals that make the Bottoms their home include beaver, opossum, shrew, badger, mink, bobcat, coyote, raccoon, striped and spotted skunk, white-tailed and mule deer, black-tailed prairie dog, gopher, cottontail, jack rabbit, wood rat, muskrat, and mouse. Birds abound as well. It is estimated that 45 percent of North American shorebirds stop at the Bottoms during their spring migration. Three-quarters of all species of birds known to occur in Kansas have been recorded at the Bottoms. And in case you can't make it during migration season, there are 100 species that breed and nest on the area, 95 that spend the winter, and 63 that are permanent residents. It is also a critical habitat for threatened and endangered birds, including the whooping crane, peregrine falcon, bald eagle, piping plover, and least tern. More than 25 species of duck and geese stop at the Bottoms. In late October, the number of Canada and white-fronted geese, mallards, pintails, wigeon, gadwalls, blue-winged teal, redheads, and ruddy ducks can reach hundreds of thousands. Waterfowl and sandhill cranes begin arriving as early as February, wading birds begin arriving in March and April, and shorebirds arrive in late April and early May. By late May, the birds that are still present will tend to nest. The fall shorebird migration can begin as early as July and extend well into September and October. Peak period for duck viewing begins early to mid-October. Whooping cranes are most likely to stop in late October into early November. Bald eagles winter here as early as November and stay as late as March.

**HIKING**—The park map indicates dikes that are accessible for foot traffic only. Before wading into the marsh, be sure you are at a foot crossing. Depths can exceed four feet. Some roads or dikes are off-limits to all activities and will be clearly marked as such. Rattlesnakes are common in warm months and mosquitoes can make traveling on foot a nuisance. Consider insect repellent mandatory. In spring, the weather changes abruptly; be prepared for anything, especially a cold wind off the water.

**FISHING AND HUNTING**—Fishing is limited to carp and bullhead. Occasionally, channel cats, crappie, and bass are available after several continuous years of high water. Check with KDWP to determine what types of watercraft are allowed, as well as where and when they are allowed.

All hunters are required to obtain and complete a daily hunting permit, which can be found at all entrances, parking lots, and boat ramps. Pools one, five, and a portion of two are refuge areas where hunting and the use of watercraft are not permitted. No shooting is allowed from roads or dikes. Waterfowl season brings heavy hunting pressure on the weekends. In addition to waterfowl and pheasant, snipe and rail hunting is usually good as well. Quail and deer are also available. In the event of whooping crane activity, the pools where the activity occurs will be closed to all hunting. The Mitigation Marsh is reserved as a hunting area for youth under 16 years of age accompanied by no more than two adults. A handicapped-accessible hunting blind is available by reservation.

**AUTO TOUR**—Enter the southeast corner of the refuge from State Highway 156 and turn right to begin the 11-mile, counterclockwise drive, following the interpretive brochure that details 13 stops. You'll find coordinating kiosks along the roadways as you travel. Stops highlight the ecosystem, history, management techniques, and wildlife nesting and feeding habits. Download the auto tour from the KDWP Web site.

**CAMPING AND FACILITIES**—Primitive camping is allowed only in designated sites, 1 mile west of the area office. Only primitive toilets are available.

**LOCATION AND DIRECTIONS**—In Barton County. There are three entrances. The driving tour enters from Highway 156 just past the KDOT rest area. (From I-70, take Exit 225 and head west). The west entrance can be accessed from U.S. Highway 281. From Hoisington go south through Kanbrick and turn east. To use the central entrance, take State Highway 4 to the town of Redwing and turn south on NE 60 Avenue.

**ENTRY**—No entrance fees. Offices are not open on weekends.

**ON THE WEB**—Maps and driving tour can be downloaded at www.kdwp.state.ks.us, search "Cheyenne." For general information, visit www.cheyennebottoms.net.

**CONTACT**—24-hour hotline, (620) 793-7730. KDWP area office, (620) 793-3066; 56 NE 40 Road, Great Bend, KS 67530.

**NEARBY**—The **WETLANDS AND WILDLIFE SCENIC BYWAY** is a 76-mile route that wraps around both Cheyenne Bottoms Wildlife Refuge and Quivira National Wildlife Refuge. Unless you're happy to spend the entire day in your car, don't plan to travel the byway and see both natural areas in a day. Instead, spend the night in a nearby community and savor a couple of days exploring the route. This byway is all about the birds—the scenery is secondary. Communities on the byway have plans to implement interesting stops for nature and bird lovers, but some are not yet fully operational. Future plans include:

Raptor Rehab Center in Great Bend

Kansas Wetlands Interpretive Center

Songbird Habitat in Hoisington

In addition to the Cheyenne Bottoms and Quivira Refuges, visitors can enjoy the following attractions along the byway:

Dozier Vineyard and Winery in Ellinwood (open 1:00 P.M.–6:00 P.M.) with footpaths and trails in wooded areas

Hike/bike path along the Arkansas River in Great Bend

Brit Spaugh Zoo in Great Bend, which offers lively, narrated bird shows

For maps and information about the scenic byway, visit www.ksbyways.org. To sign up for Kansas park and trail updates, visit www.trailsofkansas.com.

# Quivira National Wildlife Refuge

LIKE CHEYENNE BOTTOMS, Quivira National Wildlife Refuge is of significant importance to migrating birds and creatures that inhabit wetlands. Located in the Arkansas River Lowlands, Quivira sits on a bed of salt, buried by sand and silt deposited by the Arkansas River. The result is an inland body of saltwater, a rather unusual occurrence.

Twenty-one miles of canal and dams are used to manipulate the depth of more than 30 pools across 7,000 acres of marshland. Positioned on the Central Flyway, over 300 species have been known to visit the marshes, grasslands, farmlands, and sand hills that compose the refuge. As with any refuge, spring and fall are the best times for viewing a variety of migrating species, many of which nest in the refuge. Many types of mammals and reptiles make this their home year-round, as well. No matter what the season, a visit early in the morning or late afternoon will yield the best wildlife watching.

A visitor center is located near the southern entrance, featuring displays of animal pelts and mounts. Educational highlights cover the migration process and endangered species. If you have all day to explore the refuge, enter at the south end and work your way north. If you only have a few hours, enter at the middle section and head north to hit the best highlights in a shorter time. Cutting off the southern section removes about a third of the 14-mile drive. There are numerous parking pullouts where you can set out on foot to hike the tops of dikes and dams that overlook the pools. The inhabitants are skittish when visitors approach, so tread lightly.

Do not forget to stock water, food, binoculars, and bug repellent. (Sprays are less effective in the wind.) Mosquitoes will even swarm your vehicle, a preview of what's to come when you step outside. Sometimes a strong wind will keep them away.

## WILDLIFE—

**FALL:** September to December brings the greatest number of geese and ducks (over 800,000) on their way to warmer places. Shorebirds and sandhill and whooping cranes (an endangered species) make a brief appearance. According to the U.S. Fish and Wildlife Service, the western edge of the Big Salt Marsh is favored by sandhill cranes, which visit mid-October through November.

Quivira National Wildlife Refuge offers a viewing tower for bird-watching.

**WINTER:** Bald and golden eagles winter in the marsh November through March. Ducks and geese will stay until the weather drives them on to warmer places.

**SPRING:** Warmer air brings the return of ducks and geese as well as shorebirds, white pelicans, cormorants, and gulls. Whooping cranes return mid-March to mid-April.

**SUMMER:** Resident raptors include Swainson's hawk, Mississippi kite, Northern harrier, American kestrel, and red-tailed hawk. Wild turkeys, ring-necked pheasant, and bobwhite quail are often seen in the grasslands, grain fields, and wooded edges. Snowy plovers, avocets, black-necked stilts, and white-faced ibis nest in the summer. The least tern is an endangered species that nests on the northern salt flats.

Mammals found around the marsh include white-tailed deer, black-tailed prairie dogs, beavers, raccoons, badgers, and coyotes.

**HIKING**—Two trails have been established, but you can hike almost anywhere. Signs are clearly posted when areas are closed. If you have time and good weather, hike the 4-mile drive around the Big Salt Marsh. A spotting scope is available near the halfway point. The **MIGRANT'S MILE NATURE TRAIL** is located in the midsection (south of Highway 484 near the Environmental Education Classroom, stop #8 on the auto tour). The trail takes you through a variety of habitats, from grassland to woods, and alongside and over a marsh via a boardwalk. A portion of this trail is paved for accessibility.

The **BIRDHOUSE BOULEVARD** (stop #1 on the auto tour) is a short paved walkway through a wooded area that displays various types of birdhouses. It begins from a parking lot near the visitor center in the southern portion. Skip this if your time is limited.

**BIKING**—Visitors may tour the refuge by bicycle. This might be one of the best ways to see all that the refuge has to offer. The roads are flat, but they are almost all gravel-surfaced, so a mountain bike is recommended. The wind can also be fierce, which can at times make the ride a bit difficult.

**HORSEBACK RIDING**—You can tour the refuge on horseback, but the staff requires notification for safety purposes. Horses are prohibited on the nature trails, but are allowed on established roads.

**FISHING AND HUNTING**—A fishing pond for children age 14 and younger is located near the southern entrance. Adults may accompany children. An accessible fishing pond for adults is located on the north end of the Little Salt Marsh. Fishing is permitted throughout the refuge, but boats and canoes are not allowed. Federal regulations apply, as do state regulations and permits for both hunting and fishing. A regulations leaflet is available at the refuge visitor center. Hunting in designated areas is limited to waterfowl, pheasant, quail, dove, snipe, rail, squirrels, and rabbits. Hunting is not permitted March through August and may be closed at any time if whooping cranes are present.

**OTHER**—Photography blinds are located at the Little Salt Marsh and the Migrant's Mile Nature Trail. Both are accessible for people with disabilities. An observation tower and deck is also available at the Little Salt Marsh near the southern entrance. Guided tours are available to groups by appointment.

**AUTO TOUR**—The entire drive through the refuge from north to south is 14 miles. A self-guided tour brochure explains 16 points of interest, focusing on history, operational and management tools, and wildlife habitat. Visitors can easily spend a half or full day here with hiking and photography stops. Allow 3 hours minimum to tour the entire refuge. A 4-mile drive hugs the perimeter of the Big Salt Marsh in the northern section of the park, where you can find a spotting scope. This highlight is worthy of hiking. If your time is limited to an hour, start your drive there. Details of the driving tour can be found at www.fws.gov/quivira/birds&wildlife.htm.

**CAMPING**—Camping is not permitted.

**TRAFFIC**—Light: the U.S. Fish and Wildlife Service reports annual visitation of 60,000.

**LOCATION AND DIRECTIONS**—In Stafford County. The southern entrance to the refuge is located on 4th Avenue, 27 miles west of Hutchinson. Enter the midsection from State Highway 19 east out of Larned or from 95th Avenue (also called 554 Road) west from Hutchinson.

**ENTRY**—No entrance fees. Open during daylight hours. The visitor center is open Monday–Friday, 7:30 A.M. to 4:30 P.M. Boating and canoes are not permitted. Do not park on bridges or dams or block any gates. Note: Road damage occurred from extensive flooding in 2007.

**ON THE WEB**—www.fws.gov/quivira.

**CONTACT**—Department of the Interior or U.S. Fish and Wildlife Service in Stafford, (620) 486-2393 or (800) 344-WILD; RR 3, Box 48A, Stafford, KS 67578-9532.

# Cheney State Park and Reservoir

Between Wichita and Hutchison, this reservoir is a favorite for locals. Cheney State Park is above average in size and number of facilities, which may explain its popularity. Nearly 500 campsites, 22 boat ramp lanes, three courtesy docks, two fish-cleaning stations, seven rental cabins, and four beaches (one designated for personal watercraft) are enough to attract nearly a half-million visitors annually. Sailing, boating, and water sports are the main attraction. Sailors take advantage of dependable Kansas winds. One of the top sailing lakes in the United States, Cheney Reservoir is home to the Ninnescah Sailing Association, which schedules regular sailing events. If you get the chance, check out one of these events: it's quite a spectacle to see the colorful sailboats dancing on the water's shimmering surface.

In this sandy terrain where the High Plains and Lowlands alternate, a mixed-grass prairie thrives. Numerous species of trees are found near waterways. You'll also spot the occasional prickly pear cactus.

Spring Creek Observation Trail leads over a wetland at Cheney State Park.

**WILDLIFE**—Wood duck boxes have been placed to attract the colorful swimmers. Listen for woodpeckers, red-winged blackbirds, and screech owls. Signs of beaver are common, but rarely will you spot the shy rodents. A waterfowl refuge, just west of the East Shore Area, is open to wildlife-watching activities from March 15 through September 15. Deer, turkeys, pheasant, coyotes, and all the usual prairie-grass residents may be spotted on a hike or drive.

**HIKING**—GIEFER CREEK NATURE TRAIL is a short loop (under a quarter mile) located in the West Shore Area in the Giefer Creek Day-Use Area. A small parking lot marks the trailhead, where hikers embark on a short journey through riparian woodland and mixed-grass prairie. Wildlife and numerous plant species are identified with 18 markers along the route. Pick up a trail brochure or download one online prior to your hike. You might be amazed by how many species coexist in one small area: American elm, cottonwood, hackberry, catalpa, redbud, black willow, black walnut, red mulberry, blackberry bushes, Osage orange, and red cedar are all identified with trail markers. Short but sweet, this wood-chip trail hugs a clear, sandy-bottomed stream with steep banks, providing crossings on wooden bridges and planks. Butterflies and dragonflies keep you company along the way.

SPRING CREEK WILDLIFE OBSERVATION AREA AND INTERPRETIVE TRAIL is a half-mile linear route, also located in the West Shore Area, in a small wetland between the cabins and Smarsh Creek Campground. A paved trail leads through prairie grasses and shrubs to an elevated boardwalk. Views of wetland habitat allow visitors to see a lengthy beaver dam. Careful inspection will reveal frogs, turtles, and tadpoles. Muskrat, beavers, red-winged blackbirds, or woodpeckers might also make an appearance. An unsuspecting deer may approach to drink from the creek. The boardwalk parallels the lakeshore and a sandbar, where killdeers and ring-billed gulls rest. Great blue herons, great egrets, and green herons may be fishing nearby. Hike this trail in your water sandals and bring your beach attire, as a crescent-shaped beach is the perfect end to this peaceful trail.

NOTE: A new linear path is under construction in the West Shore Area. The trail will begin by the park office and end near Sailboat Cove, traversing Giefer Creek. The habitat will include woodland and mixed-grass prairie. To sign up for Kansas park and trail updates, visit www.trailsofkansas.com.

**FISHING AND HUNTING**—According to park literature, fishing is excellent for channel catfish and white bass. Crappie, striped bass, wipers, and walleyes are also prevalent. Fish for walleyes along the dam in late March and early April; look for crappie among cattails and brush in April and May. White bass spawn upriver in May, and channel cat appear at the feeders in June and July. An ADA fishing jetty is located in the West Shore Area, consisting of a fishing pier and fish attractors for crappie. An ADA boat ramp can be found in the East Shore Area. A marina is located near the dam in the East Shore Area, complete with supplies and services for boaters and anglers.

Numerous parking areas and several boat ramps allow access to the wildlife area that surrounds the lake (excluding state park areas). Waterfowl, deer, turkeys, pheasant, and coyotes are available for hunters. A shooting range is located at the northernmost end of the lake, off Parallel Road.

**CAMPING AND FACILITIES**—In the East Shore Area, three peninsulas boast numerous campsites on the water. A group camp with utilities, a restroom, and a shelter can be rented in the West Shore Area, while seven modern cabins are each designed to accommodate four. Both primitive campsites and sites with water and electric are available on either shore, a few of which can be reserved. Primitive and modern restrooms, shower houses, boat ramps, courtesy docks, a marina, dump stations, shelter houses, fish-cleaning stations, fishing jetties, and swimming beaches round out the facilities. A personal watercraft area is located at Wichita Point (in the East Shore Area). The Giefer Creek Day-Use Area in the West Shore Area has picnic tables and grills.

**TRAFFIC**—Heavy, particularly in June and July.

**LOCATION AND DIRECTIONS**—In Reno County. From Wichita, take U.S. Highway 54/400 west to State Highway 251 and turn north. To access the east shore, continue past 21st Street; the park entrance will be on your left. To access the west shore and the park office, go west on 21st Street from Highway 251; the park entrance will be on your right.

**ENTRY**—State park entrance fees apply. Open all year with limited facilities in the winter.

**ON THE WEB**—Trails are indicated on the park map, which can be found at www.kdwp.state.ks.us, search "Cheney."

**CONTACT**—State Park office in Cheney, (316) 542-3664; 16000 N E 50th Street, Cheney, KS 67025. Wildlife Area office, (620) 459-6922.

# Kingman State Fishing Lake
## and Byron Walker Wildlife Area

Although this park is just off the highway, it still feels remote and offers surprising diversity and wildlife-watching opportunities. In an area where the High Plains creep into central Kansas to meet the Wellington–McPherson Lowlands, this small fishing lake barely rates as a dot on the map. The clear, sandy-bottomed Ninnescah River winds through the park and lures wildlife. The river, small lake, ponds, and wetland area are bordered by woodlands and sand prairie where wildflowers thrive. While the scenery can be lovely, wildlife is the main attraction. The area is popular with anglers and hunters, but they may soon be outnumbered by wildlife watchers.

Lily pads are thick on the lake surface; willow leaf sunflowers and black-eyed Susans decorate the rocky shore. Follow the gravel road that runs between the river and the lake; at the end of the road, a staircase leads up to a dike for a noteworthy overlook. Shaggy-topped sand pedestals peek out

Black-eyed Susan creates a blind from which to view wildlife at Kingman State Fishing Lake.

from the wetland areas and wildflowers glow in the sun. A bench allows for patient wildlife watching or fishing. A mowed path leads along the bank for further exploration.

**WILDLIFE**—Prairie birds such as pheasant, quail, and meadowlarks love the prairie areas. Tracks of raccoon, deer, and turkeys are likely to be cast in the sand while beaver and muskrat dens may be spotted, as well. The marsh attracts mallard, teal, and nesting wood ducks. From the dikes, look for herons and cormorants as well as reptiles and amphibians. Listen carefully for bullfrogs.

**HIKING**—There was once a hiking trail surrounding the lake, but an ice storm rendered the trail useless and it is no longer being maintained. There are no designated trails, but gravel and dirt roads hug the lake.

**FISHING AND HUNTING**—Largemouth bass are rated good, while northern pike are rated excellent. The lake also holds crappie, channel cat, bluegill, redear, and walleye. Crappie spawn in April and linger around brush piles and rock jetties; northern pike spawn in weedy areas near the shore. Channel cat are caught near the feeders between April and October. The smaller ponds also contain fish and are especially good for family fishing trips. Alternatively, fish the river for channel and flathead catfish.

Permits for both fishing and hunting are required, but free. Upland birds, doves, and quail are present in good numbers, but pheasant are low. Squirrels, white-tailed deer, and turkeys are plentiful. The lake, ponds, and marshes are managed for waterfowl.

An archery range is open during daylight hours, located near the park office on the south side of U.S. Highway 54.

**CAMPING AND FACILITIES**—Primitive camping is permitted in designated areas east of the lake. Picnic tables, a group shelter, fire rings, and primitive restrooms are available. Two boat ramps are located on the east side of the lake, but motorized boating is limited to fishing purposes. Parking lots and pullouts are plentiful throughout the park; information and self-pay stations are located at both park entrances.

**LOCATION AND DIRECTIONS**—In Kingman County. From Wichita, take U.S. Highway 54/400 west. About 7 miles past the town of Kingman, signs will direct you north to the lake. To reach the park office, ignore the sign and turn left after the highway crosses the Ninnescah River.

**ENTRY**—No entrance fees. Open all year. Alcohol is prohibited. Boating is limited to fishing only.

**ON THE WEB**—A park map is available for download at www.kdwp.state.ks.us, search "Kingman."

**CONTACT**—KDWP office in Cunningham, (620) 532-3242; 8685 West Highway 54, Cunningham, KS 67035.

# Lake Afton Park

Sedgwick County's Lake Afton Park is a rural park on the outskirts of Wichita. Easily compared to Topeka's Lake Shawnee, it also began as a WPA project and offers camping, fishing, boating, skiing, swimming, and picnicking. Summer wildflowers are one of the highlights, but don't miss the Lake Afton Public Observatory on the north end of the lake. Make your first stop the park office and bait shop.

**WILDLIFE**—Great egrets, ring-billed gulls, and great blue herons are common on the lake. Migrating species may drop by in the spring or fall. A couple of picnic tables near the observatory overlook the marshy end of the lake and provide a quiet and scenic spot for a picnic and bird watching.

**AUTO TOUR/BIKING/HIKING**—A 4-mile fairly level, paved road circles the lake and travels behind the dam past shelters, coves, and beaches. A dirt road travels within the paved road and around the lake, perfect for hiking, biking, or jogging.

**FISHING**—Channel and flathead catfish, white and black crappie, sunfish, bluegill, largemouth bass, black bullhead, and walleye are prevalent. Rumor has it that the flathead catfish are huge. A fishing dock and a boat ramp are located on the northwest side of the lake. A bait store shares space with the park office. A state fishing license is required. Hunting is not permitted.

**OTHER**—A shooting range is open to the public two weekends each month, on the north end of the lake. The office can answer inquiries. Lake Afton Public Observatory sits on the north end of the lake (247th Street West at MacArthur Road, aka 39th Street South) and is a must-see. Educational astronomical programs take place at the observatory on weekend evenings throughout the year. Check the schedule online at webs.wichita.edu/lapo/events.html. A remote control airfield is located on the west side of the park.

**CAMPING AND FACILITIES**—Primitive and electric sites are available for camping. Large and small shelter houses can be reserved. A children's playground, three swimming beaches, modern restrooms and showers, dump stations, a boat ramp, fishing docks and feeders, and a grocery/bait store are available.

**TRAFFIC**—Heavy in summer months.

**LOCATION AND DIRECTIONS**—In Sedgwick County, southwest of Wichita. Head west on 39th Street South (also called MacArthur Road) toward Cheney.

**ENTRY**—Open all year. Entrance fees and county use fees apply. No jet skis, open fires, or generators allowed.

**ON THE WEB**—For maps and more information, visit sedgwickcounty.org/lake_afton or sedgwickcounty.org.

**CONTACT**—Administrative office, (316) 794-2774; 24600 W 39th Street South (MacArthur Road), Goddard, KS 67052.

# Dillon Nature Center
## and National Recreation Trail

THIS OUTDOOR TREASURE has earned two distinctions on a national level. It is considered a National Urban Wildlife Sanctuary and offers a National Recreation Trail through woods, prairie, ponds, and marsh. On the northern boundary of Hutchinson, this wild arboretum is packed with hundreds of species of trees, shrubs, and wildflowers that attract butterflies, birds, and travelers. Named for its former owners, Dillon Food Stores, the property was formerly used as a private recreation area for employees. Rather than replace species planted by Dillon, the wild arboretum maintains the exotic plants and cultivates native prairie habitat, too.

Near the entrance, look for the large bald cypress tree behind the bronze bear statue. Growing next to the pond, the cypress sends distinctive "knees" (knobby, oddly shaped roots) up through the water's surface to receive oxygen.

Inside the visitor center, large picture windows provide an up-close view of feeding birds. Black-capped chickadees, red-winged blackbirds, goldfinches, and hummingbirds all make brief appearances. A wooden deck wraps around the back of the visitor center to provide an overlook of the pond. Aquariums of native amphibians and reptiles, a natural science exhibit, and displays of nature-themed art can be found at the Education and Discovery Center. Naturally, there is also a gift shop.

The land here was given to the Hutchinson Recreation Commission in 1970 and later expanded through a partnership with Westar. Today, the city operates the center, which is funded through taxes and donations. Volunteers play a huge role in growing the center. Thousands of seedlings are grown in the basements of volunteers, who host an annual plant sale and later transplant remaining annuals and perennials to the gardens. Admission to the nature center is free, but donations are requested.

**WILDLIFE**—Birdhouses and feeders attract birds to the trail and gardens. Look for turtles, snakes, and bullfrogs around the pond, where you may also see wood ducks, herons, spotted sandpipers, cormorants, and ospreys. More than 200 species of birds have been recorded in the area. White-tailed deer, badgers, coyotes, foxes, and raptors are sometimes spotted, as well. Look for clues left behind on the hiking trail.

Fishing pond at the Dillon Nature Center in Hutchinson.

**HIKING**—Visitors can walk up to 3 miles along the National Recreation Trail, all of it easy. Trails are well maintained and marked and seem to dry quickly after rain. The **WOODARD INTERPRETIVE TRAIL** is a three-quarter-mile loop marked in blue with numbered posts that correspond to an interpretive brochure. The trail meanders through woods, mixed-grass prairie, ponds, and marsh on a surface that varies from crushed rock to grass and dirt. Some of the highlights include a tunnel of red cedar, unique Austrian and Scotch pine, sand hill plum, honey locust, and persimmon.

The **OUTER LOOP** is marked in red and follows the perimeter of the park to lengthen your hike with an additional mile and similar scenery. A concrete walkway circles the largest pond for under a half mile. Flowering and berry-producing trees and shrubs surround the pond and attract numerous birds and insects to the trails, while the water draws reptiles, birds, and mammals. For additional mileage, add the **PRAIRIE HILLS TRAIL** (one-way and just over a half mile), which heads east from the parking lot and is marked with interpretive signs through a mixed-grass prairie and prairie dog town. You'll find the squeaky critters more active on sunny days.

**FISHING AND HUNTING**—The upper pond is spring-fed and stocked with channel cat and trout as part of an urban fisheries program. You'll see frequent anglers even on rainy days. Hunting is not permitted.

**OTHER**—Nature photographers will find the park an ideal setting for their craft.

**CAMPING AND FACILITIES**—A visitor center provides restrooms, water, vending machines, and a gift shop. No camping facilities are available.

**LOCATION AND DIRECTIONS**—In Reno County. From Hutchinson, take State Highway 61 northeast to 30th Avenue and go east half a block. The entrance is on your left.

**ENTRY**—The trails are open from 8:00 A.M. to sunset on weekdays and 9:00 A.M. to sunset on weekends and holidays. The visitor center is open 8:00 A.M. to 7:00 P.M. on weekdays in high season and 8:00 A.M. to 5:00 P.M. in late fall to early spring, 10:00 A.M. to 5:00 P.M. on Saturdays, and 1:00 P.M. to 5:00 P.M. on Sundays.

**ON THE WEB**—Trail maps can be found at www.dillonnature center.com.

**CONTACT**—Dillon Nature Center, (620) 663-7411; 3002 East 30th Avenue, Hutchinson, KS 67502.

**NEARBY**—The Smithsonian-affiliated **KANSAS COSMOSPHERE AND SPACE CENTER** in Hutchinson is touted as one of the most comprehensive space museums in the world. The museum includes a rocket science demonstration, the actual Apollo 13 command module, a SR-71 spy plane, a full-scale model space shuttle, and a huge collection of Soviet space artifacts. Located at 1100 North Plum Street; phone (620) 662-2305. Open Monday through Thursday from 9:00 A.M. to 6:00 P.M., Saturday from 9:00 A.M. to 9:00 P.M., and Sunday from noon to 6:00 P.M. Visitors can purchase tickets for one feature or buy an all-inclusive ticket for the museum, IMAX, and planetarium. See www.cosmo.org for more information.

# Great Plains Nature Center
## and Chisholm Creek Park

WILDLIFE APPEARS to have adjusted to city noise and busloads of grade-school children in this urban nature education center. On a rainy fall day, great egrets, great blue herons, green herons, muskrat, painted turtles, and mallard all make an appearance under a wetland boardwalk near the visitor center. Prairie, wetland, ponds, and woodlands are managed to provide a diverse habitat attractive to birds, butterflies, reptiles, amphibians, and mammals.

Inside, exhibits illustrate the Great Plains climate and the effects of settlement. Streams and wetland, riparian, and woodland habitats are each defined. Your favorite exhibit may be the 2,200-gallon aquarium, with native amphibians on display. From the back of the Koch Exhibit Hall, a glass wildlife observatory waits with views of wetlands; a circulating stream, bird feeders, and plants lure butterflies and birds. Binoculars and spotting scopes are available upon request. A series of field guides for Kansas mammals, snakes, shorebirds, raptors, and endangered species is available without charge to visitors. The adjoining Chisholm Creek Park trails let you get outdoors and experience firsthand the numerous Great Plains characters you just learned about indoors.

**WILDLIFE**—Screech owls, great horned owls, and red-tailed hawks are common. Indigo buntings, kingbirds, herons, and egrets visit in the summer. Mink can be seen playing streamside. Look for the tracks of raccoon, deer, coyotes, and red foxes. Western painted turtles sun themselves on floating logs or hide under brush.

**HIKING**—Four successive color-coded loops lead you through each habitat. Each loop is roughly a half mile, so that when you combine all four loops, you hike about 2 miles. All trails are paved. From the kiosk at the visitor center, actual cumulative mileages are as follow:

Red—Quail Trail, 0.5 miles
Blue—Heron Trail, 0.9 miles
Green—Bluestem Trail, 1.1 miles
Yellow—Cottonwood Trail, 1.7 miles

**FISHING AND HUNTING**—Catch-and-release fishing is allowed at Island Pond just downhill from the nature center, but artificial lures must be used. Chisholm Lake (located north of State Highway 96) allows fishing with a valid Kansas fishing license. No fishing is allowed in the wetland area. Hunting is not permitted.

**CAMPING AND FACILITIES**—Parking lots, trailheads, and restrooms are located at both the visitor center at the east end of the park and at the west end. Picnic shelters can be found at the west end. A gift shop and book store can be found in the nature center. No camping facilities are provided.

**LOCATION AND DIRECTIONS**—In Sedgwick County, in Wichita. The park entrance is located a half mile south of Highway 96, at the northwest corner of Woodlawn Street and East 29th Street North. Take I-135 to Highway 96, then east on Highway 96 to Woodlawn. Go south on Woodlawn and turn west at 29th Street.

**ENTRY**—No entrance fees, but donations are appreciated. Chisholm Creek Park is open daily, sunrise to sundown. The Great Plains Nature Center is open Monday–Saturday, 9:00 A.M. to 5:00 P.M. No skateboards, bikes, or pets allowed.

**ON THE WEB**—For maps of Chisholm Creek Park or more information, visit www.gpnc.org.

**CONTACT**—Great Plains Nature Center, (316) 683-5499. KDWP regional office, Great Plains Nature Center, 8:00 A.M. to 4:45 P.M., (316) 683-8069; 6232 East 29th Street North, Wichita, KS 67220.

# NORTHEASTERN
# KANSAS

Botanical gardens are a bonus feature of Lake Shawnee.

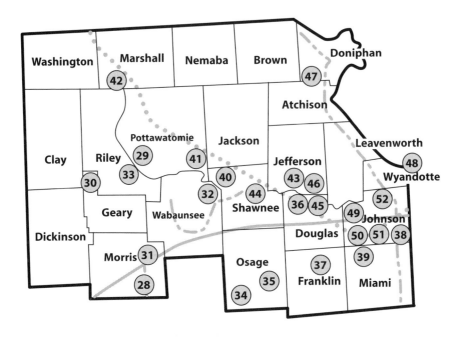

Scenic Byway
Santa Fe Trail
Oregon Trail

# NORTHEASTERN KANSAS

# Geology of the Flint Hills Region

PERHAPS THE BEST-KNOWN REGION IN KANSAS, the Flint Hills were composed of rock deposited during the Permian Period, 280 million years ago, when the climate was hot. An enormous but shallow sea covered the area and left behind deposits of limestone, a byproduct of healthy marine life. As the shallow ocean receded and advanced, it left behind layers of alternating limestone and mud, which over time hardens into shale. Over the years, the alternating layers of limestone and shale have eroded away at different rates, leaving behind the striped, layered appearance for which the hills are famous.

Rainwater continues to erode valleys, creating rolling hills with meandering creeks and streams. The low-lying areas collect sediment that runs off the slopes and provides just enough soil for trees and vegetation to grow along the creek beds. Lightning often causes fire that removes any trees and other vegetation not hearty enough to survive in thin soil or the hot, dry Kansas summers. Despite the fact that the Flint Hills may be the most well-known treasure Kansas possesses, visitors are still surprised—and rightly so—at the rolling hills and scenic beauty that blatantly defy the stereotype of "flat" Kansas.

Climbing is required in Kansas's Flint Hills.

# Flint Hills National Scenic Byway

RUNNING 47 MILES between Council Grove and Cassoday, this scenic drive offers heritage, history, and many stops for nature lovers. Visitors can easily pack a couple of days with hiking, biking, fishing, and sightseeing in the heart of the Flint Hills. If you're looking for recreation with all the amenities, make your base camp Council Grove Reservoir. If you're looking for a quiet place to rough it, choose Chase State Fishing Lake near Cottonwood Falls.

The scenic byway officially begins at Council Grove on State Highway 177. This town—still laden with Old West character—was known as the last outpost on the Santa Fe Trail, where travelers could stock up for the great westward journey. A self-guided tour features many historic sites. In fact, the city is actually designated as a National Historic Landmark. The **NEOSHO RIVER CROSSING** made the Santa Fe Trail notoriously perilous and is today marked with a paved, landscaped, and lighted walkway. Stop at the Kaw Mission State Historic Site to learn more about Native American cultures, view Santa Fe Trail exhibits and artifacts, and find information on all the area's activities.

Only 1.5 miles north of town, **COUNCIL GROVE LAKE** offers both improved and primitive campsites right on the shoreline. Short nature trails begin behind the Corps of Engineers (COE) office and at Richey Cove's group camp. Boating, skiing, swimming, and fishing are favorite ways to enjoy this setting in the Flint Hills.

A rugged, 3.5-mile segment of the **FLINT HILLS NATURE TRAIL** connects Council Grove to the **ALLEGAWAHO HERITAGE MEMORIAL PARK,** site of the last Kaw (Kanza) Indian village in Kansas, before the tribe was forced to move to Oklahoma in 1873. You can walk 2 miles in the footsteps of the Kanza on the **KANZA HERITAGE TRAIL**—a tribute to the people for whom the state was named.

Continuing south on State Highway 177, you'll also find the **TALLGRASS PRAIRIE NATIONAL PRESERVE,** with nearly 12 miles of scenic Flint Hills hiking. Schedule a ranger-guided van tour and learn all about prairie ecology and history or take the guided home tour to learn about ranching and life on the vast prairie.

In nearby Cottonwood Falls, you'll find a superb collection of Indian artifacts and arrowheads at the Roniger Memorial Museum (open 1:00 P.M. to 5:00 P.M., closed Tuesdays and Thursdays), located behind the hard-to-miss Chase County Courthouse. This stately, Second Empire, stone structure is known as the oldest, continuously used courthouse in the state. If you venture inside, you'll find an old jailhouse by walking through the courtroom, but please refrain when court is in session.

Hike, bike, barbecue, or relax with your favorite fishing pole at the **CHASE STATE FISHING LAKE** while waiting for the sun to set on a fabulous day in the Flint Hills. Located 1.5 miles west of Cottonwood Falls, the small and often calm lake reflects serene, striped hills, sprinkled with smooth limestone gravel and boulders. Picnic facilities and restrooms add to your comfort. Hike your way around the lakeshore or climb over the ridge that surrounds the lake for beautiful rural views. As a small lake, it rates as one of the best for saugeye or spotted bass. Cyclists will love riding the rolling hills and less-traveled roads.

Can't get enough of the Flint Hills? Although it is not part of the official scenic byway, a small stretch of Highway 177 between I-70 and Manhattan offers some great Flint Hills scenery in less time and distance than the byway. A pull-out and scenic overlook awaits photographers, but don't expect to stuff the sweeping vistas into one frame. Additionally, State Highway 99, west of Topeka running south from I-70, and I-35 between El Dorado and Emporia offer grand Flint Hills scenery.

**ON THE WEB**—Scenic byway maps and more can be found at www.ksbyways.org. Information about Council Grove can be found at www.councilgrove.com.

**CONTACT**—For information on Allegawaho Heritage Memorial Park, Kaw Mission State Historic Site, (620) 767-5410. For the COE at Council Grove Lake, (620) 767-5195. To rent paddleboats, fishing boats, and pontoon boats at Council Grove Lake, Council Grove Marina LLC, (620) 767-5924. For KDWP, Chase State Fishing Lake, (620) 767-5900.

# Tuttle Creek Lake and State Park
## and Rocky Ford Fishing Area

LOCATED IN THE FLINT HILLS REGION, Tuttle Creek Reservoir may be Kansas's second largest, but the scenery is certainly not second-rate. The lake is edged by long, steep slopes that sometimes climb as high as 300 feet. Limestone outcrops and evidence of the Ice Age remain. A waterfowl refuge, marshland, and riparian habitat make up the northern half of the park's acreage, while the reservoir and tallgrass prairie with wooded ravines consume the southern half, creating a diverse habitat for first-rate wildlife watching.

Eleven parks (six managed by the Army Corps of Engineers, four managed by KDWP, and one managed by Pottawatomie County) surround the lake and offer surprisingly different scenery. For example, River Pond and Outlet Park are flat, riparian areas while Fancy Creek Park on the northwest end is reminiscent of Colorado—marked by steep, rocky ravines and heavily wooded with the scent of cedar. Carnahan Creek and Randolph on the east side offer stunning Flint Hills scenery, with prairie and lake views.

Trails at Carnahan Creek Park offer stunning Flint Hills vistas at Tuttle Creek Reservoir.

**WILDLIFE**—Outlet Park and River Pond are riparian zones, which attract a great variety of birds, including herons, gulls, geese, ducks, and bald eagles. On the west side of Outlet Park lies the Blue River Trail, along which you can see waterfowl, muskrat, marsh birds, and beaver dams. The forest located on the south side of River Pond draws migrating and nesting songbirds plus warblers and vireos. Early risers may see turkeys, deer, and even owls. Protective coves such as McIntire Creek, Mill Creek, and Fancy Creek attract waterfowl and shorebirds. Herons and egrets are abundant in the summer, while pelicans make an appearance in fall. Between two marshes on the northeast end, Spring Creek attracts mink, muskrat, beavers, and raccoon. Greater prairie chicken booming grounds may be spotted among the rolling hills in the spring.

**HIKING**—**BLUE RIVER TRAIL** in Outlet Park is a popular interpretive 1-mile loop, for foot traffic only. Opportunities for wildlife viewing are abundant with spur trails that lead to viewing blinds. The trail begins near shelter #3.

**COTTONWOOD NATURE TRAIL** in River Pond State Park offers an easy quarter-mile interpretive trail with 10 items of interest along the route and an observation deck for wildlife viewing.

**CEDAR RIDGE TRAIL** is a half-mile trail that allows scenic views of a wooded ravine. Recipient of the National Americans with Disabilities Act (ADA) Trail Award in 2001, it is located in the Spillway State Park.

**CARNAHAN CREEK PARK AND RECREATION AREA** offers stellar scenery in a remote area with miles of rugged and challenging trails. If Carnahan Creek is low enough to cross, explorers may access a lakeside linear trail on the opposite side, which can be followed for 10 miles: walk 6 miles to Sunset Cove, continue up the reservoir another 2 miles to Oak Canyon, and add 2 more miles to Garrison. The first 6 miles of trail are easy to follow; beyond that, hike or ride at your own discretion. Visitors concede that while the terrain is rough, the views of the surrounding Flint Hills and coves are worth it.

When the lake is high, you will not be able to cross safely to the linear trail. Alternatively, 5 miles of mowed and gravel path wind around Carnahan Recreation Area, climbing above the cove to panoramic views of the Flint Hills. The wind will likely be merciless at the top. Bring water; primitive camping facilities and a boat ramp are the only amenities at the remote Recreation Area.

**RANDOLPH STATE PARK** is bisected by State Highway 16. Water is available in either part. Maps at the trailhead indicate various access points for the 12 miles of multi-use trail that swirl around the small, 200-acre park. These trails are well marked and should be easy to follow, although small sections in the north may be affected by water. Interesting rock outcroppings can be seen trailside, including pink Sioux quartzite left behind as glaciers melted. Picturesque views of the mile-long bridge across Tuttle Creek Lake warrant a pause.

**FANCY CREEK MOUNTAIN BIKE TRAIL** provides 6 miles of challenging trail open to hikers and bikers through dense cedar and oak forest with little open grassland. There are two trailheads. From the main trailhead, the path follows the side of a slope overlooking the north end of the lake with views of shallow mudflats, sandbars, and a mile-long bridge spanning the reservoir. Views of the rolling Flint Hills can be seen across the lake. Alternatively, if you begin from the campground, the trail enters dark woods carpeted with needles and riddled with rock. Limestone walls, ledges, and other rock formations along the trail appear to be mangled with solution holes and lichen, which creates the ambiance of a dark and magical forest. Tall red cedar trees block wind and sun, and eliminate an understory. The path ascends and descends many times with infrequent views from above. Minor stream crossings weave across the forest floor. A detailed trail map can be found at www.kansasmountainbiking.com.

**TRAIL BUILDING**—The Kansas Trails Council coordinates volunteers for the Carnahan and Randolph Trails; see www.kansastrailscouncil.org for contact information. The Fancy Creek Mountain Bike Trail is maintained by Manhattan Midwest Mountain Bike Patrol. For trailwork dates, see www.kansasmountainbiking.com.

**BIKING**—The Fancy Creek Mountain Bike Trail offers 6 miles of challenging terrain and scenic lake views for intermediate and advanced riders. Upper sections are very rocky and a few sections should be used by only the most experienced riders. Technical areas and switchbacks interrupt flowing sections. This mountain bike course is favored by the Midwest Fat Tire Series. (See Hiking for more information.) Cyclists may also use the Spillway Cycle Area. A few miles of dirt trail zigzag through the area; some stretches are appropriate for the novice, while menacing climbs await those who want a workout. A map is posted in the parking area. Multipurpose trails in Randolph and Carnahan Creek Park are also open to mountain bikes. Road bikers will enjoy the auto tour mentioned below, as the rolling park roads offer a challenge, but be aware there are no shoulders or bike lanes.

**AUTO TOUR**—For the best scenery, drive the east side of Tuttle Creek Lake from the dam to Olsburg on State Highway 43 (also called Carnahan Road). The route provides about 15 miles (one-way) of paved, winding road through ambient Flint Hills scenery of subtle canyons and private ranches. There are only a few opportunities for distant views of coves, but the remote landscape is striking enough to hold your attention. Two scenic overlooks are marked with a pullout and signage. At the midpoint, take a detour into Carnahan Creek Park and you may feel as if you alone have discovered an isolated corner of the world.

**HORSEBACK RIDING**—Equestrians will find multipurpose trails ideal for riding at Carnahan Creek Park and Randolph. Randolph offers corrals, electrical hookups, and showers in the south section of the park. Horseshoes are recommended for the rocky trails. While Randolph has water at the trailheads, there is no water on the trail. Conversely, Carnahan has no water at the trailhead, but horses can be watered at Sunset Cove, Oak Canyon, and Garrison.

**FISHING AND HUNTING**—Species include saugeye, white bass, crappie, channel catfish, and flathead. Trout are stocked all year in River Pond Park, where a special permit is required. Channel and flathead catfish can be found in both the lake and the river above and below the reservoir. Crappie and bass prefer the wooded coves where there is submerged brush and timber. Look for walleye along the face of the dam in early spring. South of the dam, the Rocky Ford Fishing Area retaining wall with walkway offers a unique angling experience. Improvements are underway to add a mile of shoreline fishing along the Big Blue, which connects the River Pond area to Rocky Ford.

Hunting on public lands that surround the reservoir may include turkey, white-tailed deer, quail, pheasant, and waterfowl. The numerous marshes (especially Fancy Creek and Olsburg) are said to be good spots for duck hunting. Deer and turkey are plentiful in the river bottoms. The Swede Creek Marsh is designated as a refuge and is closed to all activities from October 1 to January 15.

**OTHER**—An airfield for radio-controlled model aircraft is located between the Spillway Cycle Area and River Pond. At Fancy Creek Park, a state-of-the-art shooting range is open the first and third weekends each month and the fourth Thursday; this is the only place where target practice is permitted. An 18-hole disc golf course can be found in River Pond State Park.

**BOATING AND PADDLING**—14 miles of open water and wind make Tuttle Creek one of the best sailing lakes in Kansas. Wildcat Marina at Spillway provides fuel, mooring, and supplies. Pontoons and personal watercraft can be rented onsite. Canoes and kayaks can find calm water below the dam in a no-wake zone at River Pond, where they can also be rented. Swimming beaches are located at River Pond and Tuttle Creek Cove.

For a full-day, 9.5-mile float trip, you can launch from the boat ramp in Manhattan's Linear Park. Use the U.S. Highway 24/Blue River Access to begin your float through the Flint Hills to Saint George. Take I-70 to Manhattan (Exit 313), and head north on State Highway 177 for 8 miles. After crossing the Kaw River (aka the Kansas River), continue north on Highway 177 and veer east on U.S. Highway 24 toward Wamego. Linear Park's Blue River access will appear on your right (south) after 1 mile. There is plenty of parking and the single ramp is paved. You must float the Blue River for a third of a mile before you reach the Kaw. Take out at Boggs Landing in St. George. From the Blue River Access, Boggs Landing is another 7 miles east on Highway 24 and south on Military Trail Road.

**OFF-ROAD VEHICLE TRAILS**—The Tuttle Creek Off-Road Vehicle Area is open to motorized and non-motorized vehicles. The 310-acre park offers steep climbs and sharp turns over rugged terrain for day-use only. To preserve the park and trail system, the ORV area should not be used when muddy. From U.S. Highway 77 (south of State Highway 16), take Gardiner Road (County Road 893) to Secrest Road.

The Spillway Cycle Area is a smaller, 45-acre park reserved for ATVs, motorcycles, and mountain bikes. The area is located east of the dam and can be reached from either Dyer Road or State Highway 65. This area is open to vehicles with a wheelbase under 66 inches.

**CAMPING AND FACILITIES**—11 parks compose this recreational haven. Four areas make up the state park operated by KDWP: Fancy Creek, Spillway, River Pond, and Randolph. The Corps of Engineers manages six areas: Observation Point, Outlet Park, Spillway Cycle, Tuttle Creek Cove, Stockdale Park, and the Off-Road Vehicle Area. Pottawatomie County manages Carnahan Park. Campsites without utilities far outnumber the utility sites. Seven areas offer camping, but there are showers only at River Pond, Spillway, Randolph, and Stockdale. River Pond and Fancy Creek areas also offer RV hookups. The park participates in the Rent-a-Camp program, through which visitors can rent basic camping equipment such as Coleman tents, coolers, and lanterns. Softball diamonds, basketball courts, a fish-cleaning station, a playground, and an observation blind are all located in Outlet Park. Boat ramps can be found in all but the day-use areas. A full-service marina is located at Spillway Cycle. Picnic tables and restrooms are plentiful.

**TRAFFIC**—The most visited of all Kansas state parks, Turtle Creek receives heaviest traffic May through July, with the most visitors in June. It will likely feel uncrowded in September or October because of the size and number of the parks.

**LOCATION AND DIRECTIONS**—Entrance in Pottawatomie County. From I-70, take Exit 313 north toward Manhattan. Continue on State Highway 177/U.S. Highway 24 through Manhattan. Turn east on State Highway 13 and cross the dam to find the KDWP visitor center on River Pond Road.

**ENTRY**—Open all year. State Park entrance fees apply at Fancy Creek, Spillway, River Pond, and Randolph. Some areas offer limited facilities in the off-season. The waterfowl refuge is closed to all activities from October 1 through January 15.

**ON THE WEB**—Maps can be found at www.kdwp.state.ks.us, search "Tuttle," and www.nwk.usace.army.mil/tc.

**CONTACT**—Corps of Engineers Manhattan office, (785) 539-8511; KDWP Manhattan office, (785) 539-7941; Tuttle Creek Wildlife Area in Blue Rapids, (785) 363-7316. Address of KDWP: 5800-A River Pond Road, Manhattan, KS 66502.

# Milford Lake and State Park

IN ADDITION TO BEING THE LARGEST RESERVOIR with the third largest wetland in Kansas, Milford is also home to the largest state fish hatchery, the Milford Nature Center, the Kansas Landscape Arboretum, and a 21-foot-high viewing tower for wildlife watching. Milford Reservoir just might offer more educational opportunities for nature and wildlife lovers than any other state park in Kansas.

As you drive from Junction City to the state park, you'll begin a steep ascent that eventually takes you to an enormous dam. Atop the dam, you'll look upon the largest reservoir in Kansas—16,000 acres. Outlet Park is far below you, where the Republican River makes its way to Junction City. From this vantage point, you will begin to realize the size of the park and reservoir. When water is at normal levels, you'll see exposed limestone layers along the banks that glow at sunset. Kansas wind drives white caps into the rock. Prairie grass covers the hills and cedars dot the landscape, which meets an infinite sky. Within the state park, picnic areas overlook the reservoir, sand beaches, and playgrounds.

Behind the dam at Outlet Park, Milford Nature Center awaits visitors with indoor and outdoor exhibits. Live raptors, mammals, and reptiles are a major highlight. Interesting taxidermy displays are also used for education. Nearby, guided tours of the warm-water, intensive-culture fish hatchery are offered April through September on weekends or by appointment.

**WILDLIFE**—A viewing tower and a trail surrounded by fields draw many creatures at dusk and dawn. It's also the perfect place for stargazing on clear evenings. The Steve Lloyd Wetlands in the northwest corner also offer a viewing area where shorebirds and waterfowl drop in, especially during the spring and fall migration seasons. You might see a few resident pelicans in the summer. Great blue herons fishing shallow waters are a common sight. Look for the small, stocky, and less-common green herons in the wetlands. Elk have been reintroduced on the Fort Riley Reservation, which now boasts

Vibrant blooms of smooth sumac and goldenrod outline the shore on Milford Lake's Eagle Ridge Trail.

the largest free-ranging herd in Kansas. In spring you may see elk feeding during the early evening in wheat fields around Timber Creek and along State Highway 82 and U.S. Highway 77.

**HIKING**—From the nature center parking lot, you'll find the trailhead for the **TALLGRASS TRAIL** where a half-mile loop and a 1.5-mile hike both lead through wooded areas and prairie grasses to a pond and back. These easy wood-chip trails are a great way to introduce children to hiking, wildlife watching, or identifying animal tracks. Bring your fishing poles, too. Note: The length of the trail may vary according to what can be effectively maintained.

**WATERFALL TRAIL** is located near the entrance to the state park between the office and pay station, marked by a man-made waterfall. A half-mile hike on a path of mowed grass and gravel loops through cedar tunnels and prairie grasses and crosses intermittent drainage areas. Dragonflies abound on the trail. Look for painted turtles under the brush and animal tracks along the path. While the scenery is pleasant, it's a bit unremarkable; however, the trail provides a great opportunity to see wildlife for those who are quiet and patient. Benches along the trail offer quiet reflective space to enjoy nature. The trailhead sign warns of ticks and insects. The trail is open to cyclists, but not horses.

**KANSAS LANDSCAPE ARBORETUM** offers four hiking trails on the northwest corner of the lake near Wakefield. The Meadow Willow Trail is a half-mile loop featuring seven bridges. The Wild Acres Trail is a quarter-mile loop featuring a display of native wildflowers. The Woodland Trail is an easy 1-mile mulched loop that follows a creek to Milford Lake and back. The Bird Sanctuary Trail circles a small pond. Don't miss the arboretum if you're visiting in the spring, when a collection of flowering crabapple and redbud trees is stunning. Visitors can drive gravel roads through the park to view sycamores, red cedars, honey locusts, maples, and oaks, as well. Numerous species are clearly identified throughout the park.

**HIKING, BIKING, AND HORSEBACK RIDING**—Milford's trail system offers many multipurpose trails, long and short, that can be traveled independently or linked for over 16 miles of trail:

**PIPELINE TRAIL** is a series of linear paths that connect campgrounds and create shortcuts among sections of the park.

**CRYSTAL TRAIL** is a 2.2-mile loop that passes through woods to remnants of an old rock quarry. Though this trail is not as scenic as others, deer and turkey can be spotted in open fields and wildflowers bloom through fall. The trail features a few stream crossings and briefly nears a cove where you may get a peek at the nearby yacht club. In winter months, eagles can sometimes be seen. Be aware that mowed side paths may cause you to stray from the real trail.

**EAGLE RIDGE TRAIL** is an 8-mile multipurpose trail with walk-in campsites that are ideal for hikers, bikers, and equestrians alike. The trail forms a couple of loops and crosses the park road, so there are several opportunities to shorten the length if you're on foot or your time is limited. This is the most scenic trail in the park, offering panoramic views above the lake on the western half of the trail. Periodically, the trail ducks through cedar tunnels descending to and climbing from intermittent streams. The trail often skirts groves of cedar and oak along prairie flatlands where wildflowers thrive. Although it follows the shoreline, walls of cedar trees often limit lake views. Terrain is mostly easy and alternates between sand and mowed grass.

**OLD RIVER BLUFF TRAIL** is a 1.25-mile linear trail of crushed gravel that links visitors at the state park to Outlet Park and subsequently the Riverwalk Trail.

**RIVERWALK TRAIL** is a 4.8-mile linear trail of crushed gravel along the Republican River that begins at Outlet Park and leads to Junction City through Fort Riley. Access may be limited when bald eagles are present in the area.

**FISHING AND HUNTING**—Milford is sometimes called the fishing capital of Kansas. The Milford Lake Association offers a brochure with GPS coordinates for fish habitats, as well as the location of boat docks and marinas around the lake. You can pick up a copy of the brochure at the main office. The Gathering Pond is located in Outlet Park (below the dam) to provide access for bank, dock, and pier fishing. Ramps allow access for boats without engines. An accessible fishing dock and fish-cleaning station are provided at Farnum Creek Park and Curtis Creek Park. Wiper is classified as good; the lake record wiper stands at 17 pounds. White bass over 12 inches are plentiful and those over 15 inches are common. Both black bass and channel cat are fair to good. The lake record blue cat now stands at 50.2 pounds. Walleye and Crappie are rated fair.

**OTHER**—The School Creek ORV Area on the west side of the lake offers nearly 300 acres of trails for vehicles that are 50 inches wide or smaller. Packed dirt trails and extreme hills offer a challenge.

**PADDLING**—15 miles of river are available for public use. Three boat ramps along the lake (located at Broughton Bridge, Beichter, and Gatesville) offer access to 8 miles of river. Below the dam, 7 miles from the dam to the confluence of the Republican and Smoky Hill River are open. Low or high water can be an issue; call the Corps of Engineers or visit the Corps Web site to determine river status.

**CAMPING AND FACILITIES**—The largest lake in the state, Milford Reservoir boasts 13 developed areas and seven beaches. Walnut Grove and Woodland Hills Campgrounds at Milford State Park are quite scenic, resting within a cove. Cabins and group camps are available at Milford State Park, Flagstop Resort, Acorns Resort, and Thunderbird Marina. All areas offer camping (except designated day-use areas) but only the state park offers a new, top-notch equestrian camp. Most camping areas offer showers, the exceptions being Acorns Resort, Farnum Creek, School Creek, and Timber Creek. Acorns Resort offers luxury cabins and some primitive campsites. All areas have boat ramps except North Overlook and Acorns Resort, which has a launch for canoes or kayaks. Three areas are for day-use only: East Rolling Hills, North Overlook, and Outlet Park.

**TRAFFIC**—Average to heavy, with spikes in June and July.

**LOCATION AND DIRECTIONS**—In Geary County, just north of Junction City. Take I-70 to Exit 295 and head north on U.S. Highway 77. Both Milford State Park and the COE offices can be accessed from the State Highway 57 loop.

**ENTRY**—Entrance fees apply only to Milford State Park. The park is open all year, but facilities such as the park offices, nature center, and fish hatchery are limited to weekdays in the off-season. Nature center hours are 9:00 A.M. to 4:00 P.M., Monday–Friday. In high season (April through September), the hours are extended to include Saturday and Sunday from 1:00 P.M. to 5:00 P.M. The nature center is closed on Thanksgiving, Christmas, and New Year's Day. Guided tours of the fish hatchery are offered in high season on weekends or by appointment.

**ON THE WEB**—Trail maps can be found at both www.nwk.usace .army.mil/projects/milford and www.kdwp.state.ks.us, search "Milford."

**CONTACT**—Milford Lake and State Park, (785) 238-3014; KDWP Wildlife Area, (785) 461-5402; Corps of Engineers, (785) 238-8342; Nature Center, (785) 238-5323; Landscape Arboretum, (785) 461-5760; Thunderbird Marina, (785) 238-5864. Address of State Park: 8811 State Park Road, Milford, KS 66514.

**NEARBY**—There are four golf courses between Milford Reservoir and Tuttle Creek Reservoir. In Junction City, the **ROLLING MEADOWS GOLF**

COURSE is touted as one of the best values in the state. Located just below the dam, the public course offers tree-lined fairways, six small lakes, and 29 sand bunkers. Richard Watson designed the course in 1989. For more information, visit www.jcrollingmeadows.com or phone (785) 238-4303.

CUSTER HILL GOLF COURSE is located on Fort Riley Military Reservation. The 18-hole course, designed by Robert Trent Jones, is open to the public but requires a photo ID or driver's license, as well as proof of insurance and registration (or a contract if you're renting a vehicle). For more information, visit www.riley.army.mil/recreation/golf.asp or phone (785) 784-6000.

COLBERT HILLS GOLF COURSE was designed by Jeff Colbert and architect Jeff Brauer. Located in Manhattan, this course is suitable for all playing levels, with up to seven sets of tees per hole. For more information, visit www.colberthills.com or phone (877) 916-4653.

STAGG HILL GOLF COURSE is in Manhattan on the banks of the Kansas River, marked by tree-lined fairways and challenging greens. Phone (785) 539-1041.

# Council Grove Lake and
## Allegawaho Heritage Memorial Park

IN 1825, an agreement signed between the U.S. Council and the Osage Nation allowed safe passage on the Santa Fe Trail in exchange for $800. The town of Council Grove quickly acquired a reputation as one of the last places that travelers could stock up on supplies or get a bed and bath before the long journey to Santa Fe. After the railroads made the trail obsolete, the area was designated as a Kaw (or Kansa) Reservation.

Today a small reservoir on the outskirts of historic Council Grove provides many outdoor activities. While the lake itself offers only two short trails, Council Grove boasts plenty of interesting hiking and walking tours that reflect the history of the area. Additionally, the Tallgrass Prairie National Preserve is less than 20 miles away, with abundant hiking opportunities.

Cropland, pasture, and rolling hills surround Council Grove Lake. Because the reservoir is relatively small, you can get oriented quickly and see the park thoroughly in a weekend. The lake's eight public-use areas, such as the Kansa View, are clean and well manicured, offering great picnic spots and lovely views of the reservoir. As you drive over the dam, you may see anglers far below fishing the Neosho River from the outlet channel.

The COE office is located at the west end of the dam, where visitors can pick up park maps and take in a small display of local wildlife, history, and even archeological finds from the area. Continuing west, a small marina rents boats and a wetland area melds with views of the Flint Hills near Canning Creek Cove.

**WILDLIFE**—Richey and Kit Carson Coves seem to be full of colorful little birds, such as American goldfinches, eastern bluebirds, western meadowlarks, cardinals, robins, and flycatchers. Hike the short birding trail located here. As you drive over the wetland at the entrance to Canning Creek Cove, look for wildlife in the swampy areas. If you don't mind unpaved roads, follow Kelso Road for about 5 miles to the Neosho River inlet. On the east side of the park, travel north on U.S. Highway 177 to cross the Munkers Creek arm. From the wildlife areas you might see deer, quail, ducks, geese, kingfishers, and herons. KDWP manages the wildlife areas on both lake arms.

**HIKING**—A short birding trail runs between Richey Cove and Kit Carson Cove on a natural and mowed-grass surface. You'll find the trailhead marker near the group camp and restrooms. Running parallel to the shore, a row of trees and tall shrubs creates a viewing blind from which to see gulls, terns, ducks, and herons. Add a small loop of riparian woodland before returning the same way.

**PIONEER NATURE TRAIL** begins behind the COE office. Locate the kiosk from the parking lot. No map is available for this wooded path, which will take the average hiker only 30 minutes. Head through a grassy picnic area to find a path leading into the woods. A mulch-and-dirt path crosses a creek on a wooden bridge. A bench allows quiet reflection and bird-watching. The trail is well maintained and offers great opportunities for wildlife watching and wildflower viewing during summer months. The main loop is a quarter-mile long and leads upland through the woods. A half-mile extension named Buffalo Wallow travels through a portion of tallgrass prairie where it is said depressions have been left behind by buffalo that once wallowed in the dirt.

**FISHING AND HUNTING**—The Neosho River and Munkers Creek are both good fishing streams. Crappie may be your best bet, as the lake has healthy populations that congregate near underwater creek channels and around brush piles deep in the water. The COE uses cedar and evergreen in the reservoir as fish shelters marked with buoys or shoreline signs. Fish attractor location maps can be picked up at the COE office. The brochure also indicates healthy populations of saugeye, which can be up to 18-19 inches long and weigh up to 2.5 pounds. Wiper, walleye, white and largemouth bass, and channel and flathead catfish are also present in the lake. Pole-and-line fishing from the mudflats on the Neosho yields good results for catfish. Channel cats are most active just after rain. A fish-cleaning station is located near the marina, which also rents fishing boats. Boat ramps are available at all public use areas except Kansa View. Fishing is also allowed at the nearby city lake, located about a mile southwest of the reservoir.

A wildlife area is managed by KDWP for public hunting, which offers quail, rabbits, turkeys, and deer. Ducks and geese are more plentiful during migration season. With the exception of opening weekends, hunting pressure is light.

**PADDLING**—Put in at parking lots and boat ramps above the reservoir on Munkers Creek and the Neosho River to float a few miles downstream to the reservoir's public-use areas. The Corps of Engineers can provide current water levels. Paddlers should be aware that this is a wildlife area.

**CAMPING AND FACILITIES**—A high percentage of campsites are located right on the shoreline. Richey Cove has a group camp, a swimming beach, and a nature trail in addition to all camping amenities. Kit Carson Cove offers only utility campsites that cannot be reserved. Canning Creek has the widest choice of sites—group, primitive, and full-utility sites, only some of which can be reserved. All campgrounds offer boat ramps, water, and restrooms. Only Richey and Canning have shower houses and dump stations. A fish-cleaning station and marina are located at Marina Cove, which also rents pontoons, fishing boats, and paddleboats.

**LOCATION AND DIRECTIONS**—In Morris County. From I-70 take Exit 313 and follow Highway 177 south for 28 miles. Watch for small brown directional signs on your right in Morris County. Pick up the COE Tulsa District map upon arrival.

**ENTRY**—Use fees apply. Campers permitted only from 10:00 P.M. to 6:00 A.M. COE office hours are 7:45 A.M. to 4:30 P.M., Monday–Friday.

**ON THE WEB**—www.kdwp.state.ks.us, search "Council."

**CONTACT**—COE, (620) 767-5195. For the wildlife area, KDWP in Council Grove, (620) 767-5900. Marina, (620) 767-5924.

**NEARBY**—ALLEGAWAHO HERITAGE MEMORIAL PARK remembers the Kansa tribe for which the state was named with a 2-mile hike on the reservation where they lived between 1843 and 1873. A gravel path leads to a limestone tower memorial dedicated to the Kansa (also spelled Kanza or Konza), which was erected in 1925 by local citizens after the remains of a warrior were discovered in the streambed nearby. The trail changes to mowed grass as it begins a gentle climb. The payoff is panoramic views of Flint Hills pasture and ranch homes. The path descends to the country road; you can walk back to your car or continue the hike on the other side of the road.

The second half of the hike loops back to the parking lot on natural tread through riparian woodland where bottomland prairie is being restored. Glimpses of the Flint Hills appear between trees along Little John Creek. By early May, wildflowers grow tall near the stream. Killdeers nest in the fields and grasses. From the wooded trail, hikers can see the remains of stone huts, which were erected by settlers in the hope that the Kansa would live in a more "civilized" manner. A reconstruction of a bark lodge at the end of the trail provides an understanding of the accommodations the Kansa preferred. Be prepared for ticks, poison ivy, and some mud on the wooded half of the trail.

**DIRECTIONS**—From downtown, head east on Main Street (also U.S. Highway 56) to 5th Street. Take 5th Street south and travel about 3 miles. After you cross the Big John Creek Bridge, turn left on X Avenue and left again on Rd 525 to the park site. You'll see the remains of a small structure on your right. Park in the pullout just past the ruin and begin your trek on the right side of the road. Before your hike, pick up an interpretive brochure at the Kaw Mission State Historic Site or download it at www.kshs.org/places/kawmission/heritagetrail.htm.

Stone hut ruins still remain at a former Kansa Indian Reservation near Council Grove.

# Native Stone Scenic Byway
## and Flint Hills Backcountry

IF THE SURPRISING FLINT HILLS scenery from I-70 summoned the explorer in you or triggered your sense of wonder, this is your chance to get off the highway and see the rural back roads. With no semi-trucks barreling down on your bumper and no road signs to block your view, you can slow the pace and drive 48 miles through rural Flint Hills scenery on the paved Native Stone Scenic Byway. Experienced cyclists love to ride these scenic back roads, but must contend with Kansas's notorious wind and the Flint Hills' frequent elevation changes.

During the summer you'll find wildflowers, winding creeks, pasture and ranches with herds of bison, cattle, and elk along the back roads of Flint Hills. Bird-watchers can scout for prairie chicken, eastern kingbird, and bluebird. Keep an eye out for bobwhite quail, barred owl, hawk, wild turkey, killdeer, upland sandpiper, and dickcissel.

This stretch of road south of I-70 was designated as a scenic byway not only for its scenery, but for its history, as well. Because wood and trees were scarce in the Flint Hills, enterprising settlers used the plentiful stone and rock instead. As a result, many homes, walls, fences, bridges, and other buildings were constructed of native limestone. Stone fences were initiated when the government declared the open range "closed" and paid settlers to build the fences. Miles of original fence remain, serving as a symbol of the area's natural and cultural importance. A pullout and historical marker can be found along State Highway 99, where these rustic stone fences and beautiful Flint Hills scenery are on display. The byway, which was officially designated in October 2005, travels 48 miles along State Highways 4 and 99, passing through Dover, Keene, Eskridge, and Alma.

**DOVER:** Historic structures in Dover include the Dover Mercantile (now a general store and café), the Sage Inn (formerly a Stagecoach Station), and a 1920s gas station. Sandstone cliffs provide a beautiful backdrop to a rustic picnic area near Dover at Echo Cliff Park where Mission Creek flows at the base of the cliffs. To find the park, continue two miles west of Dover and detour 1 mile south on Echo Cliff Road.

**ESKRIDGE:** Impressive structures include a magnificent limestone and redwood barn and the local bank building, which is complete with turret, columns, and arches. Eskridge is also the home of Lake Wabaunsee.

**LAKE WABAUNSEE** offers camping, nine holes of golf, and access to all the usual water sports: swimming, boating, skiing, sailing, canoe/kayaking, and fishing (with city permits). Winter visitors may even get to ice skate. History provides an unusual twist: the lake area is also the site of a former POW camp for Germans captured during WWII, just one of several POW camps in Kansas. Barracks have been transformed into lakeside cabins and the army dorm is now a restaurant. Along the lake you'll find both primitive and improved campsites. A bed-and-breakfast called The Gem Resort offers a more deluxe experience, providing not only warm beds and meals, but access and equipment for many outdoor activities, as well (www.gemresort. com). The spring-fed Lake Wabaunsee is located 5 miles west of Eskridge on Highway 99. A permit office near the swimming beach, open April 1 to October 1, provides permits for boating, fishing, and camping.

**ALMA:** Give your legs some exercise with a self-guided architectural tour. Alma boasts a business district that is 98 percent native stone, earning the title "City of Native Stone." Pick up a walking tour brochure in the newspaper office at 323 Missouri Street, Monday through Friday.

**LOCATION AND DIRECTIONS**—In Wabaunsee County. From I-70 near Topeka, take Exit 353 and head south on State Highway 4. Travel

Miles of rock wall remain at the base of the Flint Hills on the Native Stone Scenic Byway.

K-4 south, then jog west and southwest, and return to I-70 by taking State Highway 99 north.

**ON THE WEB**—For maps and information, visit www.ksbyways.org. For information on Lake Wabaunsee, visit www.wabaunsee.com.

**CONTACT**—Wabaunsee County Economic Development, (785) 765-4655.

# Konza Prairie Biological Station
## and Pillsbury Crossing

AN IMMENSE TALLGRASS PRAIRIE once covered the central portion of North America. Today, this prairie is just 4 percent of its former size. Why does prairie survive in the Flint Hills Region when so much has been eradicated elsewhere? For starters, limestone and shale (flint) underlying thin soil kept settlers from plowing and planting fields in the area. It simply was not productive land for trees, crops, or shrubs that required deeper soil. Bison and wildlife, however, found the land very attractive, and great herds of bison grazed during migration. The Kansa and Osage Indians relied on the bison and understood that herds preferred new growth that quickly rejuvenated after fire.

Today, the Konza Prairie Biological Station functions as an outdoor laboratory, enabling biological research and the study of the tallgrass prairie ecosystem. Much of the preserve has never been plowed and so it retains native characteristics. Long-term research, education, and conservation are conducted on this tract of Flint Hills prairie, which was set aside in 1971 under the leadership of Kansas State University. The Nature Conservancy expanded the research station by purchasing the historic Dewey Ranch, whose house and barn now serve as the station headquarters and education center. The Conservancy also requested the property be named for the Kansa Indians who lived nearby at the confluence of the Blue and Kansas rivers.

**WILDLIFE**—Collared and horned lizards may be seen scampering on rocks or hiding under scarce shrubs. It's easy to tell them apart. The Texas horned lizard is well camouflaged by the prairie; it has a round abdomen and appears to have horns. Collared lizards come in many shades and colors, but can be identified by the rings around their necks. Wood rats pile up branches,

The Nature Trail at the Konza Prairie is a must-see.

Joseph Miriani

June is the best time to hike the Konza Prairie Biological Station for wildflower identification.

twigs, and leaves to create homes. Wild turkeys, bluebirds, Bell's vireos, and redheaded woodpeckers can be seen in the woodlands around Kings Creek, while meadowlarks and grasshopper sparrows love the open prairie.

A collage of wildflowers thrives along the trail. Look for the stunning orange blooms of butterfly milkweed, star-shaped blooms of Carolina horsenettle, dainty purple clusters of wild alfalfa, and tall purple stems of ironweed. The tall, slender stalks decorated with tiny lavender petals are woolly verbena. The number of species found on the Konza is nothing short of incredible. Complete lists of Konza Prairie plants, birds, butterflies, reptiles, and amphibians can be found on the Konza Environmental Education Program Web site at www.k-state.edu/konza/keep.

**HIKING**—Most of the property is closed to the public except by appointment. Hikers must remain on the designated public trails. As you might expect, hiking the Flint Hills can be strenuous, but fantastic views are the reward. Interpretive brochures are provided at the trailhead and parking lot. There is little shade and no drinking water. Arrive prepared with water, sunscreen, and insect repellent.

**NATURE TRAIL AND HOMESTEAD TRAIL:** Travel clockwise to follow the interpretive brochure, which you can find at the trailhead. This

2.8-mile trail begins by crossing the clear waters of Kings Creek, which are filtered by layers of limestone and shale. The trail almost immediately begins to climb and the wind works against you. Unending aerial views from the ridge are surprising. Limestone rubble and chert (another sedimentary rock) pepper the trail in unmistakable Flint Hills fashion. The Nature Trail is the most strenuous trail on the Konza, but worth your efforts. The payoff is traveling rocky ridgetops for a bird's-eye view across watersheds, ravines, and pasture. Just past the radio tower, the Kansas River valley comes into view below.

Be sure to watch for your turnoff to complete the Nature Trail, or you may double the length of your hike. The Hokanson Homestead of 1878 en route makes a lovely picnic stop. A side trail loops along native stone structures and foundations through woods along Kings Creek. An interpretive brochure is available for the side trail, as well. For your convenience, a restroom is located here, by the Hokanson Homestead, but is closed in the off-season. Take the opportunity to spot wildlife and identify wildflowers and birds on the return leg of the trail as it leads through open prairie and follows Kings Creek back to the trailhead. Perhaps a well camouflaged Texas horned lizard will make an appearance.

**KINGS CREEK LOOP:** Add an additional 2 miles to the Nature Trail with the Kings Creek Loop, for a total of 4.7 miles. Locate the trail guide in a mailbox at the start of the loop (after 1.3 miles on the Nature Trail just past the radio tower). The trail is meant to be hiked clockwise and can be difficult to follow in reverse. The interpretive guide explains that mastodons and mammoths first grazed the prairie, then bison and later cattle. A herd of 300 bison is managed here to research the effects of grazing. From the ridge above the Kansas River valley, perhaps some of the Konza's herd may be seen in the distance before the trail descends.

Burning is also used to maintain a healthy prairie ecosystem. Some areas have not been burned to study the contrast in resulting vegetation. Can you tell which? Invasive species such as redbud, rough-leaf dogwood, oak, and green ash grow where water is available and burning has been unable to control them.

The return trail parallels Kings Creek, with panoramic vistas of the Flint Hills in the distance. Wildflowers thrive in the open prairie all along the return route. Clear waters of the creek look inviting, but please don't contaminate the water by wading in it.

**GODWIN HILL LOOP:** Add another 1.4 miles to the Nature Trail and the Kings Creek Loop, for a total of 6.1 miles. In addition to the fantastic scenery you'll see on the previous two segments, this trail crosses Kings Creek and its tributaries and wanders deep into the woodlands.

**CAMPING AND FACILITIES**—Camping is not allowed. Primitive restrooms can be found on the trail in high season only.

**LOCATION AND DIRECTIONS**—In Riley County. Take I-70 toward Manhattan and take Exit 307 to follow McDowell Creek Road north for 4 miles. Turn right at the sign indicating the Kansas State University Konza Prairie (Konza Prairie Lane).

**ENTRY**—There is no entrance fee, but please consider making a donation at the trailhead when you visit this research area. No pets, horses, or bicycles are allowed. Do not wade or swim in the streams or creeks. Open daily from dusk to dawn, weather and trail conditions permitting. Trails may be closed temporarily for conservation, maintenance, or safety reasons. Bring your own water supply.

**ON THE WEB**—Visit www.k-state.edu/konza/keep for maps and Konza Prairie species lists. Or, visit www.ksu.edu/konza.

**CONTACT**—The Nature Conservancy, (785) 233-4400. Konza Prairie Biological Station, (785) 587-0441.

**NEARBY**—**PILLSBURY CROSSING,** a natural area located 7 miles southeast of Manhattan, is a flat-rock crossing that once provided settlers with a safe ford across Deep Creek. During normal stream flow, small rowboats, canoes, and kayaks may be used in the stream. Primitive camping is allowed with special permits. Bird-watching is popular and a short nature trail is provided in cooperation with a local conservation club. Alternatively, you can hike the areas along either side of the stream. Does fishing in the Flint Hills appeal to you? Channel and bullhead catfish, largemouth and spotted bass, and carp are present in Deep Creek. From Manhattan, drive south on U.S. Highway 177 for 2 miles. Turn left onto Deep Creek Road and drive 3 miles. Turn right on Pillsbury Crossing Road. For more information, call the KDWP area office in Manhattan at (785) 539-9999.

## *Geology of the Osage Cuestas Region*

THE GREATER PART OF SOUTHEASTERN KANSAS is within the Osage Cuestas Region. *Cuestas* is the Spanish word for slopes. The Osage Cuestas Region is characterized by a series of east-facing cliffs with a gentle slope or plain that falls away from the cliffs or ridges. Like waves, the crest builds while the water behind slopes away until it meets the next crest. The elements underlying these waves include Pennsylvanian Period limestone and shale that were deposited when an enormous, shallow sea covered the plains. The ridges range in height from 50 to 200 feet. Each ridge is capped with the more resistant limestone, while the gentle slopes are composed of thick layers of shale.

An illustration of the alternating layers of limestone and shale can be seen in the spillway at the dam on Clinton Lake. Construction of the dam left a cross section where you can see layers of rock that are 300 million years old.

# Melvern Lake
## and Eisenhower State Park

EISENHOWER STATE PARK is named after the only president to come from Kansas. The state park is just one small peninsula on Melvern Lake, which is 10 miles wide with many fingers and coves. Located in the Osage Cuestas Region near the edge of the Flint Hills, the park boasts especially clear water thanks to the surrounding native prairie. At the west end of the lake is a wildlife and waterfowl refuge characterized by upland habitat and marsh. The reservoir is fed by the Marais des Cygnes River, named "Marsh of the Swans" by French traders, who no doubt found the area full of wildlife.

### SELECTING YOUR BASE CAMP

Melvern Lake is composed of six park areas, five of which are run by the Corps of Engineers. Understanding the advantages and differences of each will make selecting your base camp a little easier. No doubt your favorite area will be dependent upon your favorite activities, but you can be sure there is something for everyone.

**EISENHOWER STATE PARK** is the only area managed by the Kansas Department of Wildlife and Parks. It is the largest of the six areas and has the most campsites, including one primitive cabin, two yurts, and a horse camp, as well as substantial trails for horses, hikers, and mountain bikes. Lake arms on either side of the park are suitable for sheltered flat-water paddling on calm days. Kayaks may be rented from the general store at the Doud Campground.

**OUTLET PARK** receives the most traffic. It features a fishing pond and a swimming beach on the backside of the dam. Trails encircle the sparkling ponds that sit on a manicured, flat, grassy lawn.

**COEUR D'ALENE PARK** has nature trails with an overlook and features a full-service marina for boaters.

**ARROW ROCK PARK** is touted as the most scenic park, with panoramic views. It has just 45 campsites and hike or bike trails that take advantage of expansive lake views. A picnic pavilion sits high above the reservoir and rolling hills.

**SUN DANCE PARK** offers 30 primitive campsites (no bathhouse) free of charge and is nearest the wildlife area by the town of Arvonia.

**TURKEY POINT** offers a waterfront day-use area and an isolated group campsite for privacy.

**WILDLIFE**—The refuge on the west side is a great place to look for migrating geese and ducks, shorebirds, and wading birds such as the great blue heron. Bald eagles perch on dead timber in the lake. Visitors to the wildlife area will find an office nearby in the town of Reading. Trails in Outlet Park are great places from which to inspect the canopy for nuthatches, black-capped chickadees, redheaded woodpeckers, screech owls, and red-tailed hawks. Look for the greater prairie chicken booming grounds in the outlying areas with prairie grasses.

**HIKING**—Trails long and short, paved, gravel, or primitive are scattered throughout the many park areas. The longest trails are the **CROOKED KNEE BRIDLE TRAIL** and the **FIVE STAR MOUNTAIN BIKE TRAIL** in the state park. There are many short nature trails at Melvern Lake that are worth a look, but visitors that desire lengthy trails can hike a portion of the equestrian trail that hugs the lakeshore. The Crooked Knee Bridle Trail runs through property otherwise undeveloped and is likely to yield more wildlife sightings; it is also open to exploration whether you like to follow trails or not.

**OUTLET PARK:** *The River Bottom Nature Trail* is a three-quarter-mile primitive loop of shaded trail with dense understory. A half-mile scenic but paved side trail connects with the *Marais des Cygnes Nature Trail,* a 1.5-mile gravel-surfaced trail. Marais des Cygnes leads through woods and follows a river channel to an oxbow and then traverses the river-pond shoreline. Restrooms and water are available near the trail.

**COEUR D'ALENE PARK:** *The Breakwater Trail* is a half-mile, partly wooded trail that climbs over a ridge to reach the shoreline and connects the campground with the marina. The *Overlook Trail* is a quarter mile (one-way) and serves as a connector trail between a picnic area and the overlook. The Tallgrass Heritage Trail is a mowed-grass path running 2.2 miles between Coeur d'Alene Park and Arrow Rock Park. (See below.)

**ARROW ROCK PARK:** *The Tallgrass Heritage Trail* closely follows the contour of the shoreline east for 1.8 miles within Arrow Rock Park. The western trailhead is located in the campground behind the restrooms, marked with a plain wooden post at the entrance to the woods. This linear trail has a packed-gravel surface great for both hikers and bikers. Though it weaves between thickets and brush, there is little shade mid day. Animal tracks outnumber footprints. The trail continues for another 2.2 miles to Coeur d'Alene Park on mowed grass for hikers and mountain bikers. The path is mostly flat with some minor inclines.

**EISENHOWER STATE PARK:** *The Eisenhower Interpretive Trail* is a 1-mile loop through woodland and prairie that skirts the lakeshore with 29 markers and wildflowers. The Five Star Mountain Bike Trail (see Biking) is a 5-mile wooded, rocky trail with gradual inclines. The shady path is wide enough to hike even in the summer, but lake views will be scarce in dense foliage. The Crooked Knee Bridle Trail (see Horseback Riding) offers 20 miles that alternate between mowed grass and natural surface.

**BIKING—FIVE STAR MOUNTAIN BIKE TRAIL** loop (mentioned above) begins from the Five Star Campground in Eisenhower State Park. Lake views are scarce in the summer; but the trail is shady, wooded, and secluded with minor creek crossings. **TALLGRASS HERITAGE TRAIL** is also good for biking and suitable for beginners (see Hiking).

**HORSEBACK RIDING—CROOKED KNEE,** a 20-mile bridle trail, can be accessed from three trailheads west of the park office: North Loop Horse Camp at Westpoint, Cowboy Camp, or Crooked Knee day-use area. Lake views, wooded areas, and some rocky terrain are scenic for you and fairly easy for your horse. An 11-mile southern loop skirts the lakeshore and park boundary with views from numerous coves. Blazed in blue, it crosses prairie, woods, and some minor creeks. An additional 6 miles of trail marked in orange winds within the perimeter of the blue trail, crossing creeks and traversing hills on higher ground. The orange trail is a mowed path and easy to follow; the blue trail is also well marked, but some portions cannot be mowed. Yellow flags are used to mark sections that connect the blue trail to the orange trail. Horse camps are located at Cowboy Camp and Westpoint. Utilities and corrals are provided in the latter. Hikers and bikers are also welcome, but horses have the right-of-way. A color-coded trail map can be downloaded at www.kansastrailscouncil.org.

**TRAIL BUILDING**—The Kansas Trails Council coordinates volunteers to maintain the Crooked Knee Bridle Trail and Five Star Mountain Bike Trail (Ike's Trail). If you'd like to help, visit www.kansastrailscouncil.org for contact information.

**FISHING AND HUNTING**—Anglers have 10 miles of lake to fish for walleye, crappie, saugeye, white bass, and channel catfish. Ponds located in Outlet Park are open for fishing from April 1 to October 31. Two nine-lane boat ramps and ample parking provide access to the lake from the Eisenhower State Park. All six parks have a boat ramp. The marina at Coeur d'Alene offers a heated fishing dock.

Deer, quail, turkey, duck, rabbit, and squirrel are hunted in the public lands. The upper reaches of Melvern Lake offer game-attracting crops and fields. The north side of the lake is more wooded than the south, offering more cover. Hunting and access to the refuge is restricted from October 21 to January 15.

**OTHER**—The state park rents tandem and single kayaks from a general store at the Doud Campground. As the campground is not on the water, you'll need a way to transport the kayaks to a beach or boat ramp. The coves on either side of the state park offer protected paddling along the shoreline on calm days.

**CAMPING AND FACILITIES**—Utility campsites with dump stations, as well as primitive and group campsites, are all available with picnic tables, fire rings, and shower houses. A horse camp with corrals and one primitive cabin is available at the state park. Much like primitive cabins, two yurts have also been added. Other facilities include boat ramps, docks, and a marina with boat rental and supplies, potable water, fish-cleaning stations, playgrounds, shelter houses, day-use picnic areas, and modern and primitive toilets. Three beaches are reserved for swimming only: Outlet, Coeur d'Alene, and Eisenhower State Park. The state park offers laundry facilities, kayak rentals, and a general store for basic supplies at the Doud Campground. Sports equipment such as volleyballs and horseshoes can be checked out from the camp host.

**TRAFFIC**—Below average, heaviest in May and July.

**LOCATION AND DIRECTIONS**—In Osage County, between Ottawa and Emporia, just off I-35 at Exit 155. Head north on U.S. Highway 75. For Eisenhower State Park, turn west on State Highway 278 and follow the signs. The Corps of Engineers office, with exhibits and information, is located south of the dam, a quarter mile west of the intersection of Highway 75 and State Highway 31, on Melvern Lake Parkway.

**ENTRY**—Entrance fees apply for Eisenhower State Park only. Open all year, but the waterfowl refuge is closed from October 21 to January 15.

**ON THE WEB**—For a map of the lake and COE trails, visit www.nwk.usace.army.mil/me. For KDWP and maps of Eisenhower State Park, go to www.kdwp.state.ks.us.

**CONTACT**—KDWP office in Osage City, (785) 528-4102; 29810 South Fairlawn Road, Osage City, KS 66523. Camp reservations, (877) 444-6777. Corps of Engineers office in Melvern, (785) 549-3318. Marina, (620) 256-6566.

# Pomona Lake and State Park

Pomona Lake is much smaller than neighboring Melvern Lake, but it offers some unique recreation. The lake is shaped like a turkey foot; its three long coves attract wildlife and allow ample opportunity for sheltered paddling. There are also several facilities that make group outings memorable. Wigger Campground, a primitive group site in Wolf Creek Park, offers not only privacy for your group, but also a shallow sand beach and a play area for a small fee. Wolf Creek Group Camp has 24 sites with utilities and a large picnic shelter for $100 per night. Southwind Shelter House is a group facility that can house up to 128 people; it's complete with a kitchen, a restroom, a covered porch, picnic tables, and grills with nearby swimming beach, bathhouse, and playground.

Additionally, the marina at Pomona State Park rents out ski equipment, and an All-Terrain Vehicle Area is maintained at the west end of the lake in Carbolyn Park. For golfers, a driving range is located just outside the park entrance. Multipurpose trails, both long and short, run throughout the park. With something for everyone, Pomona Lake has "group outing" or "family event" written all over it.

**WILDLIFE**—Located in the Osage Cuestas Region, the prairie is contrasted with rows of Chinquapin oak and hickory trees. Elm, cottonwood, and hackberry, as well as many other species, grow along the streams and creeks where lucky visitors may see red-bellied woodpeckers, white-breasted nuthatches, purple finches, black-capped chickadees, great egrets, or great blue herons. Migrating visitors include white pelicans, snow geese, buffleheads, mergansers, goldeneyes, and pintails. The woodlands harbor deer, wild turkeys, cottontails, coyotes, raccoon, skunks, bobcats, muskrat, and eastern wood rats. Be aware that copperhead and timber rattlesnakes also make their home near the lake.

**HIKING**—Three nature trails can be found within the state park. At the Burning Heart Campground, a path just under a mile long runs between two trailheads. You can begin from either the south end of the campground or the picnic shelter at the north end. A linear trail of just over a mile named Hedge-Wood begins just inside the park entrance and heads east to Big Bear Campground. The trail alternates between mowed grass and gravel; it is

Early morning reflections from a cove in Pomona Lake and State Park.

partly wooded and partly open through prairie grasses. Backtrack or return on the park road. A third nature trail is located on the east side of the park, just south of the Cedar Wind Campground. The trail forms a half-mile loop with extensions to restrooms and a picnic shelter. All three trails are wooded and none showcase lake views. The trails are mapped on the state park brochure provided on the KDWP Web site.

The Corp of Engineers provides **DEER CREEK NATURE TRAIL,** which is heavily wooded, winding along Deer Creek for a quarter mile, beginning in Outlet Park. Fifteen numbered stops coordinate with a brochure that you can pick up at the COE office. The route identifies many tree species.

**WITCHES' BROOM NATURE TRAIL** travels through a wooded area for a half-mile, beginning in the Corps' primitive 110-Mile Park. There are 21 numbered stops that coordinate with a brochure that identifies 18 tree species and three natural features.

**BLACKHAWK MULTI-USE TRAIL** is a lengthy trail system for equestrians, hikers, and mountain bikers. Beginning in 110-Mile Park, two parallel trails head northwest along the lake, pass through Cedar Park, and continue around Plummer Creek and 110-Mile Creek. Mature trees shade the trail as it follows the contour of the lake arm. Expect some climbs, descents, and creek crossings as you savor the lake views and celebrate having the trail all to yourself. The trail is currently about 30 miles, but expansions will make it 42. Many short loops can be formed with parallel trails marked in blue and orange. The orange route hugs the lakeshore more closely than the blue route, which skirts the park boundary. White blazes indicate passes between the two trails. For a shorter route, you can have someone drop you off at Cedar Park and hike or ride 5 miles back to camp at 110-Mile Park. Most of the trail is easy. Head north from Cedar Park for more challenging terrain. A primitive group camp called Charlie's Checkpoint is about a mile from the trailhead. Reservations can be made for a fee between April 1 and October 1. The natural-surface trail is overgrown in the summer and insects become bothersome. You can be sure there are poison ivy plants along the path. Bring some company if you are uncomfortable hiking alone. This trail passes through areas where hunting is allowed. The trail is mapped on the COE Web site and a brochure is available at the COE office.

**BIKING**—Mountain bikers can ride the multi-use Blackhawk Trail. (See Hiking.) The trail is mostly flat and does not offer much to hone technical skills, but there are still a few tough obstacles. Be aware that you share the trail with hikers and horseback riders, but most of the time you'll be alone on the trail. Bikes are also permitted on the Hedge-Wood Trail, which is perfect for children or beginners.

**HORSEBACK RIDING**—Equestrians can ride the multi-use Blackhawk Trail. (See Hiking.) A primitive horse camp (Charlie's Checkpoint) may be reserved.

**FISHING AND HUNTING**—Fish feeders and brush are strategically placed in the lake to improve habitat for crappie, channel, and flathead catfish, wiper, white bass, and walleye. Crappie fishing is best in the spring when they spawn near the shoreline. Channel cat is especially plentiful in the snags near the campground in Cedar Park. Anglers will find a fishing dock at Michigan Valley Park, marinas at Michigan Valley and Pomona, and boat ramps in all park areas. Parking lots along the creek inlets allow for convenient hunting and fishing west of U.S. Highway 75. Hunting is not permitted in park areas; however, public lands offer diverse habitat that includes prairie grassland, woodland, marsh, and lake where hunters may find rabbits, doves, quail, deer, turkeys, and waterfowl. Pick up a hunting brochure with rules and restrictions at the COE office south of the dam.

**OTHER**—An All-Terrain Vehicle Area is adjacent to Carbolyn Park on the western fork.

**BOATING AND PADDLING**—At Management Park's boat ramp, a program provides loaner life jackets for children. The main body of the lake is attractive for skiers, windsurfers, and sailors, while the sheltered fingers and coves are suitable for canoes and kayaks. Marinas at Michigan Valley and Pomona State Park offer fuel, mooring, and other supplies. The state park rents ski equipment from the marina.

Eight boat ramps and three lake arms create several options for wildlife viewing from a canoe or kayak on calm days. You must bring your own equipment.

**CAMPING AND FACILITIES**—Pomona State Park is managed by KDWP, while six more units fall under the Corps of Engineers' responsibility—Management Park, Outlet Park, Michigan Valley Park, Wolf Creek Park, 110-Mile Park, and Carbolyn Park. Group sites and improved and primitive sites are all available in the seven park areas. Any park that accepts reservations does so only from May 1 through September 30. The state park offers many campsites along the shoreline; Bunkers Cove is a shady, secluded loop with few sites, located on a ledge below the park road and hovering over the lake. Cedar Park and 110-Mile Park offer a primitive-camping experience (accessed via gravel roads) on a first-come, first-served basis. Wolf Creek Park and Michigan Valley Park offer both reservable and nonreservable sites and are the most developed of the COE parks, with dump stations, shower houses, and picnic facilities. Outlet Park is reservable and equipped for winter camping. Horseshoe pits, volleyball courts, playgrounds, a nine-hole disc golf course, and a marina are some of the extras at Pomona. Swimming beaches are located at Pomona State Park and Michigan Valley Park.

**TRAFFIC**—Below average, heaviest in May, June, and July.

**LOCATION AND DIRECTIONS**—In Osage County, north of Vassar. From Topeka, head south on U.S. Highway 75 and then east on State Highway 268 to the Corps Visitor Center. To reach the state park, take Highway 268 east to State Highway 368 north.

**ENTRY**—Entrance fees apply at Pomona State Park only. Open all year with full services May 1 to October 1. Camping reservations are accepted only from May 1 through September 30 for any park that accepts reservations.

**ON THE WEB**—Trail and park maps are available at www.nwk.usace.army.mil/po or www.kdwp.state.ks.us.

**CONTACT**—Lighthouse Bay Marina, (785) 828-4777; KDWP, (785) 828-4933; Corps of Engineers, (785) 453-2201. Address of Pomona State Park: 22900 South Highway 368, Vassar, KS 66534-9162.

# Clinton Lake and State Park

IN THE OSAGE CUESTAS REGION, just west of Lawrence, Clinton Reservoir sprawls over 8 miles of the Wakarusa Valley to provide recreation and protect the valley from flooding. The reservoir is named for the town of Clinton, which lies between the arms of Rock Creek and the Wakarusa River.

Geology buffs will want to take a closer look at the layers of limestone and shale exposed at the dam here. The cross section of rock provides an illustration of alternating deposits left behind during the Pennsylvanian Period 300 million years ago.

It is the great variety of trails that make this park shine. This natural area offers everything from short, educational nature trails and hikes to scenic overlooks and half- or full-day hikes. Some trails are lengthy and challenging enough to help hikers or backpackers train for an upcoming adventure. Add a variety of bike paths, equestrian trails, and even a ski trail to complete the picture of this Kansas gem.

## SELECTING YOUR BASE CAMP

As is the case for most reservoirs in Kansas, the Corps of Engineers and the Kansas Department of Wildlife and Parks each maintain areas around Clinton Lake. The state park is just one park of six on the lake. In addition to the state park, the city of Lawrence maintains Outlet Park and the COE operates four parks. A well-labeled map provided by the Corps helps visitors determine the governing and collecting agency.

**CLINTON STATE PARK** is situated on an 80-foot bluff on the north side of the reservoir. The park offers trails for hiking, biking, and cross-country skiing, as well as a swimming beach, four boat ramps, primitive and utility campsites, and a full-service marina. Shoreline development is purposely kept to a minimum and campsites are not on the water. Drop in on the live animal exhibit at the KDWP park office to see native reptiles and amphibians; open daily from 8:00 A.M. to 4:00 P.M.

**BLOOMINGTON PARK** is the most developed, with 400 campsites near a swimming beach, as well as picnic areas, boat ramps, playgrounds, and the Clinton Museum.

**ROCKHAVEN PARK** offers miles of trail for equestrians and hikers and 50 campsites.

**WOODRIDGE PARK** is located on the northwest corner of the lake and offers a hiking/backpacking loop. Primitive walk-in camping is allowed 100 feet from the heavily wooded circuit trail and on the grassy lawn at the trailhead.

**OVERLOOK PARK** is a day-use area at the north end of the dam. Open from 9:00 A.M. to 10:00 P.M., the park offers an observation point that provides views of the dam and lake. Visitors will find a play area between picnic sites, as well as access to the north shore trails and the two short nature trails. The COE visitor center is also located here, offering historic and natural interpretations.

**OUTLET PARK** is managed by the city of Lawrence. It offers picnic sites, a sports complex, an 18-hole golf course, a dog off-leash area, and a flying field for model aircraft.

**WILDLIFE**—High bluffs make Clinton Lake an attractive roost for bald eagles. Visitors can also drive a paved road (County Road 1023) through the wildlife refuge west of the lake for views of waterfowl. Note that the refuge is closed to all visitors from October 15 to January 15. Canada and snow geese, mallard, teal, and shorebirds sometimes drop in. Beaver and mink also make themselves at home here. Combine your drive with a hike on the George Latham Trail and you may see deer, squirrels, quail, cottontails, and mourning doves. Rocks and stone walls tend to attract snakes: keep a cautious lookout for rattlesnakes and copperheads on all the trails in Clinton State Park. Along the park's many trails, look for common signs of beaver, raccoon, coyotes, and foxes. Bluebirds and blue jays keep you company on the packed-earth surface. Eastern kingbirds linger at Lake Henry, a small body of water just south of the park office; look for the white outline on their tail feathers.

**HIKING—NORTH SHORE TRAIL SYSTEM** is a lengthy system that winds through the state park between the dam and the Coon Creek arm of the lake. The Kansas Trails Council deserves a medal for its part in designing and maintaining these trails with help from Earthriders Mountain Bike Club and the Lawrence Area Mountain Bike Club. Several trailheads allow access for day hiking. The eastern trailhead is accessed at Overlook Park. Moving west, you can also begin at a parking lot closer to Lake Henry, just south of the state park office, or the day-use picnic area and campgrounds areas. To hike the full length in a day, get an early start, leave a second car at campground #3, and begin at Overlook Park.

Two trails roughly parallel each other, traversing forests of hickory and oak and following along the lakeshore. The trails are well marked and identified with paint blazes in blue and white. Connector trails are signed in both blue and white. If you see a white blaze over the top of a blue blaze, it signifies that you are going from the white trail to the blue trail. The trails cross and join at several points, but generally the white trail climbs up and over the blue. The blue trail is considered easy to moderate at 8.1 miles in length; the more challenging white trail is 12.8 miles long. If you travel the blue trail out and take the white trail back, you will hike about 21 miles.

Often used by campers, a short trail signed in red and labeled **LANDS END** runs for 1.25 miles between campground #1 and the shoreline at the tip of the peninsula.

Wild roses adorn the trail. Snakes are a common sight on the shaded and heavily wooded areas. From the white trail, lake views are scarce through the heavy summer foliage. Watch your footing as tree roots and rocks create obstacles. Steep, rocky slopes may slow you down and recent rains can keep the trail muddy for days. The blue trail may be underwater in unusual circumstances but the white trail is almost always passable. On weekends, you'll also have to step aside for cyclists who frequent the trail. In the middle section, watch for a set of steps that lead up to campground #1. The day-use picnic area is also en route. These are good places to picnic and replenish your water. Restrooms are also available in the picnic area. If you have only a couple of hours to hike, begin at Overlook Park, hike west, and make a loop around Lake Henry and return. For a half-day of hiking, begin at Overlook Park, follow the white trail to loop around Lake Henry, continue to the day-use area or campground #1, picnic and replenish your water, and then return on the blue trail. North Shore Trail maps can be found at www.kansastrailscouncil.org. Mileage markers on the trail help you pinpoint your position on the map.

**SANDERS MOUND TRAIL** is a recently paved sidewalk in Overlook Park that leads from a shelter and overlook down toward the lake with views of the dam. It also connects to the North Shore Trail via a spur. The trail can be accessed from the North Shore Trailhead (picnic shelter #1) or from Observation Point and picnic shelter #2. The circuit is approximately 1 mile.

Two short nature trails are located behind the office for the Corps of Engineers. **BACKWOODS NATURE TRAIL** is an easy interpretive trail that loops three-quarters of a mile through woodlands. Pick up the interpretive guide at the trailhead or the visitor center. Fourteen points of interest are narrated and marked with posts that teach general outdoor observational skills. Learn to spot the nest of the eastern wood rat, how to interpret tree rings, and how human activities impact nature. **NATURE'S WAY CHILDREN'S DISCOVERY TRAIL** is a half-mile interpreted loop that can be combined with the Backwoods Nature Trail to lengthen your experience.

**SOUTH SHORE/ROCKHAVEN TRAIL** stretches between the dam and the Rock Creek arm of the lake. A system of three separate but parallel trails about a half mile apart creates over 30 miles of hiking. The official trailhead is located in the Rockhaven public-use area on the north side of the campground where the Clinton Pass extends to all three trails. Which will you choose? The Rock Bottom Trail, signed in orange, runs closest to the shore for 8 miles. The Benjamin Trail, signed in yellow, is the most challenging, at 12.5 miles. The 11-mile Rimrock Trail, signed in blue, travels the ridge above the lake. All three trails are linked with passes, or connector trails, signed in white. There are about nine passes, each roughly a mile apart, that may be used to connect the main trails and form shorter loops.

You'll be sharing this trail with equestrians, who have the right-of-way. Enjoy views of the lake and a variety of foliage from Osage orange to shagbark hickory, hackberry, red cedar, and sycamore.

**GEORGE LATHAM TRAIL** loops around the edge of Woodridge Park. For a walk-in, primitive campground, Woodridge Park is a delight. The park is surprisingly tidy, with a gravel parking circle, restrooms, and a water pump. Plentiful picnic tables, grills, and fire rings rest on a shady lawn perfect for group activities. For backpackers, trailside primitive campsites offer a perfect place to settle in to watch the limestone shores light up at sunset after an inspiring 4.5-mile hike.

You may need to wander the tree line to locate the trailheads. To hike clockwise, begin at the trailhead behind the restroom. To hike counterclockwise and follow the mile markers in order, begin at the trailhead across the grassy lot.

Traveling clockwise, hikers will see Dry Creek amble toward the lake arm. But, as its name suggests, you won't always find the creek flowing. Beaver dams and stark timber rise from the inlet, where you may also see gulls and migrating birds. Without foliage to block the view, ranch homes perched atop steep bluffs across the lake, grasses and timber, reflective streams, and rolling hills provide plenty of color in the distance, even during prespring months. The natural trail ascends and descends many times, providing views into ravines and creeks. At times, the trail closes in on the lake and offers stunning panoramic views. Rest and pay homage to George Latham at a bench dedicated to this lifelong outdoorsman who scouted and marked this trail.

Blue-paint blazes make this trail easy to follow. Hand-stacked rock walls are common and old farm machinery still remains. The trail crosses water numerous times, but will rarely cause difficulty. Occasionally, the trail skirts fields of prairie grass, but most of the course offers views of the lake from a wooded setting. Look for snakes sunning themselves on rock-wall remnants. As you parallel the lakeshore, keep an eye open for migratory birds. Gulls and geese are common, white-breasted nuthatches scamper upside down on trees, and red-tailed hawks are frequently seen soaring from branch to branch overhead.

Due to its remote location, you may have this trail all to yourself, despite its designation as a National Recreation Trail. Some sections can be steep. Plan to spend about two to three hours to complete the narrow, primitive loop. Poison ivy and insects are a problem, particularly in the summer. Watch for trip hazards, as fallen leaves cover precarious stones in the path.

**BIKING**—Mountain bikers and hikers share the **NORTH SHORE TRAIL SYSTEM,** which is composed of rocky, packed earth riddled with huge tree roots, located within Clinton State Park. (See Hiking.) A skills loop designed specifically for riders has been forged on the west end of the trail.

Road bikers can ride the paved back roads circling the lake or choose the Lawrence hike/bike path. This concrete trail parallels a section of State Highway 10 for nearly 9 miles from U.S. Highway 59 south of the city to I-70 to the northwest. The most scenic section crosses into Clinton Lake property as it passes through the spillway area. The trail is an easy, flat surface that travels mostly through suburban areas. Riders can expect to share the path with inline skaters, walkers, and joggers. Three parking lots provide access to the trail: the first on the north side of Highway 10 (North 1260 Road) at Highway 59, the second at Highway 10 and South Wakarusa Drive (east of the dam, south of 23rd Street), and the third just south of I-70, on the east side of Highway 10.

**CROSS-COUNTRY SKIING**—There are 3 miles of cross-country ski trails in an area on the north side of the lake. Visitors may access the 10-foot wide, mowed grass path near the dump station at campground #3 or begin north of the state park office. Look for the roofed kiosks that contain trail maps. The toughest stretch of the trail is an incline off the west trailhead. The payoff is panoramic views of the lake from the crest of Bunker Hill. The descent takes you past the old Barber schoolhouse and levels out as it crosses a service road and two ponds before reaching a more gradual incline at the east trailhead. Wooden bridges and a rocky creek crossing punctuate the path. Locate a trail map at www.skikansas.org.

**HORSEBACK RIDING**—Hikers and equestrians share the South Shore Trails in Rockhaven Park (see Hiking). Three trails can be combined for more than 30 miles of riding. Primitive campsites are available at the trailhead—the only sites for campers with horses.

**TRAIL BUILDING**—Volunteers meet at the state park office on the first Saturday each month from 9:00 A.M. until noon to maintain the North Shore Trail System. Visit the Kansas Trails Council (KTC) at www.kansas-trailscouncil.org for more information. The KTC also maintains the George Latham Trail and, periodically, other Clinton Lake trails.

**FISHING AND HUNTING**—Protected coves, deep river channels, rocks and cliffs, brush, and trees create a diverse habitat. Anglers may catch white and black crappie, bluegill, largemouth and smallmouth bass, white and striped bass, northern pike, walleye, channel cat, flathead catfish, and bullhead. Submerged timber in Rock Creek, Deer Creek, and Wakarusa River arms make boating more difficult, but fishing more attractive. Channel cat and white bass are rated good. The marina offers fuel, fishing supplies, a fish-cleaning station, and a restaurant; it also rents out pontoons and fishing boats. Numerous boat ramps and courtesy docks are available for anglers.

Land surrounding the lake is a mix of cropland, grassland, and timber, providing excellent habitat for game. The parks and the dam are closed to hunting, but most of the remaining land surrounding Clinton Lake is open to hunting deer, quail, turkey, waterfowl, dove, rabbit, and squirrel. Waterfowl hunters can take advantage of the Coblentz Marsh, located on the Wakarusa River arm of the lake near the Shawnee/Douglas County line. The refuge is closed annually from October 15 to January 15.

**WATER SPORTS**—Boating, skiing, windsurfing, personal watercraft, and swimming are all accommodated at Clinton Lake. The marina offers boat slips, fuel, and equipment rental. The main body of the lake is substantial enough for motor boats and skiing, but submerged timber makes skiing and boating perilous in the river arms. Boundaries are marked for your safety. Windsurfing and sailboats are popular with Kansas's frequent winds, but be sure to check conditions and water level before you venture out. The Bloomington Park swimming beach is open May through September from 8:00 A.M. to 10:00 P.M.; another beach can be found at Clinton State Park in a small cove near campground #3.

**CAMPING AND FACILITIES**—Four park areas offer camping. Because the state park rests on a bluff, there are no campsites on the water; however, there is plentiful space for improved and primitive camping with grills and fire rings, shower buildings, and dump stations. A full-service marina provides fuel, bait, supplies, mooring, dry storage, a restaurant, and seasonal pontoon and fishing boat rentals. Unlike many state parks, Clinton State Park offers a heated shower house year-round in campground #3, along with frost-free water hydrants. Rockhaven Park and Woodridge Park offer primitive camping only. Bloomington Park also offers all the amenities of the state park, with the addition of group camps and a museum. Because sites are plentiful, reservations should be needed only on holiday weekends. Boat ramps, a courtesy dock, picnic areas, and a swimming beach round out state park amenities.

**TRAFFIC**—Average to heavy, with spikes in June and July.

**LOCATION AND DIRECTIONS**—In Douglas County, just west of Lawrence. Take I-70 to State Highway 10 (Exit 197) and go south about 3.5 miles, then veer right at the fork and watch for park signs on your right.

**ENTRY**—Entrance fees apply at the state park only. Open all year. Day-use area is open from 9:00 A.M. to 10:00 P.M. The offices are closed on weekends (except during high season). Access to the wildlife and wetland areas is periodically limited.

**ON THE WEB**—Campsites may be reserved at www.reserveusa.com. For state park information, visit www.kdwp.state.ks.us, search "Clinton." The COE offers the most information, at www.nwk.usace.army.mil/cl. In addition, trail maps can be found at baldwin-city.com and at www.kansas-trailscouncil.org.

**CONTACT**—KDWP state park office, (785) 842-8562. For camping, fishing, or lake-level information, call the Corps of Engineers, (785) 843-7665. For the wildlife area, call (785) 887-6882. For more information on the Clinton Marina, call (785) 749-3222 (closed Sunday and Monday). Address: 798 North 1415 Road, Lawrence, KS 66049.

# Prairie Spirit Trail

ALTHOUGH IT'S LESS THAN AN HOUR AWAY from Kansas City, you'll be surprised to find that this converted rail trail receives very little traffic. Originally, the railway ran from Leavenworth all the way to Galveston. Now the railbed is just a nice way for bikers to spend their day or weekend. An observant rider or hiker will see wildflowers growing right alongside the trail as it rolls through rural U.S.A. You'll roll past small towns and see clean fishing lakes, farmland, and wooded areas, reminding you that life is just as it should be. This experience is pure Americana.

Though some sections are covered with trees that form lovely tunnels and archways overhead, don't expect much shade. Numerous bridges cross over creeks and streams, but many will be dry. Views are enhanced by rolling hills, despite the fact the trail is mostly level as it follows the converted railway bed. Thirty miles of trail are currently open for use with another 20 miles of trail under construction. There are five official trailheads: from north to south, trailheads are found in Ottawa, Princeton, Richmond, Garnett, and Welda. The better trailheads are in Ottawa and Garnett, where rail depots have been converted into visitor facilities. The Garnett depot offers restrooms, vending machines, a covered picnic area, and a barbecue grill. (It's also on the edge of downtown where you can find restaurants, shops, museums, and antique stores.) Just north of town, North Lake Park surrounds Lake Garnett and offers even more options for outdoor recreation. Ottawa is a more sizable town with more lodging and dining options and a local history museum in the depot.

The trail is made of fine, hard-packed limestone reserved for bicyclists and hikers. It seems an unnecessary luxury to have a 12-foot-wide trail when you rarely encounter others, but you can bring a friend and ride side by side on the Prairie Spirit Trail. Prolonged drought caused deep ruts in the trail in 2006 and flooding caused significant damage in 2007. Check the Web site for current conditions before planning a trip. A nominal per-person fee is payable at any of the five trailheads. Choose among the following segments or combine them all for one long trip: Ottawa to Princeton is 6 miles, Princeton to Richmond is 7 miles, Richmond to Garnett is 9.4 miles, and Garnett to Welda is 8.3 miles. Welda to Iola, which is still under construction, will be 20 miles when complete.

**WILDLIFE**—Scat is extremely common on the trail, which is indicative of all the wildlife that dwells here. Walkers may have opportunity to sneak up on wildlife, particularly if hiking early or late in the day. Deer, rabbits, wild turkeys, ground squirrels, quail, and many songbirds frequent the streams and woods. You may also find evidence of coyotes and foxes on the trail. Look for snake tracks and patterns left in the limestone dust. Wild berries and prairie grasses, blooming wildflowers, and shrubs are common spring through fall. Smooth sumac, purple prairie clover, and wavy-leaf thistle are prevalent trailside. Smooth sumac is the low-growing shrub with a dark red feathery bloom, which is also responsible for bright foliage in the fall. Look for a Kansas wildflower guide at the trailhead before you set out.

**HIKING**—The **GARNETT TRAILHEAD** is a favorite start for hikers. In either direction you'll see city parks and lakes before the trees thicken to block the scenery. Inside Garnett city limits the trail is paved, landscaped, and lined with vintage-looking street lamps. Heading north, the trail soon passes by Lake Garnett at North Lake Park before it becomes immersed in the trees. Heading south, the much smaller Crystal Lake comes into view before the trail finds rolling farmland and pasture.

**BIKING**—If you're looking for the least difficult section, begin at Garnett and head south to Welda. The grade is easy and the section is shorter. First passing Crystal Lake, the trail offers wooded areas that peek out to rolling hills and pasture with prevalent wildflowers along the way. The northern-most scenery from Ottawa to Richmond is less wooded and more open through farmland and small towns. Ride the entire trail for the ultimate Kansas sampler platter.

**FISHING**—Two lakes appear along the trail's midsection in Garnett. Crystal Lake and Lake Garnett (at North Lake Park) are stocked with wall-eye, wiper, channel and flathead catfish, bluegill, bullhead, white bass, green sunfish, white crappie, black crappie, black buffalo, redear sunfish, largemouth bass, and rainbow trout. City and state permits are required. There is no hunting allowed along the trail and possession of firearms is prohibited.

**CAMPING AND FACILITIES**—You may not find working facilities at the lesser trailheads in the off-season, but the depots at Garnett and Ottawa are always open. Primitive and RV camping is allowed at North Lake Park and RV camping is allowed at Crystal Lake. Neither have shower houses. Camping permits are required and available through the Garnett Police Department at 131 West 5th Street or can be purchased from a park ranger.

**TRAFFIC**—Little or below average, heaviest in July and October.

**LOCATION AND DIRECTIONS**—In Franklin County. Take Exit 183 from I-35. To reach the Ottawa Depot, go north on U.S. Highway 59 to the junction with State Highway 68. The depot is one block west and 1 south of the junction at 135 West Tecumseh. For all other trailheads, go south on Highway 59. For the depot at Garnett, turn east on Eighth Avenue and look for the red caboose.

**ENTRY**—Open all year during daylight hours. A daily per-person fee is payable at the trailheads. Check the Web site for trail closures and conditions.

**ON THE WEB**—Maps and more can be found at www.prairiespirit trail.org and www.garnett-ks.com.

**CONTACT**—Garnett Area Chamber of Commerce, (785) 448-6767 or (785) 448-5496.

**NEARBY**—A typical recreation area, **CEDAR VALLEY RESERVOIR** is 7.5 miles west of Garnett and provides boating, skiing, fishing, RV and wilderness camping facilities, floating boat docks, loading ramps, restrooms, and picnic areas. Bring your own water. The lake is perfect for paddling, as it is long and narrow like a river. From Garnett, head west on 7th Avenue and follow the signs.

# Overland Park Arboretum and Botanical Gardens

YOU CANNOT TRULY KNOW the Overland Park Arboretum until you have visited in all four seasons. Eight ecosystems are identified within 300 acres. As you hike, test your senses. Can you identify where one system ends and another begins? The trail map is an educational resource that will open your eyes and hone your senses to hiking in Kansas. As you pull into the parking lot, you'll be immersed in dry oak savanna. Walk along Wolf Creek to see riparian woodland; these woodlands are unique from those you'll find on higher limestone bluffs just a quarter mile away.

The variety of species is what makes each season unique. Spring brings the blooms of wildflowers and redbud. In fall, sumac turns glaring red while pawpaws and oaks transform to yellow. Spring and summer wildflowers attract attention to the understory. (Visitors should note, though, that summer can be intolerable due to mosquitoes.) Winter brings a stark contrast between the limestone bluffs and the dark banks of Wolf Creek adorned by smooth, bleached bark of sycamores towering overhead.

In addition to numerous ecosystems within the natural area, there are botanical gardens that create colorful, creative, and restful spaces. The Erickson Water Garden combines plants that attract birds and butterflies with benches and tumbling water. Rare regional butterflies are sometimes spotted. The Monet Garden uses a reflective pond and scenic bridges along with soft color to pay tribute to the famous French artist who turned gardens into works of art.

Owned by the city of Overland Park, this charming arboretum is supported and maintained by Overland Park Department of Parks and Recreation along with the Friends of the Arboretum and many private donors and volunteers.

**WILDLIFE**—Deer linger in the clearings. Turtles lay claim to floating logs. Frogs, toads, and water snakes are common. Watch for copperhead snakes, which are less common. Cottontails and fox squirrels hide in the brush. Red-bellied and downy woodpeckers are easier to spot in the winter. Great blue herons and mallard ducks can be spotted in Wolf Creek. Birds of prey in nearly every form scout the creek and woodlands.

**HIKING**—6 miles of mulch, asphalt, and cement trails traverse the Arboretum. Pick up a trail map at the visitor center. Most trails are fairly level; however, as the names indicate, the Bluff Loop and the Rocky Ridge trails offer a view of the lowlands from limestone bluffs and outcroppings with some short but steep climbs. The majority of trails are mulched; natural paths and are marked as follows:

**ASPHALT TRAIL:** Less than half a mile long, this easy loop is paved in asphalt. It begins in the parking lot and circles the picnic area through dry oak savanna.

**WEST TRAIL (BROWN):** Interpretive signs placed along this easy, level 1-mile loop help you identify the many trees in the dry oak-hickory forest.

**BLUFF LOOP (GREEN):** 1 mile long, this trail is mostly level with some minor climbs. The Bluff Loop follows the contour of the creek below limestone cliffs and rock outcroppings in riparian woodland. Huge cottonwood and sycamore trees stretch overhead while buckeye and pawpaw thrive in the understory. Leatherwood trees are found here at the western edge of their range. Water seeping from the cliffs above can make for some muddy areas year-round.

**BIRD WATCH AND COTTONWOOD TRAIL (ORANGE):** Less than half a mile in length, this trail is easy and level, connecting the paved trails to the backcountry trails. Bird-watching is enhanced with a feeder station.

**ROCKY RIDGE TRAIL (YELLOW):** 1 mile long, this trail leads up and over the limestone cliffs and rock outcropping for the highest view. Two spur trails lead to overlooks where prairie restoration is an ongoing process. You must access the yellow trail from the green trail.

The remaining mileage is found on cement and asphalt trails that meander through the gardens and among waterfalls, ponds, pools, and streams.

**OTHER**—The arboretum offers docent-guided group tours if prior arrangements are made. Special events such as a holiday luminary walk are popular.

**CAMPING AND FACILITIES**—There are no camping facilities. Near the parking lot you'll find a picnic area with grills, pavilions, and shelters that can be reserved. To the right of the parking lot, the Environmental Education Visitors' Center accommodates social events and learning programs. It is well stocked with trail maps and information about native wildlife. You'll find modern restrooms and water behind the center, as well as patio tables and chairs. During the summer, water coolers are placed along the trails. You'll often find a can of bug spray at the visitor center—consider bug spray mandatory throughout warm months.

**LOCATION AND DIRECTIONS**—In Johnson County. From Overland Park, take U.S. Highway 69 to 179th Street. Turn west (right) on 179th and go a half mile to the entrance, which will be on your left just past Antioch Road (8909 West 179th Street).

**ENTRY**—No entrance fees, but donations are suggested. Hours are 8:00 A.M. to 7:30 P.M.; April 10 to September 30. The arboretum closes at 5:00 P.M. from October 1 to April 9 and is closed on Christmas Day. Dogs must be kept on a leash and are not allowed on the cement trails.

**ON THE WEB**—Maps and more can be found at www.opkansas.org and www.overlandparkarboretum.org.

**CONTACT**—For information, call (913) 685-3604. For reservations or private events, call (913) 895-6390 or write 8909 West 179th Street, Overland Park, KS 66085.

# Hillsdale Lake and State Park

Located near south Kansas City, the modern facilities and a wide range of activities make Hillsdale State Park a popular recreation destination. Rolling hills and wooded areas compete for your attention, which will no doubt be focused on the dazzling lake. Lovely scenery can be attributed to a mixed habitat: here in the northeast corner of Kansas, the stately hardwood forest of the east meets and mingles with the prairie of the Great Plains. You'll find an example of the two habitats coming together at your first marker on the Hidden Spring Nature Trail. It is this mixture of prairie, forest and stream that sustains a great variety of wildlife.

The northwest corner of the Hillsdale Reservoir is designated as a wetland. While this habitat primarily attracts migrating waterfowl, you may see herons and shorebirds on the banks, breakers, and beaches anywhere in the park. When the Corps of Engineers constructed the dam and filled the lake, 70 percent of the timber was left standing to create an attractive habitat for fish and waterfowl.

Two offices are located across from each other at the entrance to the park. On the north side of the street is the Corps of Engineers visitor center, which includes an educational exhibit, restrooms, maps, and a trailhead for the Hidden Spring Nature Trail. Across the street is the state park office, where visitors can obtain permits and reservations and speak with KDWP rangers.

**WILDLIFE**—Visitors can expect to encounter white-tailed deer, raccoon, beavers, squirrels, rabbits, coyotes, bobcats, shorebirds, and waterfowl. There are three wetlands that require some walking to access. From October 1 through January 15, a refuge on the Rock Creek arm provides migrating birds with an area to feed and rest undisturbed.

**HIKING**—**HIDDEN SPRING NATURE TRAIL** is a self-guided trail that forms two three-quarter-mile loops for a total of 1.5 miles. The first loop is an easy and fairly level interpretive trail beginning at the end of the sidewalk outside the Corps of Engineers visitor center. Pick up the brochure at the kiosk out front or just inside the front doors. Hike the loop clockwise to follow the brochure. A park sign warns trail users of ticks, so be sure to bring bug spray. In fall and spring you may not be bothered by ticks, but spiders and their large, ornate webs will keep you alert. You may want to lead with a stick to clear the webs of industrious inhabitants while exploring.

Prairie grasses adorn the entry of the trail, which leads you through forest, lichen-covered rock, and moss-covered trees. Watch for animal tracks or scat on the trail; perhaps you'll even encounter the creatures that left them. The trail guide illustrates the numerous varieties of trees and shrubs found in the park. The well-maintained trail is shaded by a tall canopy. Wooden staircases, benches, bridges, rock terraces, and numerous wildflowers decorate the natural path. Wildflowers are most prevalent in the spring and fall when sunlight filters through the trees. Look for fossils in the limestone out-croppings. The additional Eagle Loop descends to lake level and later climbs back out. The hidden spring is roped off so as not to invite further human interference, but is visible from the path.

**BIKING AND HIKING THE MULTI-USE TRAIL**—Inside the park, nearly 49 miles of multi-use trail are available for cyclists, equestrians, and hikers alike. Much of the trail is a crushed-gravel surface that winds in and out of grassy fields and wooded areas to provide peeks at the lake and surrounding hills. A section even leads along the spillway stream and through a wetland area behind the dam. Some sections are mowed grass. Metal stakes mark entry points along the route. The trail will be soggy with some standing water after heavy rainfall. Be sure to pick up current litera-ture, as four color-coded loop routes have been mapped out for users. The trail system can be confusing and changes occur as the system is upgraded. You'll likely need a couple of publications to get the big picture. In addition to the state park map, you'll want the brochure labeled *Saddle Ridge Equestrian Area* for illustrations of the colored-coded loop routes (not shown in color). The trail leading west of the marina (labeled "Outlet Blue Loop") is reserved for cyclists and hikers, as horses are not allowed in the picnic areas, campgrounds, or beaches. Get brochures in advance or you may spend a lot of time at the park trying to plan your route.

There are four parking lots convenient for trail users. They are located at the swimming beach, Jayhawker Marina, R.C. Flying Field, and the Saddle Ridge Equestrian Area. Ride or hike partial sections for shorter routes or combine them for a longer journey. The Northwest Blue Trail is 10.7 miles, the Southeast Red Trail is 12.4 miles, the Southwest Red Trail is 16.6 miles, and the Outlet Blue Loop is 9 miles. (Note: This is not actually a loop; it's an out-and-back trail, but you can return on park roads to make it a loop.)

**ROAD BIKING**—Aside from the multi-use trail, cyclists may ride the paved park road, which begins at the park office, crosses the dam, and veers right into the park. En route you'll see the marina, day-use areas, and swim-ming beach. At the end of the road, you'll weave through the Russell Crites Recreation Area and campground. Return along the same route for approx-imately 15 miles of road biking.

**HORSEBACK RIDING**—32 miles of multi-use trail are designated for horseback riders. A campground especially for horse owners (Saddle Ridge Campground) can be accessed from the road behind the COE office. Primitive camping with water and showers is available.

**FISHING AND HUNTING**—All 51 miles of shoreline are open to fishing, with the exception of designated beaches and boat ramps. The marina rents fishing and pontoon boats, and a heated fishing dock offers comfort in the winter. The lake is known for its largemouth bass and crappie. Walleye are also wellstocked. Catfish and bluegill are present, as well.

Hunting waterfowl, big and small game, and upland game birds is allowed within park boundaries, excluding any developed areas. Boat ramps, beaches, campgrounds, and the dam are safety zones where hunting is prohibited. Three wetland areas require some walking to access. All three are open to hunting during waterfowl season. The waterfowl refuge is closed to all activities from October 1 to January 15.

**OTHER**—There are two developed beaches, one for swimming and one for windsurfing. Additionally, a breaker separates a watercraft beach from the swimming beach. The R.C. Flying Field for model airplanes is located behind the dam.

**CAMPING AND FACILITIES**—One of the youngest state parks in Kansas, the facilities at Hillsdale are clean and modern. Both primitive and improved campsites are provided, many with lake views. Restrooms and shower houses are open during the camping season (April 15 to October 15) within the Russell Crites Recreation Area. The park offers ten boat ramp lanes, two beaches, four campgrounds, a day-use picnic area, reservable group shelters, and a heated fishing dock. Pontoon boats and fishing boats can be rented from the marina.

**TRAFFIC**—Heavy, particularly in June.

**LOCATION AND DIRECTIONS**—In Miami County. From Kansas City, take I-35 south to U.S. Highway 169 south. Exit on 255th Street and turn west. After passing the town of Hillsdale, you'll see the COE office on the north side and the park office on the south side of 255th Street. Continue on 255th Street, taking the first right after crossing the dam for most recreational opportunities. For the windsurfing beach and the horse camp, take the gravel road behind the COE office toward Saddle Ridge Campground. The waterfowl refuge is best reached from a different exit. From Highway 169, exit west on 223rd Street after the town of Spring Hill. Turn south on Cedar Niles Road (for Cedar Niles access) or Waverly Road for Antioch Access.

**ENTRY**—State park entrance fees apply. Open all year, but restrooms and shower houses are closed after October 15. Beaches are open from sunrise to sunset.

**ON THE WEB**—Lake maps can be found on the COE Web site, www.nwk.usace.army.mil/hi. Trail maps can be found on the KDWP Web site, www.kdwp.state.ks.us, search "Hillsdale."

**CONTACT**—KDWP office in Hillsdale, (913) 783-4507; COE office, (913) 783-4366. Address of KDWP: 26001 West 255th Street, Paola, KS 66071.

# Geology of the Glaciated Region

KANSAS WAS COVERED not once but twice by advancing glaciers during the Pleistocene Epoch (the period from 1.6 million to 10,000 years ago). The first event covered the northeast corner; the second advanced all the way to north-central Kansas. The force of these glaciers, which were up to 500 feet thick, was strong enough to break off and move large boulders across the country as it advanced. The weight and friction of the massive, moving sheets of ice were capable of pulverizing rocks and sediments in their path. Most of the evidence left behind by glaciers has been erased with time and erosion, but two features remain as proof in the Kansas soil.

First, loess soil deposits can be found prominently along river- and streambanks in the Glaciated Region. Look for a very fine, almost powderlike substance with a yellowish cast in places where the earth has been exposed or cut away. You can find some examples in Kansas City area parks and trails. The farther north you travel, the deeper the deposits.

Another reminder of glacial activity is rock brought all the way from distant states, sometimes called *glacial erratics*. Although many types of rock were left behind as glaciers melted, the most obvious was a pink quartzite. Quartzite is sand cemented with silica and is therefore quite resistant to erosion. Keep your eyes open as you hike in northeast Kansas and you'll find pink rocks and boulders embedded in the earth. This pink or red stone is named Sioux quartzite because it comes all the way from the Sioux Falls area of South Dakota.

## REMEMBERING THE OREGON TRAIL

Beginning in Independence, Missouri, the Oregon Trail cuts across the northeast corner of Kansas, ambles through Topeka, and then curves north of Manhattan. Wagon-wheel ruts still remain as silent evidence of the weary yet hopeful travelers who sought new life or fortune in the expanding United States. Several parks celebrate the memory of the famous Oregon Trail near or on the original route.

# Herbert Reinhard Green Memorial Wildlife Area

J UST WEST OF TOPEKA AT WILLARD, this land made its place in history as a Potawatomi trading post named Uniontown on the Oregon-California Trail in the mid 1800s. The town was abandoned and burned after two cholera outbreaks; but years later, in 1877, the Herbert Reinhard Green family built a home using remnants of Uniontown. Gravesites nearby are reminders of the hardships endured before the turn of the century.

**WILDLIFE**—A brochure provided by KDWP at the trailhead offers an extensive wildlife list. Mammals include all the usual suspects as well as muskrat, badgers, eastern moles, woodchucks, plains pocket gophers, big brown bats, long-tailed weasels, and mink. Look for numerous varieties of toads, frogs, snakes, turtles, skinks, and salamanders. More than 50 species of birds may be spotted along Post Creek, in the uplands and prairies or soaring in the sky.

**HIKING**—Two short, self-guided nature trails begin from the parking area. The **POST CREEK RIDGE TRAIL** is a 1-mile loop that features the site of the Green family home, which is still strewn with old farm implements and rock-fence remnants. The trail winds along a ridge above Post Creek up and over some steep hills through prairie now overtaken by woods. Located on the southernmost edge of the Glacial Hills Region, the trail offers fantastic examples of the pink Sioux quartzite left behind when advancing glaciers melted. The **OREGON TRACE TRAIL** offers an additional loop of three-quarters of a mile that is easier to walk than the Post Creek loop. The original Oregon Trail ruts are indicated with a marker along the route. Maps are available at the trailhead.

**LOCATION AND DIRECTIONS**—The Green Memorial Wildlife Area is in Shawnee County, west of Topeka. From I-70, take Exit 346. Head north on NW Carlson Road to Willard. In Willard, go east on 2nd Street until it ends at Gilkerson Road and then go a half mile south. (Follow the signs.) A gravel parking lot is provided at the trailhead.

**ENTRY**—Access is free. No water or facilities are provided.

**ON THE WEB**—www.kdwp.state.ks.us, search "Green."

**CONTACT**—KDWP office at Valley Falls, (785) 945-6615.

# Oregon Trail Nature Park

A PICTURESQUE SILO painted with scenes from the Oregon Trail identifies the parking lot and picnic area at this small but lovely nature park.
Riparian habitat and rolling hills create scenic highlights that meld seamless-
ly into endless views of farmland. Water, restrooms, and picnic tables can be
found at the trailhead.

**WILDLIFE**—White-tailed deer, rabbits, squirrels, raccoon, coyotes, quail,
turkeys, and prairie chickens may be seen in the park or wildlife area.
Migrating geese and ducks can be seen on the ponds.

**HIKING**—Exploring every inch of the park would total only 1.5 miles.
Visitors can expect to spend an hour walking three connected loops. One
section of the trail is steep enough that railroad ties and a rope have been
installed to help climbers reach an overlook. The climb won't pose any prob-
lems to people in good health. The Jeffrey Energy Center sits below in the
sites of the overlook on the north side of the park and offers an interesting

Climb for the best views at Oregon Trail Nature Park.

Admiring the still lake at Oregon Trail Nature Park.

contrast to natural elements, bring your binoculars. In fall, large flocks of snow geese may make an appearance at the pond with cement smoke stacks as a backdrop. Hikers can continue down the hill and around the pond for more mileage. The pond has a natural blind of wildflowers, buckbrush, bittersweet, and cedar growing around it. Stumps gnawed by beavers suggest their presence, but it's difficult to imagine that a power plant provides an attractive habitat for them. An example of fine loess soil with its greenish-yellow hue can be seen in a cross section of a hill just off the trail.

**LOCATION AND DIRECTIONS**—In Pottawatomie County, west of Topeka. Take U.S. Highway 24 west toward Saint Mary's. About 4 miles beyond, before reaching Belvue, turn right on Schoeman Road and left on Oregon Trail Road. The parking lot will be on your right.

**ENTRY**—There is no entrance fee. Picnic tables and modern restrooms can be found at the trailhead. The park is open from May to September, 7:00 A.M. to 9:00 P.M.; from October to April, 8:00 A.M. to 6:00 P.M.

**ON THE WEB**—www.kdwp.state.ks.us, search "Jeffrey."

**CONTACT**—The park is a joint venture between KDWP and Westar Energy. It lies within the property borders of the Jeffery Energy Center, (785) 539-9999.

# Historic Trails Park

AN IMPRESSIVE NUMBER of historic trails once crossed through Marshall County—eight, to be exact: Oregon, Overland, Pony Express, Military, Mormon, Otoe-Missouria, Saint Joseph-California, and Pike's Peak-California. It's likely you've never heard of some, while others are pretty renowned. Located in Marysville, the Historic Trails Park pays homage to them all. Maps and plaques are used to explain and remember each trail and its significance. The park also offers a life-sized replica of a rope ferry. Pioneers once paid a handsome toll and sometimes waited days for their turn to safely cross the Big Blue River, which you can still see here today. Native wildflowers of the plains are displayed and the history of the first civilian post office in territorial Kansas is explained.

**WILDLIFE**—Look for the very distinct coal black squirrel, once unique to this area, but whose populations are increasing.

**LOCATION AND DIRECTIONS**—Located in Marshall County, in the town of Marysville. From U.S. Highway 36, go south on U.S. Highway 77. Watch for a directional sign within four to five blocks. The park entrance will be on your left after two overpasses.

**ENTRY**—No entrance fees. Always open.

**ON THE WEB**—skyways.lib.ks.us/towns/Marysville/.

**CONTACT**—Marysville Chamber of Commerce, (785) 562-3101.

# Perry Lake and State Park

PERRY LAKE is the result of impounding the Delaware River in the Glaciated Region where prairie and woodlands commingle along its shores. The Ice Age helped contour this park, leaving high bluffs and boulder-strewn hillsides in its wake. Adding further distinction, one of the largest trees in the state—a cottonwood—happens to be located just a mile west of Perry Lake at Ozawkie. Perry Lake also boasts a National Recreation Trail nearly 30 miles in length. If you can't do all 30 miles, several short trails for day hiking provide delightful options for any nature lover. There are also bike, equestrian, and ATV trails.

The options at Perry Lake seem endless, with 1,000 campsites, 16 group picnic shelters, and eight boat ramps. Eleven marshes form a wildlife area, with two marshes providing refuge for waterfowl and shorebirds. This park is big! So, pick up trail maps at the information office before proceeding to the trailheads or download them in advance—and get going!

**WILDLIFE**—Marsh and mudflats attract migrant waterfowl, shorebirds, and mammals such as muskrat, mink, and beavers. Raccoon, coyotes, opossums, skunks, and bobcats take cover in the woodlands. Wild turkeys, pileated woodpeckers, and rose-breasted grosbeaks thrive in the riparian woodland. Near the dam, watch for bald eagles, blue herons, and cliff swallows. Hike the Delaware Marsh for the opportunity to see amphibians and reptiles. Take advantage of a trailside observation blind to view waterfowl and shorebirds. Paradise Point is a loop drive that extends into an oxbow where the Delaware River meets the open waters of the wildlife refuge, combining forest, grassland, and shoreline. Because the area receives less traffic and is so diverse, it may offer your best opportunity to view wildlife. Be aware of hunting season before hiking or heading out into remote areas on foot.

**HIKING**—**PERRY LAKE NATIONAL RECREATION TRAIL,** a 30-mile circuit traversing three parks, is tucked into the east side of the reservoir. The official starting point is located in Slough (pronounced *slew*) Creek Park. There are three official trailheads, but three more parking lots near the trail double your options. Maintenance typically occurs in late fall and early spring, great times to view fall foliage and peak migration seasons. The trail is blazed in blue with spur trails marked in white, most leading to campgrounds.

The most popular day hike is **SECTION 1,** which begins at Slough Creek and heads north along the reservoir to Longview Park. Fairly easy, the trail has gentle slopes, woodlands, and some open field crossings with generous views of the lake. This 6-mile section of the trail gets much use and is maintained more frequently. For an additional half mile, pass through Longview Park, a public-use area that has all the necessities for a break.

**SECTION 2** begins on more difficult terrain, with frequent elevation changes in the next 7.7 miles. It is closer to the lake and offers small coves, rest areas, and rock outcroppings as well as panoramic views. Nearing the Lakewood Hills subdivision, the trail turns east at about the 10-mile marker and offers high bluff views. The toughest terrain is yet to come. Over the next 3.5 miles, the trail follows Little Slough Creek, with spectacular bluff views. At Solitude Point, located near large rock outcroppings, the Dorothy Moore Memorial Park Bench is a great place to rest. Just a couple more miles will take you to Old Military Trail Park, which was named as such because this valley was part of a passage from Fort Leavenworth to Fort Riley.

**SECTION 3** is a remote area covering 3.5 miles into the backwaters of Little Slough Creek. In nearly a half mile, you'll reach the 94th Street bridge, which has been washed out due to flooding. Cross the gravel road a few hundred feet down trail, climbing to a hilltop view of the lake. The trail follows the creek until it reaches Kiowa Road. (Note: Follow the gravel road south for an additional 4 miles to reach Section 4.)

**SECTION 4** is 6.5 miles, in which remote conditions prevail again for 4 miles along the creek and through wooded areas and small fields. You will reach the Ferguson Road Trailhead about 2.5 miles from the Slough Creek Trailhead. Turn left when your trail intersects with Section 1 to complete the half-mile walk back to Slough Creek Trailhead.

Though this 30-mile loop trail cannot be hiked in one day, backpackers can camp at Old Military Trailhead, Slough Creek, and Longview Park. Hiking between May and September will require permethrin clothing treatment to repel ticks. As areas surrounding the trail are open to hunting, hikers should avoid visiting during deer rifle season (early December). Orange hats, vests, or T-shirts are recommended if hiking during hunting season. Long sleeves and pants are highly recommended because of poison ivy, nettles, and thorns.

**THUNDER RIDGE EDUCATIONAL TRAIL:** Located in Slough Creek Park, the trail offers a challenging yet rewarding way to learn about the natural elements and habitat found in the park, with 30 interpretive markers along the trail. The 2.5-mile trail is blazed in white and follows a ridgeline through a forest with frequent elevation changes. Spur trails are usually marked with signposts and lead to campgrounds that surround the trail. Panoramic views of the lake are frequent in early spring or late fall. Giant boulders strewn haphazardly on hillsides are covered with moss and lichen. Two trailside ponds create great habitat for bird-watching. Look for white-tailed deer, raccoon prints, wild turkeys, and red-headed woodpeckers.

**DELAWARE MARSH TRAIL:** Behind the dam, a marsh was created by natural runoff. Mounds of soil were placed in the wetland to provide attractive resting and nesting areas for birds. The trail meanders through open grasslands of the Delaware Marsh for 1.75 miles of hiking. Marked with blue blazes, the trail is fairly level and rated easy. Interpretive stations and a wildlife blind are located on the trail. Keep your eyes open for shorebirds and waterfowl as well as amphibians and reptiles. Water is lowered during spring and fall migrations to attract shorebirds such as sandpipers, plovers, and willets. When flooded, the wetlands attract ducks and geese. Waders such as great blue herons and egrets stalk the shoreline for food.

**STATE CHAMPION TREE TRAIL:** This 1-mile loop offers a view of one of the state's largest eastern cottonwood trees. You might see birds of prey as well as the small mammals they stalk in the heavily wooded area just 1 mile west of Ozawkie on State Highway 92.

**BIKING**—Originated to provide Kansans with a competitive course, mountain bike trails were established by volunteers under the direction of the Kansas Trails Council. Many avid riders agree that the **PERRY BIKE TRAIL** is the best and most challenging bike trail in Kansas. With the exception of some recent additions, nearly all mileage can be considered moderate to difficult, with steep successive climbs, switchbacks, and many technical areas. Some warn not to ride this trail without a "real bike" and a quality helmet. To find the trailhead located within Perry State Park, follow State Highway 237 across the bridge over the lake into the Delaware Area, then veer right on Kimberly Road. The trails consume the peninsula and head up the lakeshore. Eleven named trails combine for more than 20 miles of single-track, all signed in blue or white. Blue denotes the high road; white indicates that the trail is closer to the water. Following is a list of trail segments with rating and mileage taken from the park brochure provided by KDWP and the Kansas Trails Council:

> Kid Rock—blue, 0.25 miles, very easy, loop
> Skyline—blue, 3.5 miles, easy, loop
> Knot Head—blue, 1 mile, easy, loop
> Willow—blue, 1 mile, easy, loop
> Wild West—white, 1 mile, easy/moderate, linear
> Great White—white, 2.5 miles, difficult, loop
> Mad Mile—white, 1 mile, difficult, loop
> Blackfoot—blue, 2.5 miles, difficult, linear
> Logan's Run—white, 2 miles, moderate, linear
> Copper Head—white, 2 miles, difficult, linear
> Twin Peaks—blue, 2.5 miles, moderate, linear
> Carlyle—white, 2 miles, moderate, loop

**HORSEBACK RIDING**—About 25 miles of riding trail have been designed and maintained by equestrian groups. A primitive campground with a restroom and shower is located near the trailhead at the Wild Horse area. Flagged with red or white, the sections within the state park are suitable for riders of average experience. Trails that wander into the adjoining

Rock Creek Park are designed for advanced riders and trail-wise horses, covering more difficult terrain where water is not readily available. Improvements are currently in process.

**OTHER**—Located behind the dam in Outlet Park, the 140 acres of ATV riding terrain are rated easy to difficult for beginners and experienced riders alike. The trail follows blue blazes and makes two stream crossings. The ATV area has been improved recently and now offers loading/unloading ramps, a children's area, a parking lot, and vault toilets. Shelters and cosmetic improvements are still to come. The trail will be closed during wet conditions. A brochure at the office provides trail rules and a map.

**TRAIL BUILDING**—The Kansas Trails Council works with the COE to coordinate trail work in sections, in cooperation with groups such as the Kansas City Outdoor Club, the Sierra Club, the Lawrence Mountain Bike Club, Boy Scouts, and the Kansas ATV Association. To volunteer, visit www.kansastrailscouncil.org or phone the COE.

**FISHING AND HUNTING**—An angler's best bet for crappie is in the Slough Creek, Rock Creek, and Old Town areas. Channel cat is prevalent in the Delaware River and on mudflats in the upper end of the reservoir. White bass chase schools of shad. Largemouth bass can be found in the creek arms. Walleye are present, but scarce.

Hunters may be interested to know that pheasant are more abundant in the public area north of Valley Falls. Quail, white-tailed deer, wild turkeys, cottontail rabbits, fox squirrels, and mourning doves call the woods and grasses home. A mentor/youth hunting area is open all year for those 16 years or younger accompanied by an adult.

**CAMPING AND FACILITIES**—Nine park areas surround Perry Lake. Note that two of the parks have similar, thus confusing names. Perry State Park is the only park operated by KDWP. Located west of the dam, it is divided into two areas: Jefferson Point and Delaware. Perry Park is located east of the dam and is operated by the Corps of Engineers. To avoid confusion, it is often referred to as Perry COE Park. The COE operates eight parks: Thompsonville, Outlet, and Perry COE Parks provide day-use areas, while Old Town, Longview, Slough Creek, Old Military Trail, and Rock Creek Parks offer camping. Improved, primitive, and group camping are available with or without a reservation. Slough Creek Park and Perry State Park offer the largest campgrounds, with all facilities and access to trails. Camping along the National Recreation Trail is not permitted, but walk-in camping areas for hikers can be reached via spur trails at Old Military

Trailhead and Longview Park. Group campsites are located in Longview, Slough Creek, and Old Military Trail Parks.

Additional facilities include sanitary dump stations, showers, water, restrooms, boat ramps, picnic areas, two swimming beaches, and two marinas. The swimming beaches and marinas are located in both Perry State Park and Perry COE Park.

**TRAFFIC**—Average, heaviest in May and July.

**LOCATION AND DIRECTIONS**—In Jefferson County, between Topeka and Lawrence. From U.S. Highway 24, turn north on State Highway 237 to reach the Perry State Park office. To reach the COE office, take Highway 24 to Perry and turn north on Ferguson Road (1029).

**ENTRY**—Entrance fees apply at Perry State Park's Delaware and Jefferson Point Areas. The park is open all year, but road closures in the wildlife area occur from November 1 through February 28. The wildlife area is closed to all activities from October 1 to January 15. Camping is prohibited in the wildlife area. Some campgrounds are seasonal.

**ON THE WEB**—Trails are mapped out at www.nwk.usace.army.mil/pe. Also see www.perrylaketrail.net. State park maps can be downloaded at www.kdwp.state.ks.us, search "Perry."

**CONTACT**—For the Corps of Engineers at Perry, (785) 597-5144. For the Kansas Department of Wildlife and Parks at Ozawkie or Perry State Park, (785) 246-3449. For the wildlife area at Valley Falls, call (785) 945-6615. Address of KDWP: 5441 West Lake Road, Ozawkie, KS 66070-9802.

# Lake Shawnee
## and Dornwood Park
## National Recreation Trail

Beginning as a WPA project, this 450-acre lake on the east edge of Topeka was once a fair distance away from civilization, but suburbs are now closing in. Even so, it's a great place to spend the day or weekend relaxing with family or teaching children to enjoy the outdoors. Much thought and effort have gone into providing extras such as Ensley Botanical Garden, which the Shawnee County Department of Parks and Recreation continues

Waterfalls and lily pads at the botanical gardens at Lake Shawnee.

to expand. Both open-air and enclosed air-conditioned shelters and grills are available for luxury outings. You'll be surprised when you see the shelter houses, which resemble rustic stone cabins. Even annual events hosted at the lake are quite unique. The Huff 'n Puff Hot Air Balloon Rally is held for a full weekend in early September (www.huff-n-puff.org) and the Topeka Tinman Triathlon is held in June (www.topekatinman.com). Visitors can stop at the Shawnee County Department of Parks and Recreation office for maps and appropriate licensing.

There are no wooded trails at Lake Shawnee, but nearby Dornwood Park offers 7 miles of trails popular with both hikers and mountain bikers.

**WILDLIFE**—Canada geese and mallards nest on the lake. Herons can be spotted fishing the shallow coves.

**HIKING AND BIKING**—The **LAKE SHAWNEE TRAIL** will eventually be a 5-mile, multipurpose sidewalk that circles the entire lake. The trail leads through the botanical gardens, skirts the marina and the picnic and overlook areas, and passes behind the dam. At present, 3 miles are complete; the final 2 miles near the golf course are currently under construction. To sign up for Kansas park and trail updates, visit www.trailsofkansas.com.

**FISHING AND HUNTING**—A recent agreement with Kansas Department of Wildlife and Parks has boosted fishing in Lake Shawnee. Populations of bass, trout, crappie, catfish, bluegill, stripers, and walleye have been increased. A state license is required; for some activities, a county license may also be required. Fishing and boating licenses can be purchased at the marina. Concrete boat ramps are provided on the southeast corner of the lake. Hunting is prohibited.

**OTHER**—A marina offers paddleboat, canoe, and kayak rentals, in addition to food and drinks. An easy disc golf course is free. Open daily, an 18-hole public golf course complete with driving range lies on the southeast corner of the lake and can be accessed from East Edge Road. The par-70 course features bent-grass greens and zoysia fairways with Lake Shawnee as a scenic backdrop. Boating and skiing are allowed in a small area near the dam. The remainder of the lake is designated for no-wake boating activities.

**CAMPING AND FACILITIES**—A campground situated on a small peninsula offers waterfront views for RVs, two ADA sites, and upland tent camping. Facilities include shower houses, laundry facilities, and a dump station. A swimming beach and a limited number of boat slips are available for registered campers. The park has a liberal 30-day camping limit. Recreational facilities include lighted tennis courts (which close at 11:00 P.M.), softball fields, sand volleyball courts, picnic areas with grills, a public swimming beach, a windsurf beach, and boat ramps. Paddleboats, canoes, and kayaks can be rented at the marina, where there are also concessions.

**TRAFFIC**—Heavy, especially on summer weekends.

**LOCATION AND DIRECTIONS**—In Shawnee County, east of Topeka. Take I-70 to Exit 365 (Rice Road). Turn east through a roundabout onto SE Cyprus Drive. Turn south onto SE Croco Road. Turn west on 29th Street to locate the administrative office.

**ENTRY**—Open all year, with some limitations. The marina is open from May 6 to September 24 on weekends only, from 9:00 A.M. to 8:00 P.M., but open daily from Memorial Day through August 12. The campground is open all year, but reservations are taken only during high season (excluding the week of July 4th).

**ON THE WEB**—Maps and more can be found at www.co.shawnee. ks.us/parksandrec.

**CONTACT**—Administrative office, (785) 267-1156; campground, (785) 267-1859; shelter house rentals, (267) 267-1156; golf course, (785) 267-2295; marina, (785) 267-2211; swimming beach, (785) 266-8557. Park address: 3137 SE 29th Street, Topeka, KS 66605.

**NEARBY**—**DORNWOOD PARK NATIONAL RECREATION TRAIL** is well maintained for hiking and mountain biking by the Kansas Trails Council. A total of 7 miles of natural path has three loops that can be hiked independently or consecutively. The trail is rated moderate due to some steep climbs and descents through thick woods along Deer Creek, which feeds Lake Shawnee. The foundation of an old stone dairy can be seen from the trailhead. The northwest loop offers views from high above the creek, while the longer, southern loop boasts rocky sections, prairie vistas, and several stream crossings. For riders, this section is considered more technical. Access the northeast loop by crossing a footbridge just past the dairy ruins.

Trail building takes place on the fourth Saturday of each month at 9:00 A.M., weather permitting, and you are invited to participate. You can sign up to volunteer or download a trail map at www.kansastrailscouncil.org.

**DIRECTIONS**—From I-70, exit onto SE California Avenue (364A) and turn south. Turn east on SE 25th Street. The trailhead is located just past city baseball diamonds. The ballpark may be a safer place to leave your car, as theft has been a problem at the trailhead in the past.

# Riverfront Park and
## Kaw River National Recreation Trail

BECAUSE OF THICK LOESS DEPOSITS and its shallow depth the Kansas (or Kaw) River is more like a ribbon of mud than a sparkling waterway. Nonetheless, the slow, meandering ribbon rolls through charming rural landscapes and has much to offer hikers, wildlife lovers, and recreational enthusiasts.

The city of Lawrence's Riverfront Park offers an easily accessible, centralized trailhead marked by the Kansas River bridge, as well as a visitor center located in the renovated Union Pacific train depot. Today, trains still run on the tracks behind the depot. A wealth of information about Kansas is available at the visitor center, as are modern restrooms and a brief historical film about the city on the river and its vital role in the Civil War. A parking lot just across the street from the train depot will provide access to the Riverfront Park trail system. A picnic table on the deck at the visitor center and the surrounding gardens tended by Lawrence Parks and Recreation Department tempt you to linger. Home to some remarkable architecture (such as the Douglas County courthouse), as well as historical sites, museums, and the University of Kansas, Lawrence (nicknamed "the City of the Arts") is definitely worth exploring before or after your hike.

**WILDLIFE**—Because there is much activity along the recreation trail, wildlife may be scarce unless your outing is early or late in the day. Even so, many small mammals and birds are drawn to surrounding croplands near the riverfront. Naturally, numerous birds and mammals are also drawn to the Kaw's life-sustaining waters. Even in the middle of the day, you may see bald eagles soar across the river from a high perch. Raccoons and deer leave footprints along the trail. Blue herons scour the banks for fish. Gulls, Canada geese, and mallards enjoy sandbars when water levels are low. Songbirds and woodpeckers can be heard among thick foliage along the trail. Turtles and snakes sun themselves on timber in the river.

**HIKING**—The levee surrounding the north bank of the river safeguards residents against flooding and provides a lengthy, flat, multi-use trail that offers big vistas of farmland and rural Lawrence. On the plus side, you likely won't come into contact with poison ivy or ticks; on the minus side, there is no shade and at times views of the river are scarce even though the trail sits only feet above the lazy Kaw River. The one-way levee trail runs for a total of 10 miles, roughly 5 miles in either direction from the visitor center.

**BIKING**—The **KAW RIVER MOUNTAIN BIKE TRAIL** offers 4 miles of packed dirt and sand as it meanders along the edge of the riverbank and provides outstanding views of the Kaw River. The one-way bike trail sometimes deviates from the river's edge to take advantage of ravines and hills. Log jumps have been added for challenge, but the trail is rated easy for mountain bikers. The trail connects with the levee trail in numerous places to shorten or vary the route. The trailhead is located a mile east of the visitor center. Go east on Locust Street, then south on 8th Street and follow the road over the levee to the parking lot, where you'll also see a boat ramp. Trail maps are available online at www.lawrencemountainbikeclub.org/map_river.shtml.

**TRAIL BUILDING**—The Lawrence Mountain Bike Club maintains the natural trails. If you'd like to help, see www.lawrencemountainbike club.org.

**PADDLING**—If you don't own canoes, a KOA in Lawrence (1473 U.S. Highway 40, [785] 842-3877) offers full- and half-day float trips on the Kaw. (See camping and facilities section for the location of two boat ramps.) The Kaw is sometimes shallow and placid, but when reservoirs upstream release water or heavy rains persist, conditions can change rapidly. Paddlers must beware of dams and know how to ford them. See www.kansasriver.com for great information on navigating the Kansas River.

**OTHER**—An 18-hole disc golf course starts at the entrance to Riverfront Park; it's a challenging course that winds through wooded sections of the park.

**CAMPING AND FACILITIES**—Primitive camping is allowed in Riverfront Park. Campers are also welcome at the KOA, located at 1473 U.S. Highway 40, (785) 842-3877. Clinton Lake and State Park is only minutes away. Two boat ramps are provided within Riverfront Park. One is located a mile east of the visitor center (see Biking section) and the other is located at the intersection of U.S. Highways 24, 40, and 59, just north of I-70.

**LOCATION AND DIRECTIONS**—In Douglas County. From I-70 take the east Lawrence exit (204). Make a left at Massachusetts Street/U.S. Highway 40/59 and then turn left onto Locust Street. The visitor center is located just ahead on 2nd Street.

**ENTRY**—There are no entrance fees. Riverfront Park is open daily 6:00 A.M. to 11:30 P.M. Once you leave the visitor center, there are no facilities on the trails. Visitor center hours are 8:30 A.M. to 5:30 P.M., Monday–Saturday, and 1:00 P.M. to 5:00 P.M. on Sundays. Winter hours are shortened Monday –Saturday to 9:00 A.M. to 5:00 P.M.

**ON THE WEB**—Maps and more can be found at www.lprd.org or www.lawrencemountainbikeclub.org.

**CONTACT**—Lawrence Parks and Recreation Department, (785) 832-3450; Visitor Center, (888) 529-5267; Lawrence KOA, (785) 842-3877. Visitor center address: 402 North 2nd Street, Lawrence, KS 66044.

# Floating the Kansas River

ONE OF ONLY THREE publicly accessible rivers in the state, the Kansas River originates in Junction City, where the Republican and Smoky Hill Rivers converge. It meanders eastward for 170 miles. The last accessible point is in Johnson County, Kansas, southwest of Kansas City.

Much of the Kansas (Kaw) River is pleasant for beginners, but there are several stretches that should be avoided. Dams in Lawrence, Topeka, and Edwardsville create hazardous conditions. Only the experienced should attempt these areas after carefully scouting the hazards and being fully prepared to portage. Controlled release from reservoirs into the river should also be monitored before floating.

There are many points of access: some facilities are optimal, while others make launching more difficult. Information becomes outdated quickly and the struggle to improve paddling opportunities in Kansas is ongoing. Paddlers would be wise to reference the Friends of the Kaw Web site for detailed information before planning a float trip on the Kansas River. Paddlers wanting to gain experience can also sign up for group floats and enjoy a "sandbar seminar" on river ecology for a very reasonable fee.

About 10.7 miles of river roll between Lecompton and Lawrence, where concrete boat ramps provide an uneventful launch. Early fall is an excellent time to paddle, especially for those less experienced. If you can wait for mid- to late October, you'll be treated to prolific yellow, red, and orange foliage of the hardwoods that grow along the banks. Climbing vines create the illusion that tree trunks and branches are bright red. Slow and wide, the Kansas allows beginners time for corrections and experimenting with strokes and landings. Anyone looking for a whitewater thrill might be bored paddling the Kansas River, but if a lazy day of solitude and wildlife watching is what you're after, you'll find the experience very satisfying. You're likely to find wide sandbars for picnicking, exploring, and photography. Geology and archeology buffs can hunt for bones, arrowheads, and artifacts left behind long ago by the Kansa tribes. You may also find remnants tossed aside by glaciers. Test your knowledge and try to identify the wildlife tracks that abound in the sand when you stop to explore. Great blue herons are prevalent on the four- to five-hour float. Keep your eyes open for beavers and watch for eagles in the trees as you approach the power plant and the take-out near Lawrence.

The power plant near Lawrence makes for a noisy companion you'll want to speed past. If it's windy, you might swear you're going backward. After passing the power plant, be aware that your take-out will be on the left (north) bank. The ramp is not highly visible: you don't want to miss it or you'll encounter the hydraulic dam under the Lawrence Bridge in a mile and a half. Plan to stay within the banks of the river or you'll likely be treading on private property.

Paddlers take a sandbar break while canoeing the Kansas River.

**WILDLIFE**—Great blue herons will follow you downriver. Watch the canopy for eagles and woodpeckers. Canada geese, gulls, and mallards can be seen on the sandbars. Coyotes, while-tailed deer, turkeys, and beavers may be spotted from the river.

**FISHING**—The Kansas River is known to yield enormous channel and flathead catfish.

**CAMPING AND FACILITIES**—Primitive camping is permitted in Riverfront Park in Lawrence. There are no facilities. (See Kaw River National Recreation Trail.)

**LOCATION AND DIRECTIONS**—Put in at Rising Sun Access Park at Lecompton (just south of Perry). Take I-70 to Exit 197. Head north for a quarter mile to Lakeview Road (North 1800th Road). Turn west on Lakeview and then north on Lecompton Road (East 600th Road/1029). Follow 1029 through Lecompton and cross the Kansas River. After crossing the bridge, follow signs for the park on your left.

Take out at the Lawrence Riverfront Park access. From I-70 take the east Lawrence exit (204). Turn right onto U.S. Highway 24/59. Proceed 1 mile to the junction at U.S. Highway 40. Take the road on your left, which goes over railroad tracks and the levee into the park. The park is patrolled and maintained by Lawrence, but there are no facilities.

**ON THE WEB**—Find an interactive map of boat ramps, facilities, and group float information at the Friends of the Kaw Web site, www.kansasriver. com. Also visit www.lprd.org for information on Lawrence facilities and parks.

**CONTACT**—Lawrence Parks and Recreation Department, (785) 832-3450.

# Glacial Hills Scenic Byway

FOLLOWING THE WEST BANK of the Missouri River and the east border of Kansas, the Glacial Hills Scenic Byway travels State Highway 7 and connects Leavenworth, Atchison, Troy, and White Cloud. Vistas of scenic, rolling hills are strung together with longer stretches of farmland and ranch. During the summer, chicory, black-eyed Susans, sunflowers, and prairie clover tint the hillsides and even grow from roadside ditches. Rows of corn trace the curve of the blacktop while windmills keep watch over the flatlands.

Mid-fall or early spring is ideal to travel the byway, because in summer thick foliage obscures the river. Because the forest is predominantly hardwoods like hickory and oak, fall conditions catapult the lesser vistas into explosions of color.

The byway begins at the "first city of Kansas." Leavenworth still has a very active downtown during the week, featuring many federal sites, such as the Leavenworth Penitentiary, Fort Leavenworth, and a federal cemetery. A 21-site, interactive walking/driving tour awaits visitors. (The itinerary is available online at www.lvks.org.) History buffs may be tempted to spend an entire day at Leavenworth, but Atchison is just as alluring.

Atchison plays up its role in the Lewis and Clark Expedition; but thanks to its location on the river and the railroad industry, it also became a thriving commercial center. A trolley tour will help you get oriented with this city of beautifully restored Victorian homes and historic churches, a nicely developed riverfront, a scenic campus, and no fewer than five niche museums. Outdoor enthusiasts will enjoy the International Forest of Friendship, the Atchison State Fishing Lake, and the Independence Creek Recreation Trail.

**WILDLIFE**—Deer are likely to bound across the road, so drive with care. Beavers, muskrat, raccoon, skunks, opossums, mink, foxes, bobcats, and weasels may also be seen, as water is a nearby companion to the drive.

**HIKING AND BIKING**—The **INTERNATIONAL FOREST OF FRIENDSHIP** pays tribute to aeronautic heroes (such as native Amelia Earhart); at the same time it educates, celebrating all 50 states and 35 countries with trees that symbolize each. Test your knowledge of tree species in a pleasant setting at Warnock Lake. A sidewalk just under 1 mile zigzags through the memorial setting and across a wooden footbridge within a small, 2.5-acre space that includes a gazebo and benches for rest and reflection. The small lake offers additional walking or biking on narrow blacktop roads that wrap around the water. Group shelters, grills, and primitive restrooms are on hand for day use; areas for both primitive and RV camping are available, as well. The property is surrounded with private farms and cropland. From downtown, take U.S. Highway 73 south (K-7), turn right on Patriot Street and left on Price Boulevard; follow it to Rawlins Road and then turn west on 274th Road.

**INDEPENDENCE CREEK RECREATION TRAIL** is 5 miles of multipurpose trail extending north from Riverfront Park in Atchison to Independence Creek, where hikers will find the restoration of a former Kansa Indian village. Along the route is the Benedictine Bottoms, a wetland restoration project on the east side of the trail. The path begins on road

Tribute to Amelia Earhart at the International Forest of Friendship on the Glacial Hills Scenic Byway.

(look for the "share the road" sign at the north end of Riverfront Park) and eventually changes to gravel levee. From the Chamber of Commerce Visitors Center at 200 South 10th Street, go north a block and turn east (right) on Commercial Street to reach the Riverfront Park, which offers restrooms, showers, and your choice of riverfront restaurants. Historical exhibits pay tribute to local heroes Lewis and Clark.

**ROAD BIKING**—Few sections of State Highway 7 have shoulders, but generally the road is great for riding. The best time to bike is on weekdays between 9:00 A.M. and 3:00 P.M., when traffic is light. Alternatively, you may piece together a route within Atchison by beginning at Jackson Park and heading north to Riverview Drive, where you'll be impressed by river bluff views on the east side and gorgeous turn-of-the-century homes on the west side. Follow Riverview Drive north to 4th Street and make a right on Commercial Street, and then follow Riverview Road through the developed Riverfront Park. Add the Independence Creek Recreation Trail for more scenic miles. Stop at the visitor center along Highway 7 for city maps and information or download a city map at www.atchisonkansas.net.

**FISHING AND HUNTING**—**ATCHISON STATE FISHING LAKE** is located a few miles northwest of Atchison. Take Highway 7 north 3.5 miles, turn west on 318th Road, go 2 miles to Pawnee Road, and then go north 0.5 miles. The 66-acre lake is shallow on the west end, but up to 30 feet deep near the dam. Angle for largemouth bass and crappie in brush piles. Bluegill enjoy grassy edges and channel cat hang out at the fish feeders. Walleye, redear sunfish, and flathead catfish are also stocked. A boat ramp, water, restrooms, parking, fishing piers, and the office are all located in the public-use area east of the dam. Fish attractors have been placed around the perimeter of the lake. Cross the dam to find a fishing trail on the north side of the lake.

Three acres of food plots sustain wildlife such as deer and waterfowl in the winter. Hunting is allowed in a small area of about 46 acres of grassland and 90 acres of timber in an area that follows the outlet creek behind the dam.

**OTHER**—Boat ramps allow access to the Missouri River from Riverfront Park in Atchison (for the experienced paddler only). At the northernmost end of the Glacial Hills Scenic Byway, White Cloud offers a small riverfront park that provides access to the Missouri River, as well. Here you'll find a riverside dock, a boat ramp, a fish-cleaning station, a restroom, and a covered pavilion. Turn left at the park and follow signs toward an overlook, from which you can see Kansas, Missouri, Iowa, and Nebraska. A gravel drive leads to a wooden viewing platform.

**CAMPING AND FACILITIES**—Primitive and RV camping are available at Warnock Lake on Atchison's southwest side. Fees are payable to a groundskeeper who lives at the lake. Primitive restrooms, grills, group shelters, and a public water hydrant are the extent of amenities. All roads are paved.

Atchison State Fishing Lake (see above, Fishing and Hunting) offers primitive camping in designated areas on the south shore of the lake. Drinking water, picnic tables and grills, primitive restrooms, fishing piers, and parking lots can be found in the public-use area. Dirt roads are closed late fall through winter, limiting access to a majority of the campsites.

**LOCATION AND DIRECTIONS**—Atchison is in Atchison County. From Leavenworth, follow State Highway 7 north about 30 miles. White Cloud is in Doniphan County. From Atchison, follow Highway 7 north for 33 miles, almost to the Nebraska border.

**ON THE WEB**—Find maps and information about Atchison at

www.atchisonkansas.net, Leavenworth at www.lvks.org, the Glacial Hills Scenic Byway at www.ksbyways.org, Doniphan County at www.dpcountyks.com, and Atchison State Fishing Lake at www.kdwp.state.ks.us, search "Atchison."

**CONTACT**—Atchison visitor center, (800) 234-1854; Leavenworth visitor center, (800) 844-4114; Atchison State Fishing Lake, (785) 793-7730.

**NEARBY**—About 2 and a half miles west of the scenic byway in Highland, the **NATIVE AMERICAN HERITAGE MUSEUM** illustrates the journey of the Great Lakes Indians, who were forced to relocate from northern woodlands to Kansas prairie. Originally, the museum building was designated as a mission to educate Native American children. Located on the California-Oregon Trail, the setting provides a nice place for picnics and hikes. Quillwork, baskets, artwork, and handicrafts help demonstrate the culture of Native American tribes, while exhibits tell personal stories handed down by descendants. Learn how the four Indian nations presently living on reservations in Kansas—Potawatomi, Iowa, Kickapoo, and Sac and Fox—differ in lifestyle, food, and art with interactive exhibits. You can even explore a bark-house dwelling.

From Highway 7, turn west at the town of Sparks on County Road 2128 toward Highland. Drive approximately 2.5 miles and follow signs to the museum at 1737 Elgin Road. Open Wednesday–Saturday from 9:00 A.M. to 5:00 P.M. and Sunday from 1:00 P.M. to 5:00 P.M. Closed on state holidays. Appointments needed December to February. Visit www.kshs.org/places/nativeamerican or phone (785) 442-3304. Small per-person entry fees apply.

# Wyandotte County Lake Park

ALTHOUGH WYANDOTTE COUNTY LAKE PARK, just northwest of Kansas City, is a pleasant surprise amid suburbia, the park was here long before the suburbs. Originally a WPA project, the park's dam was built by as many as 2,000 people in the mid-1930s. If the numerous shelters and structures around the lake remind you of your last visit to a national park, it's because they were patterned after National Park Service plans. Native stone and timber were used in the construction to provide a handsome but primitive look. Some may describe the park as an Ozark-like setting, but the characteristics of the Glacial Hills Region are clearly on display; deposits of fine loess soil are easy to spot by their strange yellowish hue. Pink quartzite rocks and boulders carried by glaciers from as far away as South Dakota are present. Both loess and quartzite can be seen along the bridle trail circling the lake.

If ever you find yourself with cabin fever in the winter, this park may be one of a few that are just as lovely during winter as summer. Around 3:30 P.M. every day, the dramatic winter light hits yellow limestone banks. When the lake reflects blue sky, winter's chilly grip melts away. The spillway creates a lovely stream and marshy area attractive to waterfowl. When it's too cold to walk or bike, a 7-mile drive around the lake may hold you over till spring. Keep your eyes open for bald eagles, whose populations are plentiful enough to beget the regional "Eagle Days" events held every January.

Near the entrance of Wyandotte County Lake Park, you'll find a Korean-Vietnam War Memorial. After passing the memorial, go left at the fork to find the administrative office, restrooms, a playground, and parking lot. Continue up the road to reach the official visitor center, located near the marina and boathouse. You can acquire park and trail maps at the administrative office or the visitor center. Rangers patrol the park and can answer your questions.

Limestone bridge at Wyandotte County Lake.

**WILDLIFE**—Geese frequent the visitor center lawn. Do not feed them, as it causes a significant problem for the park. Besides the usual Canada geese, you may also see the less common white-fronted geese; their orange bills and feet give them away. Sightings of white-tailed deer are almost guaranteed. Dusk and dawn might bring sightings of wild turkeys, great blue herons, ospreys, beavers, opossums, raccoons, and foxes. The coves and lookouts are great places to pull out your binoculars and look for migrating pintails, green- or blue-winged teals, goldeneyes, and common or hooded mergansers.

**HIKING**—The bridle trail circles the park road, which in turn circles the lake. An 8-mile trail ascends and descends over and over again. The path is quite wide, about six feet on average. While it is relatively easy to follow, there are many side trails, which are typically only half as wide as the main trail. If you find yourself on a path just wide enough for one person, you've probably strayed from the main trail. Backtrack until you find the wider segment again. Watch for pink or red ribbons in the trees that sometimes mark the path, but they're not always where you need them.

This trail can be treacherous in the winter. Even on a warm day, there may be plenty of ice left on the trail, which can be dangerous on downhill slopes. Much of the trail resembles a dirt road, but at times it becomes a ditch or trough where water, snow, and ice accumulate. A hiking stick certainly comes in handy. You may not be able to avoid mud. But if you come prepared, you'll still enjoy this hike, which climbs surprisingly high and descends unexpectedly low, twisting and turning through oak and hickory forest. Stepping stones are placed in a stream crossing on the east side of the park. The trail occasionally brings you to clearings along the edge of the woods where you may get a look at the rolling hills across the park road. Look for metal trail signs up the road that point the way back into the woods.

Winter offers more views of the lake, which can scarcely be seen through foliage during the rest of the year. Because of the trail's moderate rating, you can expect to hike about 2 miles per hour. The park road makes a faster return, but be aware that it lacks a shoulder and has hairpin turns that limit visibility for drivers.

**BIKING**—The park road provides a 7-mile paved circuit that will offer a significant challenge to most road bikers. The speed limit is 20 mph, which won't be a problem for you! (See Auto Tour below.)

**HORSEBACK RIDING**—8 miles of riding trail circumnavigate the park road with switchbacks and steep descents. The east side is somewhat less scenic than the west side, but less traveled. (See Hiking section for more information.)

**FISHING AND HUNTING**—The lake is stocked with trout and catfish. Most all the region's usual species are self-sustaining, as well. A children's fishing area is also provided near the marina on the east side. There is no hunting allowed in the park.

**OTHER**—A model railroad offers free rides every second Saturday of the month, from April through November. An archery range is located on a spur road in the northwest corner of the park.

**AUTO TOUR**—The park road provides a 7-mile loop tour of the park. If you can take your eyes off the challenging road, you'll enjoy lovely scenery like limestone cliffs, rustic buildings and shelters, beaches, coves, and scenic overlooks. Snaking creeks feed the lake, which is often dotted with geese and fishing boats. With over 300 picnic tables, you should never be without a good place to rest or picnic. Allow 20 to 30 minutes for the drive without stops. Hairpin turns sometimes limit visibility and will confine you to the 20-mph speed limit. Take a break at Davis Hall Lodge and make your way to the back deck, where a stone patio with picnic tables overlooks the lake.

**CAMPING AND FACILITIES**—There are no camping facilities. The marina rents small motorboats and provides a snack bar. Boat ramps and docks, restrooms and water pumps, public picnic areas and tables, playground, reservable shelter houses, and an archery range are among the amenities. Davis Hall can accommodate up to 150 people.

**LOCATION AND DIRECTIONS**—In Wyandotte County. Take I-435 to Leavenworth Road (County Road 5) east (Exit 15). Continue east on Leavenworth Road to North 91st Street and turn left. At the war memorial, veer left toward the administration building and continue past to reach the boathouse and visitor center.

**ENTRY**—No entrance fees. Open 6:00 A.M. to midnight. The boathouse is closed on Tuesdays. Boating and fishing are limited to March through November.

**ON THE WEB**—www.kckpl.lib.ks.us/wyco/parks/wylake.html.

**CONTACT**—Wyandotte County Administration, (913) 596-7077; ranger headquarters, (913) 596-7085; marina, (913) 299-8488. Park address: 3488 West Drive, Kansas City, KS 66109.

# Kill Creek Park

Another of Johnson County's parks makes the list of outdoor treasures for its variety and length of trails. Kill Creek Park is in a rural setting outside De Soto, but it is predicted to become suburban as it is wedged between quickly growing Overland Park and Lawrence. Plans to expand the park are in motion. Currently, there is no visitor center, but a marina, a beach area, and a playground are the centerpiece from which most trails radiate. The parking lot for shelter #1 provides access to the mountain bike connector trail, the 3-mile hiking trail, and the paved trails. Because there are so many trails, many of which cross in numerous places, consider the trail map a necessity. The map is well done and trails are well marked with both metal stakes and colored flags in the trees and grasses, but pay attention to remain on your chosen path. Visitors should arrive prepared for numerous stream and creek crossings.

**WILDLIFE**—Hikers may not see wildlife, but the evidence is everywhere. Owls, hawks, deer, foxes, coyotes, rabbits, raccoons, and opossums leave tracks and scat on the trails.

**HIKING**—Two hiking trails flagged in pink are maintained by the Kansas City Outdoor Club. Maintenance usually occurs early spring and late fall.

A short section of trail runs along the southern perimeter of the lake between segments of paved trail. Beginning at the marina parking lot, continue on pavement toward the marshy end of the lake. The trail winds through wooded area, with occasional views of timber standing in the shallow end of the lake. Take advantage of wildlife viewing during peak migration seasons. You can walk this section out and back or continue on asphalt trail to circle the entire lake.

The second hiking trail winds for approximately 3 miles through woods and prairie. This trail meanders across a minor creek many times and, depending on recent rainfall, you may get your feet wet. Most crossings have stones on which to cross, but many of these rocks are unstable and slippery with moss. Pay attention to pink flags in the trees that indicate creek crossings or you may have a difficult time finding your way. The trail is well marked, but when foliage peaks, flags may become more difficult to spot. Hikers will find bluffs of layered limestone outcroppings, some look as though they were crafted by hand, and a dripping rock alcove that resembles a grotto. Remnants of mortar-free, lichen-covered rock walls can be seen throughout the park, a reminder that there was once a private homestead on the land. The 3-mile trail ends on asphalt. You will make a 4-mile loop by walking back on the asphalt; alternatively, you can follow the mountain bike connector trail back to the parking lot.

**BIKING**—Two mountain bike trails are maintained by Earth Riders and flagged in orange. **EDDY**, for advanced riders, begins with a stream crossing and then parallels Kill Creek with some technical challenges. This 1.5-mile linear, singletrack route has a short loop at the end. Follow the loop counterclockwise for a greater challenge, dubbed "Killer Creek." **HANK** is a 1.8-mile circuit for beginners and intermediate riders, containing some challenging rocky sections. A 1-mile connector trail leads cyclists to Hank and Eddy from the parking lot at shelter #1 along wider, fairly level ground suitable for children and beginners. There are rocks, roots, and a grade at the end of the connector to get you warmed up.

**HORSEBACK RIDING**—Once inside the park entrance, take the first right for the horse parking area near a small pond. A looping gravel road allows trailers to pull through and hitching posts are found on the gravel loop. Access to the trailhead may be closed when conditions are muddy or wet. Five miles of riding are maintained, with some rocky stretches and some mowed prairie areas where wildflowers are outstanding. During the summer, though, insects here can be intolerable. The trail marked with metal stakes and blue flags leads along the north side of the pond and then crosses the hiking trail. It nears a minor creek, then crosses the bike trail before beginning a loop. The loop crosses Kill Creek twice and the paved trail three times before bringing riders back the way they came.

**TRAIL BUILDING**—Earth Riders Trails Association and Earth Riders Mountain Bike Club partner to maintain bike trails; see www.earthriders.org for more information. The Kansas City Outdoor Club maintains the hiking trail. If you'd like to help, see www.kcoc.info.

**FISHING AND HUNTING**—A state fishing license and a Johnson County fishing license are required to fish the 30-acre lake and neighboring streams. Small watercraft are available for rent at the marina during summer months only. The lake is stocked with walleye and smallmouth bass. Anglers may also catch channel cat, bluegill, and crappie. Hunting is not permitted.

**OTHER**—Possum Trot Orienteering Club offers competitive events for various levels of skill at Kill Creek Park. For those unfamiliar, orienteering is a sport that involves the use of a map and compass to locate designated points on a preplanned course. Competitors are timed to determine the winner. There are also 3 miles of paved trail for walking, jogging, skating, or biking.

**CAMPING AND FACILITIES**—No camping is available. Facilities include paved parking lots, water, restrooms, a beach, four picnic shelters, and a marina with canoe and pedal boat rentals.

**LOCATION AND DIRECTIONS**—In Johnson County. Take State Highway 10 to the Kill Creek Road exit. Turn south on Kill Creek Road and west on 115th Street. Proceed to Homestead Lane and turn left. The park entrance is on the right.

**ENTRY**—No entrance fees. There is no visitor center, so locate park maps online. The marina is open only during the summer.

**ON THE WEB**—Find maps and more at www.jcprd.com or www.earth riders.com.

**CONTACT**—Johnson County Park and Recreation District, (913) 831-3355; 11670 South Homestead Lane, Olathe, KS 66061.

# The Olathe Prairie Center

THE OLATHE PRAIRIE CENTER could be described as the Tallgrass Prairie National Preserve's little sister. The center does not match the National Preserve in size and sophistication, but makes up for this in many ways. There are no underlying Flint Hills or ranger-guided tours, but 6 miles of trail lead through open swells of tallgrass prairie edged by riparian woodlands that are punctuated with creeks, wetlands, and ponds. Like its big sister, the Prairie Center is rich with wildflowers and decorated with handmade structures made of native stone from the property. The surviving homestead, chicken coop, and barn were erected in 1925 and are currently used by KDWP as an office and equipment storage facility.

Hickory, sycamore, walnut, Osage orange, cedar, and redbud are all found on the property. Meade's milkweed, an endangered species, blooms in late spring. Yucca grows along the trail, as do spiderwort, wild strawberry, and prickly poppy. Eight ponds dot the grounds and Cedar Creek divides the park in half. Limestone outcroppings along the creek look as if skillfully crafted by stonemasons. Glacial deposits of quartzite boulders are present on the property, and limestone boulders display solution holes worn smooth over the ages. Quiet and private, this little park offers solitude for hikers only, though dogs are allowed on a leash.

**WILDLIFE**—White-tailed deer are abundant. Bluebirds, meadowlarks, grasshopper sparrows, American kestrels, and mourning doves explore the grasses and woodlands. Watch for glass lizards on rock walls, as well as snakes and box turtles around the ponds and streams in warmer months. Mallards and herons may briefly visit the ponds. Coyote and fox scat is common on the trail, but it is unlikely that any of these animals will make an appearance.

**HIKING**—6 miles of trail crisscross the 300-acre property. As the trails frequently intersect and bisect one another, it's advisable to pick up a map at the trailhead before you begin. A triangular circuit named the **OSBORNE TRAIL** explores the eastern half of the park and measures 1.6 miles. This trail leads to the largest of the eight ponds, which is trimmed with cattails.

Several ponds and abundant yucca dot the landscape at Olathe Prairie Center.

It also offers a fishing pier with views of prairie and mortar-free stonewall remnants as old as 1850. Just beyond the pond are a lovely picnic area and a restroom.

If you skirt the outer edges of the property by piecing together trails, you will hike about 3 miles. This involves crossing Cedar Creek twice, which can be treacherous after heavy rain. The creek crossings are underlaid with concrete and have stepping stones in place. Under normal circumstances, the crossing is slick. You may not get your feet wet, but exercise caution. In high or fast water, do not attempt to cross; you can drive to the other end of the park to access the remaining trails with ease. Trails are composed of gravel roads and mowed grass, and while most of the park is easy to navigate, paths in the northwest corner can all but disappear. As homes along Moonlight Road come into view, make your way south until you find the pond located near the western trailhead.

**FISHING AND HUNTING**—Catch-and-release fishing is allowed on the banks of Cedar Creek. A five-acre pond supports bluegill, catfish, largemouth bass, and sunfish. A Kansas fishing license is required. No hunting of any kind is allowed.

**OTHER**—Ecology workshops for teachers are conducted throughout the year and school groups are welcome with advance reservations. Call (913) 856-7669, ext. 1 for more information.

**CAMPING AND FACILITIES**—At each end, parking and restrooms are provided at the trailhead. The park office, buildings, and maps can be found at the east trailhead. Primitive camping is allowed with special permission.

**LOCATION AND DIRECTIONS**—In Johnson County, in Olathe. Take either I-35 or State Highway 7 to 135th Street (Santa Fe Street/State Highway 150) and head west for 3 miles from Highway 7. Turn left on Cedar Niles Road to find the east trailhead. Continue on 135th Street to turn left on Moonlight Road to begin at the west end of the park.

**ENTRY**—No entrance fees. Trails are open daily from dusk to dawn. Dogs must be leashed. There is no water available.

**ON THE WEB**—www.kdwp.state.ks.us, search "Olathe Prairie Center."

**CONTACT**— KDWP office in Olathe, (913) 856-7669; Grassland Heritage Foundation, (913) 262-3506. Address of prairie center: 26325 West 135th Street, Olathe, KS 66061.

# Ernie Miller Nature Center and Park

I N EARLY SPRING, this natural area comes alive with bright green understory, wildflowers like jack-in-the-pulpit and spiderwort, and cheerful blooms of the redbud. Summer brings prairie wildflowers and winter offers the holidaylike berries of bittersweet and buckbrush. Fall brings glorious colors from bur oak, hickory, western buckeye, and pawpaw. Be wary of poison ivy in any season.

Wildflowers in a windstorm at sunset.

Joseph Miriani

Ernie Miller Nature Center has the distinction of the first nature center in Johnson County. The nature center offers many books, guides, and other educational resources concerning local habitat and wildlife. Live raptors and reptiles are on display in the center, which offers educational programs throughout the year, most of which are geared toward children and families. A bench positioned in front of a plate glass window creates a birdwatching haven from within the center.

**WILDLIFE**—Watch for cardinals, scarlet tanagers, and redbellied and downy woodpeckers. Also look for animal tracks on the trail; you will undoubtedly find deer and fawn prints and maybe even coyote and bobcat tracks. As you walk along the stream, look for beaver dens and the mounds of dirt they use to mark their territory.

**HIKING**—A combination of paved and natural trails weaves through forest and prairie alongside Little Cedar Creek. About 3 miles of trail can be completed in 1.5 hours if you take your time and keep your eyes open for wildlife. First, pick up a trail map inside the front doors of the nature center. Outside, an illustrated trail guide can be borrowed or purchased for a dollar. The pocket-sized guide illustrates the seasonal changes found in this small, but charming park

Begin the natural path by passing the picnic shelter in the lower parking lot. The paved path quickly changes to dirt on the **SOUTH TRAIL,** which meanders through woods for about 1.5 miles and brings you to a confusing intersection. Cross the wooden footbridge and climb the hill to continue on the natural path. The **UPPER RIDGE TRAIL** may be littered with brush piles after winter maintenance, which delights the birds. The trail brings you back down to a second crossing on the Little Cedar and, depending upon season and water levels, you may not be able to cross without getting wet. If you are unable to cross, you can return to the footbridge on the **LOWER RIDGE TRAIL,** which hugs the creek.

There are numerous side trails that appear to lead nowhere, but the park is small enough that you don't have to worry about getting lost. Eventually, you'll end up at the nature center. The paved trail offers 12 numbered stations that pass the amphitheater, a small pond, and the backside of the viewing station from within the center.

Once upon a time this park had a rural feel to it, but now seems more suburban. Noise levels have picked up from State Highway 7, which borders one side of the park. In the winter, noise from traffic is more noticeable without foliage to muffle it.

**FACILITIES**—Modern restrooms and water can be found in the nature center.

**LOCATION AND DIRECTIONS**—In Johnson County. The entrance is on the west side of State Highway 7, about 3 miles south of State Highway 10 and just north of West Santa Fe Street (West 135th Street).

**ENTRY**—Trails are open dawn to dusk every day of the year. The nature center is open Monday-Saturday, 9:00 A.M. to 4:30 P.M., and closed for lunch from noon to 1:00 P.M. There are no fees.

**ON THE WEB**—Maps can be found at www.erniemiller.com. For more information, see www.jcprd.com.

**CONTACT**—Ernie Miller Nature Center, (913) 764-7759; 909 North Highway 7, Olathe, KS 66061.

# Shawnee Mission Park
## and Gary Haller Trail

S HAWNEE MISSION PARK is a standard for south Kansas City residents. Although surrounded by suburbs, it's a respite for locals who crave fresh air and time away from their daily routine. Its popularity stems from the range of amenities and the convenient location in a highly populated area. Well maintained and staffed, the park is operated by Johnson County Parks and Recreation District. The 120-acre lake that empties into Mill Creek forms the centerpiece and focal point of the park. The largest park in Johnson County has ambitious plans to improve and expand throughout the coming years. (To sign up for Kansas park and trail updates, visit www.trails of kansas.com.) The master plan includes a canoe trail, a wetland boardwalk with an overlook, and an improved fishing trail.

A 5-mile, paved park road wraps around the lake, providing access to the numerous amenities. Tennis courts, a theatrical stage, softball fields, a seasonal swimming beach, and a marina are all found on the north side of the lake between a visitor center on the east side and the dam on the west side. An archery range, an observation tower, an off-leash dog area, and a flying field for model aircraft are all located on the south shore.

West of the dam, visitors can extend their recreation with access to Mill Creek Streamway Park's Gary Haller Trail. Pick up a Shawnee Mission Park map at the visitor center (located at Renner Road and 79th Street), which also offers many nature books, local park maps, and the coveted Johnson County trail map. You can refill a water bottle and use the modern facilities before packing in all the day's activities.

**WILDLIFE**—You may think wildlife would be scarce in a heavily used area such as this, but white-tailed deer, mallards, Canada geese, red-winged blackbirds, bluebirds, cardinals, blue jays, great blue herons, and woodpeckers are commonly seen. Raccoons, opossums, and wild turkeys are somewhat common, while foxes, beavers, ospreys, kingfishers, and bald eagles are seen infrequently.

**HIKING**—**SERTOMA WOODLAND TRAIL:** This narrow trail loop enters a wooded area, descends across a creek on a boardwalk, and then climbs to a clearing along a wood-chip path. The presence of water and lack of traffic draw wildlife to this charming loop, which has a fairly thick understory. On a lovely fall day, robins feverishly ready themselves for winter and wild turkeys flutter from tree branches to find hiding places in the brush. You may see a deer leap from the underbrush and a great blue heron make its way back to the lake. Take a break on a bench and watch bluebirds, blue jays, and cardinals go about their business. In a matter of minutes, the show magically unfolds before you. You can start from the parking lot at the end of Small Lakes Road (shelter #2) and head north up the hill to the trailhead clearly marked on your left. The entire route is just under 1 mile.

**SOUTH SHORE TRAIL:** Beginning at shelter #10 and ending at shelter #8 just south of the dam, this rocky, natural, dirt path runs 3 miles one-way on a ridge above the lake. Good hiking boots are recommended, as this trail never leaves the woods and frequently crosses creeks and drainage. After heavy rains, crossings may be a challenge and the path can be quite muddy. In fact, when the ground is saturated, the trail will fill with standing water. From the shelter #10 parking lot, head west to the sign marked "no bicycles." Hikers are almost instantly treated to aerial views of the creeks that feed the lake. The trail is fairly wide with uneven terrain. In some places, railroad ties have been used to terrace steep slopes and prevent erosion. As you hike along the ridge overlooking the lake, you'll find many side trails that lead to views of the marina and picnic areas below. Early spring brings

Reflections on Small Lakes at Shawnee Mission Park.

vibrant contrast between pink blooms of redbud and the bright green understory. Winter is a good time to hike this trail, which is usually overgrown in the summer and even in late spring. A stream crossing falls near the halfway point. You may be misled by game trails, so watch for the carefully placed stepping stones in the creek and steep stone staircase on the other side. Pass through the red gates marked for the off-leash area. This is a very popular feature at the park and you are likely to see several hikers with dogs running loose. You may also hear the whine of model aircraft from the R.C. Flying Field, located just south of the trail. Expect to spend about an hour hiking in each direction, unless muddy conditions slow you down.

**MULTI-USE ASPHALT TRAIL:** This 2.5-mile, one-way asphalt trail begins at the visitor center and follows the north side of the park, ending at the dam with a gradual but definite grade. Views are fairly scenic passing the reflective ponds called Small Lakes, through open rolling hills, passing by the sparkling lake, the beach, and marina until the dam comes into sight. Return the way you came, or continue west of the dam to connect to the Gary Haller Trail just outside the park.

**BIKING**—Mountain biking is popular in a wooded terrace north of the lake between the tennis courts and the dam. A challenging system offers bikers a path riddled with obstacles such as tree roots and rocks with hairpin turns and switchbacks. The mountain bike route was recently redesigned, expanded, and mapped for hikers and bikers. Two separate loops can be combined for 4.5 miles of riding. There are 3 trailheads from which you can choose; the park road or paved trail will connect you to your preferred starting point. Extending from the north end of the dam, the purple loop marks 2 miles of more difficult terrain. Cyclists should note that the horse trail intersects the purple loop at the north end; avoid the horse trail and always yield the right-of-way. Beginning at the west edge of the tennis courts, the orange loop is 2.5 miles long, but rated easier than the purple loop.

The 5-mile, paved park road is also popular with cyclists and offers a challenge on gradual and steep rolling hills. Lake views as well as green hillsides and fields of wildflowers are the reward. Riders will have to contend with traffic as there are no shoulders.

**HORSEBACK RIDING**—An equestrian trail traverses the perimeter of the park, offering approximately 8 miles of trail. The trail is a mowed-grass path, passing mostly through wooded areas and back out into the open near the theater and the park offices. Park at Walnut Grove or the Archery Range (on the south side of the lake) to access the horse trail.

**TRAIL BUILDING**—A volunteer coordinator can help match you to a suitable project. Call (913) 894-3321 or see www.jcprd.com. Earth Riders Trails Association coordinates volunteers for the mountain bike trail. See www.earthriders.org.

**FISHING AND BOATING**—The marina on the north side of the lake provides a large parking lot near a boat launch and a swimming beach. During summer months you can rent pedal boats, fishing boats, canoes, and sailboats. A state fishing license and a district fishing permit are both required to fish in the lake. The marina operates from10:00 A.M. to 7:00 P.M. in the summer only. Phone (913) 888-1990.

**OTHER**—The park offers an archery range, an off-leash dog area, and an 18-hole disc golf course (par 54). Live theater performances are given on summer weekends at Theatre in the Park (visit www.theatreinthepark.org for current schedule and more information).

**CAMPING AND FACILITIES**—10 picnic shelters are available by reservation and usually mark spots where you can find parking, public restrooms, water, and barbecue grills. There are three designated play areas for children. Organized youth groups may camp on the northwest boundary of the park with permission. The marina and swimming beach are available in-season.

**LOCATION AND DIRECTIONS**—In Johnson County. In Shawnee, just west of I-435, south of Shawnee Mission Parkway, and north of 87th Parkway. The main entrance and visitor center are at the intersection of 79th Street and Renner Road. A secondary entrance can be accessed on the north side of 87th Parkway (also west of I-435).

**ENTRY**—No entrance fees. In winter months, the marina is closed and modern restrooms are locked.

**ON THE WEB**—Park and trail maps are available online at www.jcprd.com.

**CONTACT**—Visitor center and ranger headquarters, (913) 438-7275; 7900 Renner Road, Shawnee, KS 66219.

**NEARBY**—Running north to south for 17 miles from the Kansas River all the way to Olathe, the **GARY HALLER TRAIL** (at Mill Creek Streamway Park) is the most scenic and diverse of Johnson County's paved trails. Views alternate from streams to wetlands from wildflower prairies to pasture and wooded areas. From Shawnee Mission Park, the trail can be accessed at the midsection. Heading north from Shawnee Mission Park, the path encounters strenuous hills and then levels out, ending at the Kansas (or Kaw) River. Watch for beaver dams as you near the river. Heading south from Shawnee Mission Park, the trail is easy to moderate, with a few strenuous hills. Modern or primitive restrooms and water are available at designated trailheads. The south end extends to the historic Mahaffie Farmstead (1100 East Kansas City Road), a nice place to rest before your return. Most of the trail is shady, with a few exceptions.

Deer are commonly seen near Shawnee Mission Park. Great blue herons frequent the banks of Mill Creek and the pond at the 10-mile marker. Bluebirds are common, thanks to nesting boxes. Beaver may be spotted near wooded edges or along the streambanks and skittish bobcats are occasionally spooked from the brush.

Train whistles frequently intrude on this otherwise peaceful trail which is a favorite for cyclists, but it can be crowded with dog walkers, joggers, and skaters. Friday nights are the best time to ride without crowds. Finish your ride with a barbecue at the group shelter at the 87th Lane Access, which overlooks a pond. Pick up the trail guide for hiking and biking in Johnson County at the Shawnee Mission Park visitor center or request one online.

# SOUTHEASTERN KANSAS

Toronto Lake's sandstone shoreline glows in the sun.

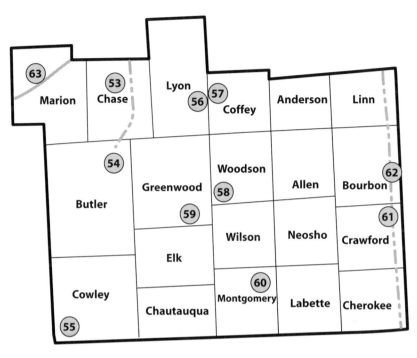

Scenic Byway

Santa Fe Trail

# SOUTHEASTERN KANSAS

# Tallgrass Prairie National Preserve
## and Chase County State Fishing Lake

You've likely heard the prairie described as a sea of grass. Imagine unending vistas of green or gold with scarcely a tree in sight, let alone buildings or other man-made structures. Either you're in awe or you feel slightly exposed. It's not a beauty that screams of exhilaration. Rather, it's a beauty derived from peace and solitude. This ancient land has seen cultures and generations come and go. Once spanning the entire central portion of North America, the tallgrass prairie is now reduced to only 4 percent. However, thanks to a partnership of many organizations, the 11,000-acre Tallgrass Prairie National Preserve will still be here when you or your grandchildren return.

Overlook Trail at the Tallgrass Prairie National Preserve.

Previously considered a useless, treeless wasteland, the Flint Hills tallgrass prairie may not have been useful for farming, but proved to be perfect for ranching and grazing. Cattleman and rancher Stephen F. Jones and his wife Louisa relocated to Kansas from Colorado and built a stone ranch house in 1881. Located near Fox Creek, the terraced land provided a natural spring and thus a perfect location for a stock ranch. As limestone is abundant and wood scarce on the prairie, Jones constructed an 11-room home, a three-story barn, a one-room schoolhouse, a fence, and various outbuildings all from hand-cut limestone. Visitors can tour the surviving ranch, which is now cared for by the National Park Service, and explore the Flint Hills prairie and ridges up close for a very personal experience. There is no entrance fee, but donations are suggested.

**WILDLIFE**—Red-tailed hawks and owls perch high on branches over Fox Creek, looking for resident mice and snakes. Grasshopper sparrows and western meadowlarks flit about the grasses. Coyote, as well as collared and Texas horned lizards are present, but make themselves scarce. Booming grounds for prairie chickens can be spotted on hills in open grassland. Look for the large and colorful lubber grasshoppers, which appear to be wearing armor.

**FRONTCOUNTRY HIKING TRAILS**—Two short nature trails require no permit. Pick up a map at the barn or stone ranch house. Be sure to use bug spray and sunscreen in the summer months.

**SOUTHWIND NATURE TRAIL** begins behind the ranch house and meanders for 1.75 miles through prairie wildflowers to a scenic overlook, crossing a tree-lined creek that leads to the picturesque one-room schoolhouse. The trail brings you back to the front yard of the ranch home. If you have limited time, choose this trail, as it packs Flint Hills views and prairie life into one condensed tour. The path can be soft and muddy after rain.

**BOTTOMLAND NATURE TRAIL** is a wheelchair-accessible trail. It begins behind the Saint Anthony Cemetery. The packed trail loops through bottomland prairie and along the edge of Fox Creek, with options for either a half- or a three-quarter-mile trip. Trailside exhibits tell the history of the land currently being restored to prairie. This trail is probably the least scenic of all the trails, but extends great opportunities to see wildlife early mornings or late in the day.

**BACKCOUNTRY HIKING TRAILS**—Backcountry trails follow ridges where hikers are treated to amazing scenery and endless vistas. Daylight plays on softly eroded hilltops and clouds cast dramatic shadows on the valleys below. Seasonal wildflowers add streaks of color to the steep hillsides. Even in winter, monochromatic views are inspiring. Nearing the trailhead, hikers get a bird's-eye view of the impressive limestone homestead, where cattle linger around watering holes and sometimes become hiking companions. On a clear day, observant hikers may spot the lonely one-room schoolhouse on a distant ridgeline. As the ranger-guided tour buses are limited to three tours per day, you are likely to have these stunning views all to yourself.

All backcountry trails begin beside the barn and follow color-coded routes. You must pick up a free permit and trail map in person at the stone barn. Access to backcountry trails is allowed daily from 9:00 A.M. to 3:30 P.M. during tour season (the last Saturday in April to the last Sunday in October). After tour season, backcountry hiking is limited to weekends.

**SCENIC OVERLOOK TRAIL** is 3.2 miles one-way; it is the route of the ranger-guided bus tour. Signed in blue, the trail climbs 300 feet through rolling prairie pasture to an overlook. Since it is not a loop, you'll be hiking 6.4 miles. To shorten the route, catch an early bus tour to take advantage of the narrative, then hike your way back. You'll have the best of both worlds with this plan.

**RED HOUSE TRAIL,** signed in red, joins two loops for 6 total miles of hiking. It first loops through pasture with views of the ranch and homestead and then leads through prairie grass and flowers to a grove of cottonwood trees in a low-lying drainage area.

**3 PASTURE LOOP,** signed in green, is a 3.8-mile loop that is a shortened circuit of the Red House Trail. The loop circles through adjoining pastures in upland prairie on old ranch roads and mowed paths. It's softer underfoot, but less scenic than the blue trail. In early summer, cattle graze here. Can you recognize the difference between grazing damage and water erosion?

**OTHER**—A ranger-guided bus tour provides outstanding value. Five dollars gets you 1.5 hours of education on prairie plants and animals, history, and geology, as well as panoramic views of the best scenery the park has to offer. Rangers let you wander around a limestone outcrop and they highlight fossils, identify plant life, and explain burn and graze management. Can you tell flint from limestone? The route follows the blue-signed, Scenic Overlook Trail. Tours leave at 11:00 A.M., 1:00 P.M., and 3:00 P.M. Guided bus tours operate only from the last Saturday in April to the last Sunday in October. Outside of the summer season, you may get your own private tour. Reservations are not necessary, but recommended.

Volunteers narrate a brief tour of the ranch house interior. Visitor information and a gift shop are also available at the ranch house. Enter from the back porch. Maps are available for a self-guided tour of the ranch complex.

**CAMPING AND FACILITIES**—No camping is allowed within the Tallgrass Preserve. Restrooms are limited to an outhouse at the ranch and a modern, accessible restroom at the Bottomland Trail parking lot. There are no picnic tables or water. A 10-minute orientation film can be viewed in the barn, which is also the place to get your free backcountry hiking permits and maps for the self-guided tour of the ranch complex.

**LOCATION AND DIRECTIONS**—In Chase County. Tallgrass Prairie National Preserve is 18 miles west of Emporia and 2 miles north of Strong City on State Highway 177. The park entrance is clearly marked. All trails can be accessed from the Preserve headquarters, with the exception of the Bottomland Trail. To access the Bottomland Trail, turn in from Highway 177 at the Saint Anthony Cemetery just south of the preserve. Follow the dirt road to the parking lot and trailhead.

**ENTRY**—There are no entrance fees. Frontcountry hiking is allowed daily during daylight hours, weather permitting. Self-guided tours of the ranch are available daily from 9:00 A.M. to 4:30 P.M. (except holidays). Access to backcountry trails is allowed from 9:00 A.M. to 3:30 P.M. during tour season. After tour season, backcountry hiking is limited to weekends.

**ON THE WEB**—www.nps.gov/tapr.

**CONTACT**—National Park Service (U.S. Department of the Interior) at the Tallgrass Prairie National Preserve, (620) 273-8494; Route 1, Box 14, Highway 177, Strong City, KS 66869.

**NEARBY**—**CHASE COUNTY STATE FISHING LAKE** is a small lake and wildlife area nestled in the Flint Hills just 1.5 miles west of Cottonwood Falls and managed by the KDWP. The lake reflects the serene, striped hills sprinkled with smooth limestone gravel and boulders. Geese waddle across the rustic roads. One boat launch is provided for fishing use only. Anglers will find several fishing piers for channel and flathead catfish, crappie, bluegill, saugeye, and white and largemouth bass. A park brochure offers tips for best results. Facilities include a primitive toilet, fire rings and grills with picnic tables, and a shelter house. Primitive camping is allowed. Hunting is permitted outside the fishing and camping area, but is not popular because of its small animal population. Hiking is allowed, though there are no maintained trails. For the best views, hike the ridge surrounding the lake or follow the lakeshore. The park office is located in Council Grove at (620) 767-5900. Maps can be downloaded at www.kdwp.state.ks.us, search "Chase State Fishing Lake."

# El Dorado State Park

CAMPING IS KING at El Dorado, the largest of Kansas's state parks. With the most land and over a thousand campsites ranging from primitive to full-service, and 10 cabins (primitive and deluxe), camping is the park's greatest attraction. There are four park areas that all have campgrounds available on a first-come, first-served basis. Group camping and horse camping can be arranged in designated areas. El Dorado is also one of the state's most handicapped-accessible parks.

## SELECTING YOUR BASE CAMP

With four areas and over a thousand campsites, where should you set up camp? **BOULDER BLUFF** is where you stay if you're an equestrian. This northwest section of the park has many miles of trail that hug the shoreline and campgrounds that accommodate horses. **BLUESTEM POINT** is a peninsula on the northeast side with a swimming beach, a play area, and both deluxe and primitive cabins. There are no maintained trails, but you can follow game trails and explore the shoreline. On the peninsula, you'll likely see deer, coyotes, owls, and hawks. The **SHADY CREEK** area in the southeast corner is primarily open prairie with a marina for those who favor boating. In season, the marina rents pontoon boats for your leisure. If you love to hike or bike, choose **WALNUT RIVER.** Situated behind the dam, this area doesn't have prevalent views of the lake, but pleasant trails meander along creeks and prairie. Walnut River also allows you quick access to hike or bike the equestrian trail in adjoining Boulder Bluff. The area resembles a large, flat, grassy lawn but has blacktop roads and surfaced paths especially nice for biking. Walnut River's Linear Trail takes you into the town of El Dorado for a supply run or quick dose of Western culture.

**WILDLIFE**—A variety of habitat brings a variety of wildlife. With farmland, creeks, wetlands and drainage areas, standing timber in the reservoir, wooded areas, and prairie, you're likely to see many species. Listen for coyotes at night. Watch for belted kingfishers near Walnut Creek. This large blue bird has a ragged crest and white band around its neck. It dives headfirst for fish and then brings its prey back to the trees to eat. The northern harrier is also a resident at El Dorado—it's the only hawk with an owl-like face. It tends to rock back and forth in the wind like a vulture.

**HIKING**—El Dorado Reservoir lies in an open plain east of Wichita. Trails are easy and mostly level through tallgrass prairie tracing Bemis Creek or Shady Creek.

**TETER NATURE TRAIL**—Between the park office and the dam, a parking lot with a large trail sign marks the spot where the trail first traverses prairie and provides many opportunities to spot wildflowers and interesting shrubs. Look for the pink dripping hearts of the Wahoo shrub and the red feathery blooms of the smooth sumac. Take a right at the first fork to follow the interpretive trail in order. Short but sweet, this three-quarter-mile natural path heads down a steep ravine and travels along a creek into hardwood bottomland, past a large patch of pawpaw trees with leaves bigger than the human hand. Huge, twisted, and gnarly bur oaks are impressive. While some interpretive signs can be found along the way, most are in disrepair and no longer legible. Between the trees, you can spot the dam on one side and a steep bank on the other. After climbing back out, stay right at the fork to take the prairie path back to your car.

**WALNUT RIDGE TRAIL**—If you're staying in the Walnut River Campground, cross the wooden Walnut River bridge on the west end to locate the trailhead. If you're here for the day, you can park at the west end of the dam and follow the cement path (the El Dorado Linear Trail) through prairie grasses and take the left fork to find the trailhead. The hike is a three-quarter-mile loop of wood-chip path that leads through woods along Walnut River and into a clearing that nears the paved trail before returning.

**SATCHEL CREEK COVE LOOP**—On the park map, you may notice a loop trail near the entrance to Bluestem Point. The trail was recently added for cross-county run/walk competitions. This is a 1-mile, mowed loop maintained only in October when competitions are scheduled.

**SHADY CREEK NATURE TRAIL**—According to park literature, this trail begins across the road from the self-pay station at the entrance to the Shady Creek Area; however, while there is a park kiosk, neither the trail nor a trailhead sign is apparent. It seems a low-lying woodland area provides riparian habitat to follow for three-quarters of a mile. Hikers can retrace their steps or return on the park road. The park office advises that a 1-mile trail is planned, with interpretive markers and a profusion of wildflowers along a prairie path. Trail work has not yet begun.

**BIKING**—Paved and cement paths meander the Walnut River Area, while the **EL DORADO LINEAR TRAIL** leads into the town of El Dorado. You may prefer riding the 12-mile equestrian trail or the roads that circle the park. The **DOUBLE BLACK DIAMOND MOUNTAIN BIKE TRAIL** runs for 2 miles. In spite of a sign at the trailhead, you may not be able to identify the trail when falling leaves obliterate the narrow dirt path. The trailhead is located just across the wooden footbridge in Walnut River Campground. The trail, which loops in a ravine between the linear trail and a stream, is rated challenging, as it leads through dense timber with water crossings.

**HORSEBACK RIDING**—Begin at horse camp #1 in Boulder Bluff and head north. The trail first makes a loop near an old rock quarry. From there, it heads south through prairie, edging the shoreline and avoiding the campgrounds. Lake views abound, with little to no shade on the 12-mile, relatively flat mowed trail. (Eventually, the trail will span 20 miles.) Wildflowers will delight the observant rider late spring through early fall. The return trail runs between the park road and railroad tracks. Riders and hikers might prefer returning along the lakefront instead. (Note: Some portions of the trail may be erased after high water. Improvements are planned for the equestrian camp.)

**TRAIL BUILDING**—See www.kansastrailscouncil.org to help with the Boulder Bluff horse trail.

**FISHING AND HUNTING**—Six boat ramps are convenient to all four areas. A youth fishing pond is located in the Bluestem Point Area. There are two piers or docks, one at Shady Creek and one at Boulder Bluff. Anglers may catch bluegill, black crappie, channel and flathead catfish, largemouth bass, white bass, and white crappie. Smallmouth bass and walleye are your best bet. The Shady Creek Marina rents pontoon boats in season.

**OTHER**—Somewhat like a treasure hunt for GPS users, geocaching is gaining in popularity. Eight caches (or containers) lie camouflaged within the park and seven more are in the wildlife area, with more being added.

**CAMPING AND FACILITIES**—1,100 campsites of all types are available on a first-come, first-served basis. A few campsites can be reserved within Bluestem Point and Walnut River. Seven cabins can be reserved from one year to one week in advance. A laundry area and ice are available in the Walnut River Area near two deluxe cabins. Two swimming beaches with bathhouses and picnic tables are available in Bluestem Point and Walnut River. Boating, skiing, sailing, and personal watercraft are allowed from boat ramps in each of the four areas. The Walnut Valley Sailing Club operates a sailboat pier for its members in the Boulder Bluff Area. The Shady Creek Marina rents pontoon boats to visitors.

**TRAFFIC**—Heavy, especially through summer, and heaviest in July.

**LOCATION AND DIRECTIONS**—In Butler County, northeast of Wichita. The Bluestem Point Area is on the northeast side of the park. Take State Highway 177 from I-35 to NE Bluestem Point Road. For the Boulder Bluff or Walnut River Areas, take U.S. Highway 77 from I-35. Enter from either North Myers Road, or East 12th Avenue. The Shady Creek Area and the park office can be reached from either direction.

**ENTRY**—State park entrance fees apply at all areas. The park is open all year, but restrooms and bathhouses are locked and the marina is closed after October 15.

**ON THE WEB**—Trails are mapped at www.kdwp.state.ks.us, search "El Dorado."

**CONTACT**—El Dorado State Park office, (316) 321-7180; 618 NE Bluestem Road, El Dorado, KS 67042-8643.

# Chaplin Nature Center

Located in the Arkansas River Lowlands Region, Chaplin Nature center is an educational and inspirational experience for nature lovers, providing both indoor and outdoor exhibits. Originally, the Chaplin family managed a farm with the vision of protecting natural areas for a public nature center. Later, the Wichita Audubon Society purchased the property and is credited with development and preservation of the nature center. A full-time naturalist is on staff at the visitor center to facilitate group, student, and public education programs. Nature displays, a nature library, a bookstore, and gift shop are all onsite, as well. Check the online calendar for special events and educational programs. Hiking trails and the visitor center are open to the public at no charge, although donations are appreciated.

**WILDLIFE**—The canopy and dense understory of the diverse woodland attract white-breasted nuthatches, Carolina chickadees, wrens, tufted titmice, cedar waxwings, warblers, vireos, and the seldom-seen pileated woodpeckers. An observation deck at the visitor center makes bird-watching and wildlife photography easy. Bird feeders attract goldfinches and humming-birds. From sandbars of the Arkansas River, explorers can identify a multitude of wildlife tracks. Look for the prints of herons, turkeys, bobcats, foxes, deer, and raccoons.

**HIKING**—Maps can be obtained only at the visitor center. Well-marked trails lead through dense woods, bottomland timber, prairie, wetlands, and even sandbars of the Arkansas River. Begin your hike by descending the wooden staircase from the viewing platform behind the visitor center. Trails begin at the base of the stairs and can be hiked independently, or linked for 4 miles of hiking:

**WILDLIFE HOMES TRAIL** identifies nesting habitat on a quarter-mile loop. **LOST PRAIRIES TRAIL** meanders prairie grasses and wildflowers for three-quarters of a mile. Walk wooded riparian areas on the half-mile **SPRING CREEK TRAIL.** The half-mile **BLUFF TRAIL** climbs to views over Spring Creek and looks into the wooded valley below. Save the 2-mile **RIVER TRAIL** for the grand finale. This branch extends to sandbars along the scenic Arkansas River for outstanding wildlife watching and identification of animal tracks.

**CAMPING AND FACILITIES**—Parking, restrooms, and water are your only facilities. Camping is not allowed.

**LOCATION AND DIRECTIONS**—In Cowley County. From Arkansas City, go west on U.S. Highway 166 and then north on 31st Road to 27th Drive.

**ENTRY**—No entrance fees, but donations are appreciated. The visitor center is open on weekends throughout the year: Saturday from 9:00 A.M. to 5:00 P.M. and Sunday from 1:00 P.M. to 5:00 P.M. Weekday hours vary seasonally. Always closed on Mondays and holidays. Trails are open daily from sunrise to sunset.

**ON THE WEB**—www.wichitaaudubon.org/cnc.html.

**CONTACT**—Chaplin Nature Center, (620) 442-4133; 27814 27th Drive, Arkansas City, KS 67005.

# Flint Hills National Wildlife Refuge

J UST 8 MILES FROM THE INTERSTATE, this convenient refuge near Emporia offers a quiet and reflective escape to observe migratory and resident wildlife on foot or from your vehicle. Fertile farmland, prairie, riparian, and wetland habitat summon migrating wildlife. The refuge offers serene beauty unique in all four seasons. This 18,500-acre refuge of shallow marshes and ponds is located in a floodplain up the Neosho River from the John Redmond Reservoir. Don't be fooled by the name: you won't find Flint Hill scenery here in this relatively flat, open area.

For some, a marsh or a swamp may not be a thing of beauty, but on a warm fall day, ponds on the Burgess Marsh Trail reflect cobalt blue sky and yellow foliage from trees that line the ponds. When the sun is low, opaque prairie grass glows copper. Wildflowers taller than people create a natural

Burgess Marsh at Flint Hills National Wildlife Refuge.

blind from which to view the marsh. Even so, the birds are keenly aware of any presence on the trail and launch overhead to escape. Flocks of American coot are common on the refuge; their shiny black feathers and white bills make them stand apart from the mallards. You may see a startled water snake make a break for the pond. Turtles bask in the sun atop floating logs. A northern harrier swoops after smaller prey, but great blue herons are shy. At the edge of the pond, the wake is all that's left behind as a small deer bounds away. Fresh tracks are common atop the grass-covered dike, which is reminiscent of an emerald green ribbon.

**WILDLIFE**—Early spring brings snow geese and turkeys. Warblers, bluebirds, scissor-tailed flycatchers, snowy egrets, and shorebirds can be spotted in April and May. Summer brings the added bonus of wildflowers, most notably sunflowers, while great blue herons, green herons, wood ducks, and blue-winged teal nest on the refuge. Fall is peak season for migrating waterfowl, including redheads, canvasbacks, and white pelicans. Deer rutting and brightly colored foliage are highlights in the fall. Winter brings stark views, with more opportunity to see birds of prey, including red-tailed hawks, American kestrels, and northern harriers. Ducks and geese fatten themselves in marshes, luring elusive bobcats. Numerous bald eagles hunt the wetlands and are more easily spotted in the winter.

**HIKING**—**BURGESS MARSH TRAIL** allows wildlife lovers to wander atop a dike to view wetlands on either side for about a quarter mile. A paved path first leads to a boardwalk that extends into one of the larger ponds, creating a great platform for viewing. Nervous waterfowl will scatter as you approach. Continue on the mowed path, which meanders between two wetland areas. Unless you arrive after a hard freeze, don't forget your bug spray.

**TOWNSITE TRAIL** (also known as the HQ or Hartford Trail) is a three-quarter-mile path that ambles through river bottom timber and follows the Neosho River. A winding natural path leads you through pecan and pear trees, across bridges and past old remnants of a home site, and eventually on an old, surviving road. It's the old town site remnants that give this trail its name. You may see common deer, ducks, and herons on this lovely wooded trail; but if you've come for bird-watching, the other trails will suit you better.

**DOVE ROOST TRAIL** is a little harder to reach, but offers a 1-mile hike around a pond in both woodland and prairie habitat. An observation tower can be found in the parking lot.

**BIKING**—Most of the park roads are maintained gravel and flat. A bicycle might be a great way to cover more ground with a clear view of the habitat.

Though gravel roads bring dust from passing vehicles, there will be little traffic along the path. The **INDIAN HILL LOOP** provides a short and scenic 5-mile ride or you can ride from headquarters to the **DOVE ROOST TRAIL** and back for approximately 18 miles. Much of this scenery will be farmland, prairie, and woods, rather than marsh.

**FISHING AND HUNTING**—Fishing access is provided at the Hartford Recreational Area and the Dove Roost Trail, both located on the Indian Hill Loop road. Boat ramps can be found at Jacobs Creek (on the southeastern end) and at the Hartford Recreation Area. The Neosho River has been known to yield some record-setting catches, including channel and flathead catfish, crappie, and even paddlefish and spoonbill. Hunting for quail, turkeys, deer, and waterfowl is allowed, but a great portion of the refuge is closed to hunting November 1 through March 1. Be sure to locate a map online or request one through the mail prior to planning a hunting or fishing trip. State hunting and fishing regulations apply.

**AUTO TOUR**—The Indian Hill Loop auto tour is a 5-mile loop on gravel roads, beginning on cropland and winding through marsh area and prairie. Croplands help attract and feed some species, so keep an eye to the fields as well as the marshes. As it is a low-lying floodplain, roads can be closed at any time. Park officials ask you to respect any road closures for your own safety.

**CAMPING AND FACILITIES**—Primitive camping is allowed on areas open to public access. Campfires are permitted, but must be attended to at all time. There is no restroom or water available.

**TRAFFIC**—Very light: the U.S. Fish and Wildlife Service reports 40,000 visitors annually.

**OTHER**—Wild food gathering, mushroom hunting, and bait collecting are allowed.

**LOCATION AND DIRECTIONS**—In Lyon and Coffey Counties. East of Emporia, take Exit 141 from I-35. Head south on State Highway 130 for 8 miles to Hartford. You'll find the Burgess Marsh Trail on your right, about 2 miles before Hartford. To reach headquarters and the Townsite (HQ) Trail, turn west in Hartford on Maple Avenue and go three blocks to the entrance. The Townsite Trail can be accessed just north of headquarters. To reach the Indian Hill Loop auto tour, continue on Highway 130 through Hartford and turn east on 18th Lane. Follow the signs. The Dove Roost Trailhead is about 8 miles east of headquarters on gravel roads. From Highway 130, turn east on 19th Lane and go about

3.5 miles to Emmer Road, turn right to continue east on 19th Road, and then make a right onto Garner Road to the trailhead.

**ENTRY**—There are no entrance fees at the refuge. Note that portions are closed to the public from November 1 through March 1. The park headquarters in Hartford offer maps, information, and restrooms, but are open only Monday–Friday, 8:00 A.M. to 4:30 P.M. (closed federal holidays). Weekend visitors can pick up maps, as well as plant and bird checklists, at a kiosk outside headquarters and at the Burgess Marsh Trailhead. If you plan to visit on weekends, phone ahead for road closures and visitor information.

**ON THE WEB**—Maps and more can be found at flinthills.fws.gov.

**CONTACT**—Call the U.S. Fish and Wildlife Service, (620) 392-5553, for information or the current bird count; or write 530 West Maple Avenue, P.O. Box 128, Hartford, KS 66854.

# John Redmond Reservoir
## and Otter Creek Game Management Area

Located in the floodplain of the Neosho River valley, John Redmond Reservoir is adjoined to the Flint Hills National Wildlife Refuge. While all NWR areas are limited to wildlife-related activities, Redmond Reservoir offers all of the traditional recreational pursuits, including camping, boating, and skiing, with a lengthy multipurpose trail for hikers, bikers, and equestrians. An area west of the dam is designated for off-road vehicles while Otter Creek Game Management Area is managed for hunting and fishing.

**WILDLIFE**—Native prairie grasses, woodlands, wetlands, and cropland attract waterfowl, shorebirds, bobwhite quail, greater prairie chickens, rabbits, and deer. A 15-acre marsh attracts shorebirds and waterfowl within the Otter Creek Game Area.

**HIKING/BIKING/HORSEBACK RIDING**—**HICKORY CREEK TRAIL** can keep hikers happy for days with 14 miles of trail. Blazed in blue paint, the main trail is 8 miles long, with an additional 6 miles of side loops blazed in white or orange—white for loops that run lakeside and orange for upland detours or shortcuts. There are four official trailheads and park roads that cross the trail seven times, creating additional access or exit points. Overlook and Dam Site Trailheads have restrooms with water during warm months only. Campgrounds have restrooms, but will require a detour. A trail map can be requested over the phone, but the over-copied version is barely legible. (Note: The trail will be closed during deer hunting season.)

For a shorter hike, follow the blue trail from the Overlook Trailhead and hike to the Redmond Cove Trailhead, which is 2.2 miles if you avoid the side trails. Add the orange loop between the trailheads for an additional mile. Designated campgrounds can be found along the trail at Dam Site, Redmond Cove, and Hickory Creek, which enable backpacking or day hiking in either direction. Riders should be able to complete the trail in a day, but hikers cannot. Most of the trail is dirt tread; it can become slick when wet and may take days to dry after rain. Lake views are infrequent on this wooded trail that straddles prairie areas and ponds. Except for a section toward the end that leads to a bluff overlooking the creek, most of the trail is fairly level.

Remember that horseback riders have the right-of-way. Hikers yield to bikers. To estimate hike times, park officials suggest 2 miles per hour for the average hiker in good health. As sections are periodically flooded, ask a ranger for current trail conditions before you begin. Poison ivy and nettles provide good reason to wear long pants. Ticks will be a problem in warm months. (Note: Trail conditions suffered after extreme rainfall in 2007. Considerable time may be needed to make repairs.)

**TRAIL BUILDING**—The COE staff works in cooperation with volunteers and work crews. Workdays are scheduled throughout the year. If you would like to help, please contact the lake office at (316) 364-8613.

**FISHING AND HUNTING**—Frequent flooding causes fish to be flushed through the dam into the spillway, where anglers find success. Anglers must wear life jackets to fish in the spillway. A rearing pond has helped produce good wiper. Channel cat, crappie, flathead, white bass, and sunfish can also be found.

Bobwhite quail, greater prairie chickens, rabbits, and deer are attracted to the Otter Creek Game Management Area, where a 15-acre marsh also attracts shorebirds and waterfowl. Note that target practice is not allowed. Be sure you are aware of the boundaries between the John Redmond Reservoir and the Flint Hills National Wildlife Refuge.

**OTHER**—An off-road vehicle area provides 140 acres of trail for dirt bikes and ATVs in Otter Creek Campground at the southwest end of the dam. Trails are open from sunrise to sunset.

**CAMPING AND FACILITIES**—Most park areas have designated campsites, picnic facilities, boat ramps, water, and restrooms. Only Dam Site and Riverside West have showers. Group shelters are located at Dam Site and Riverside East. A swimming beach, a changing house, and a dump station can be found at Dam Site.

**LOCATION AND DIRECTIONS**—In Coffey County. Take I-35 to Exit 155 and head south on State Highway 75 to New Strawn and follow the signs.

**ENTRY**—The park is open all year, but water is unavailable from late October to mid-March. COE use fees apply.

**ON THE WEB**—Lake maps are online, but trail maps are not. Visit www.swt.usace.army.mil, choose "recreation" and then "John Redmond."

**CONTACT**—Trail and lake maps can be acquired from the COE Tulsa District, (620) 364-8613. KDWP operates the Otter Creek Game Management Area, (316) 637-2748; 738 Fegan Road, Toronto, KS 66777.

# Geology of the Chautauqua Hills Region

KANSANS HAVE ANCIENT HISTORY and geology to thank for some of the best trails in the state and three spectacular parks. The Chautauqua Hills Region, a pie-shaped wedge of land that was formed by thick sandstone, interrupts the Osage Cuestas Region. During the Pennsylvanian Period, rivers emptied into shallow seas at this location. Sand and other sediments piled up at the mouths of rivers and deltas. After the seas dried up, the sands were compacted into sandstone and mud was compacted into shale. Uplift and erosion exposed low hills capped by more resistant sandstone. Today, the Verdigris, Fall, and Elk rivers continue to erode and expose the sandstone bluffs through which they pass, impacting the scenery you see at Elk City, Fall River, and Cross Timbers State Parks in the southeast region of Kansas. Characteristics of the Chautauqua Hills Region may be most obvious at Elk City State Park, known for its imposing rock outcroppings and interesting formations.

# Cross Timbers State Park
## and Toronto Lake

TRAILS AT CROSS TIMBERS STATE PARK radiate a magic that can only be derived from age. Although it's difficult to pinpoint why, the trails seem to be steeped in "Old World" charm. Early pioneers labeled the area the Cross Timbers Region—a reference to its thick stands of post and black-jack oak. The region forms a great ecotone as it transitions between the deciduous forest of the east and the grasses of the Great Plains. One of few places where old-growth forest remains, the park's ancient post oaks have been analyzed by scientists from the University of Arkansas Tree-Ring Laboratory. The Ancient Trees Trail was subsequently designed to showcase these trees and educate the public. You might imagine the old trees as tall and stately, towering overhead. Instead, they are slow-growing and slender; the trees remain small, but grow straight as broomsticks.

The land was once a favored hunting and campground for the Osage Nation. Visitors can walk in the footsteps of the Osage by obtaining special

Cambi Colley

Bridge to Chautauqua Hills Trail at Cross Timbers State Park.

**195**

permission to camp in the backcountry on segments of the Chautauqua Hills Trail.

Park areas would not be described as manicured and well groomed, but cabins at Toronto Point are nicer than many state park accommodations. Three cabins are perched on a rocky shore facing the dam, complete with a flagstone walkway, a porch overlooking the lake, a fire pit, and a picnic table. A full-sized refrigerator, a two-burner stove, a microwave, a kitchen table for six, and a full bath make this an inexpensive luxury camp that offers convenient access to hiking and biking trails with privacy and great views.

**WILDLIFE**—Cross Timbers State Park is heavily wooded, with less open prairie than its neighbor, Fall River State Park. Birds include eagles, turkey vultures, wild turkeys, doves, bobwhite quail, migratory birds, and waterfowl such as mallards, pintails, mergansers, buffleheads, and white pelicans. You might see sandpipers and plovers, too. White-tailed deer, beavers, foxes, coyotes, raccoons, skunks, and snakes are typical resident mammals and reptiles. An extensive birding list is provided at the information station.

**HIKING**—All trails are open to foot traffic. Hikers should note that all but the Ancient Trees Trail are open to cyclists as well. During excessive wet periods, trails may be closed when deemed hazardous or impassable.

**ANCIENT TREES TRAIL** is a 1-mile, self-guided educational trail that showcases old-growth post oaks with interpretive markers that describe the ages of the trees and historic events of the time period. The loop lowers to lake level with views of a cove, while the remainder leads through grasses, native plants, and wildflowers. The trailhead is located northwest of the Sandstone Campground, behind the pay station at the entrance to Toronto Point.

**CHAUTAUQUA HILLS TRAIL** offers four color-coded, connecting loops that wrap around the Miller Creek arm of the reservoir. The main trailhead is accessed from Toronto Point, east of Point Road. To reach the longer trails on the eastside of the arm, take Coyote Road south from State Highway 105. Note that archery hunting is a seasonal option on the Chautauqua Hills Trail. Signs will be posted at the trailhead during hunting season. Backcountry camping is allowed along the trail with special permission. All the trails are rated moderate. The Blue Trail travels 1.5 miles along the scenic and narrow lake arm that resembles a wide river. Wooden bridges, sandstone slab stream crossings, and rugged stone staircases lead hikers through a heavily shaded area on a relatively wide path. This trail is quite scenic and is the perfect option for those with limited time. The Yellow Trail is 5 miles, curving around a riparian and sometimes swampy area and through woods and prairie with sandstone outcroppings. This trail is more secluded than the Blue Trail and may offer more opportunity for wildlife watching. Backcountry campsites are located along the trail. The West Red Trail covers 6.75 miles, partly over open shoreline and lake arm scenery, partly through wooded area and prairie. A scenery synopsis includes post and blackjack oak forest, tallgrass prairie, sandstone boulders and steps, ridges, and a healthy dose of lake views. Backcountry campsites are located along the trail. The East Red Trail is an 11-mile loop that runs close to the open shoreline and back into wooded areas, sometimes nearing private lands. This section of trail traverses public land where hunting is allowed.

Beginning at the Blackjack Campground in the Holiday Hill Site, the **BLACKJACK TRAIL** is 1 mile of moderate hiking through woodlands that offer the opportunity to spot wildlife such as wild turkeys and deer. Compared with other options in the park, the trail may seem ordinary until fall, when sunlight filters through the trees, or spring, when wildflowers, redbud, and rough-leafed dogwood put on a show. Add another half mile to your hike with an adjoining loop on the **OAK RIDGE TRAIL.**

Highly recommended is the **OVERLOOK TRAIL** in Woodson Cove. Although only 1.25 miles long, the hiking is rated moderate, as the trail climbs steep ravines, crosses streams and sandstone outcroppings, and peers into sandstone caves. The trail is fairly wide, with emerald green moss as thick as carpet and lichen-covered boulders (some the size of cars) scattered trailside. The loop path eventually leads to a rocky ledge that overlooks the lake and trolling anglers below. This peaceful trail and lovely overlook are well worth the inclines. There are two trailheads for the Overlook Trail: at Woodson Cove there are stone picnic tables and primitive restrooms; at Overlook there is a shelter, but no restrooms. While the trail is easy to follow, the exit can be easy to miss. The trail is blazed in blue, but to exit look for a white blaze that begins a connector trail and marks the end of the Overlook Trail.

**BIKING**—All trails but the Ancient Trees Trail are open to mountain biking. Each path is rugged, with sandstone and limestone boulders and steps, tree roots, and stream crossings. During excessively wet periods, trails may be closed if deemed hazardous or impassable or if conditions are detrimental to the trail. Note that archery hunting is a seasonal option on the Chautauqua Hills Trail. Signs are posted at the trailhead during hunting season.

**FISHING AND HUNTING**—Fishing is allowed on the rivers and the reservoir. Both provide excellent fishing for white crappie, white bass, and channel and flathead catfish. Anglers may also catch black bass, bluegill, and sunfish. A fishing pier can be found at Toronto Point. Archery hunting is available seasonally on the Toronto Point trails. The wildlife area is managed for both hunting and viewing wildlife.

**CAMPING AND FACILITIES**—Four park areas compose the state park. Traveling clockwise, they are: Toronto Point, Mann's Cove, Woodson Cove, and Holiday Hill and Dam Site. The park offers primitive camping in all park areas. Improved campsites are located at Toronto Point and Holiday Hill. A limited number of sites are located along the lake. Cabins and a group campsite can be reserved at Toronto Point. With prior permission, backpackers can find primitive, walk-in campsites just off the Chautauqua Hills Trail system. Spur trails lead to several designated backcountry sites on both the Yellow Trail and the West Red Trail.

Restrooms are available in all areas, but only Toronto Point and Holiday Hill have showers. A swimming beach is located on Toronto Point near the Sandstone Campground. Boat ramps are located at Manns Cove, Holiday Hill, and Toronto Point.

**TRAFFIC**—Below average, heaviest in May and June.

**LOCATION AND DIRECTIONS**—In Woodson County. From Wichita take I-35 north to Exit 71. Take U.S. Highway 54 past El Dorado and Eureka. Turn south on State Highway 105 toward Toronto. State Highway 105 circles the lake providing access to each of the 4 park areas. The park office is in the Holiday Hill and Damsite Area on the south shore, just across the dam on the right.

**ENTRY**—State park entrance fees apply at all areas. Toronto Point has the most amenities and campsites, as well as a frost-free water hydrant for winter. Some areas will be closed seasonally.

**ON THE WEB**—Parks and trails are marked on the park brochure at www.kdwp.state.ks.us, search "Toronto." The COE Tulsa District is a secondary source of information, at www.swt.usace.army.mil, select "recreation" and then "Toronto Lake."

**CONTACT**—KDWP in Toronto, (620) 637-2213; 144 Highway 105, Toronto, KS 66777-9749.

# Fall River Lake and State Park

Fall River State Park and Wildlife Area is remote and rustic. In fact, many of the roads are unpaved. One of the oldest projects in the state, its reservoir was completed in 1949 under the Flood Control Act. About a mile wide at the dam, the lake spreads nearly 15 miles, surrounded by rolling Flint Hills scenery. In addition to the lush green prairie and tree-lined streams that paint the background, glittering sandstone boulders and limestone outcroppings provide interest along the hiking trails and stream-banks. In late spring, Fall River rivals any state park with its wildflower display. Scurfpea, leadplant, purple coneflower, wild rose, catclaw, beardtongue, spiderwort, and spider milkweed can all be found in the open prairies and fields beside easy hiking trails. Later in summer, daisy fleabane, fringe-leaf ruellia, and evening primrose take their turn. Bird-watching is superb on the prairie, with little canopy to conceal your view.

Perhaps because of its remote location, this gem is also one of the least visited state parks in Kansas. A lengthy new trail system is currently being planned and created by the Kansas Trails Council with help from the Kansas Singletrack Society. New trails may spark more interest and draw visitors, boosting visitation. So, in the meantime, enjoy the solitude while you can.

**WILDLIFE**—Fall River Lake is ideal for bird-watching. Keep your eyes peeled for bald eagles, great horned owls, wild turkeys, doves, bobwhite quail, prairie chickens, pileated and downy woodpeckers, scissor-tailed fly-catchers, dickcissels, orioles, bluebirds, barn and tree swallows, red-winged blackbirds, and brown-headed cowbirds. When viewing from the wildlife area, you might see migratory waterfowl such as mallards, pintails, mergansers, and buffleheads. Sandpipers, plover, and white pelicans pass through, as well. White-tailed deer, beavers, foxes, coyotes, raccoons, skunks, and snakes also reside here.

**HIKING AND MOUNTAIN BIKING**—Fall River State Park is composed of two areas separated by the dam. On the east side of the dam is Quarry Bay. On the west side of the dam is Fredonia Bay. State park trails add up to 6.5 miles of hiking or biking. Don't forget your bug spray and sunscreen.

**FREDONIA BAY**—**CASNER CREEK TRAIL:** Two trailheads access this 1.5-mile loop. One trailhead is posted at the Casner Creek

Campground and the other at the youth fishing pond. Counterclockwise from the fishing pond, this rather easy trail follows a mowed path through woods that line an intermittent creek and then continues through prairie heavy with wildflowers and open views of the surrounding landscape. It crosses the park road and continues through prairie marked by tall blinds. At the opposite end, hikers will find restrooms at the Casner Creek Campground before returning through woodlands that skirt a shallow cove or riparian area when rainfall has been sufficient. This is a great place to watch for birds, snakes, turtles, deer, and small mammals looking for a drink.

**TURKEY RUN TRAIL:** Locate the trailhead at the day-use area named Gobbler's Knob (a right turn after the permit station). The 1-mile trail passes through a gate on a mowed path that leads through wildflowers and into woods, where you'll see interesting trees. Look for the giant thorns of the ominous-looking honey locust. The path interrupts an enormous Osage orange so hikers can pass. Blackjack and scrub oak hardwoods shade the trail. Multicolored sandstone boulders litter the path and some large specimens are carefully placed as stepping stones for a stream crossing. The sandstone boulders are the result of rivers that once emptied into the great inland sea during the Pennsylvanian Period. The striking colors are formed from quartz grains cemented together with calcium carbonate, iron oxide or silica. The trail leaves the woods to continue through upland prairie to panoramic views of Fall River Lake and the surrounding croplands and ranches before returning to the woods.

**QUARRY BAY**—A series of color-coded trails add up to 4 miles of hiking, beginning at the Post Oak Trailhead just inside the park entrance (across the road from the maintenance building). A drawing of the trail system is posted at the trailhead, along with a warning about ticks, chiggers, and mosquitoes. The trails may be hiked in succession, as a loop. or independently. **OVERLOOK TRAIL** is less trail and more overlook. **POST OAK TRAIL** is three-quarters of a mile long, signed in red. The rugged path leads away from the lake downhill to views of Craig Creek, which is laden with lichen-covered limestone, and then climbs back out. **CATCLAW TRAIL** is 1.75 miles long. Signed in yellow, this trail leads through tallgrass prairie, sloping sandstone ridges, and woods to panoramic views of the reservoir. **BLUESTEM PRAIRIE TRAIL** can be combined with the Catclaw Trail for a total of 3 miles. On its own, the Bluestem Prairie Trail is a 1.5-mile loop through prairie grasses. Can you distinguish among Indian grass, switchgrass, and bluestem?

**TRAIL BUILDING**—Trails in the park are being extended by as much as 30 miles. The first phase connects the Bluestem Trail to the COE's Whitehall Campground on the north side of the lake. Eventually, two more loops will be added and the Casner Creek Trail will also be connected. The Kansas Trails Council coordinates workdays on the third weekend each month. Visit the Web site for contact information: www.kansastrailscouncil.org. The COE is also requesting volunteers to help with cleanup and other light duties.

**FISHING AND HUNTING**—Fall River Lake is stocked with largemouth bass, bluegill, crappie, walleye, white bass, and channel catfish. White bass fishing is excellent, especially in early spring above the reservoir in Otter Creek and Fall River. Hunters may pursue prairie chicken, deer, turkey, dove, quail, rabbit, and squirrel in the wildlife area. Although there are no maintained trails in the wildlife area, gravel roads allow access.

**PADDLING**—An access area for Fall River can be found east of Eureka on State Highway 99, south of U.S. Highway 54. A scenic float, ranging in classification from flatwater to class II, meanders for 12 miles through the wildlife area to Fall River Reservoir. Boat ramps will be found on your right for take out at the State Park's Fredonia Bay Area. Paddlers can rent equipment in Eureka, northwest of the park. An outfitter at Fall River Boat and Canoe Rental specializes in group trips (6 to 8 miles, three hours) and offers guided backpack trips in March, April, and October. Call Lloyd Funk in Eureka at (620) 583-6481.

**CAMPING AND FACILITIES**—The COE manages the Dam Site, Whitehall Bay, Brown's Cove, and Rock Ridge Cove Areas, while KDWP manages Fredonia Bay and Quarry Bay. Both primitive and improved camping sites are available, complete with trailer dump stations. Primitive camping is available in the wildlife area, as well. A swimming beach is located on Quarry Bay. Boat ramps can be found in all areas. A lovely day-use area located at Gobbler's Knob in Fredonia Bay overlooks the lake and offers shelters, picnic tables, and grills. Facilities also include modern restrooms and showers, an amphitheater for summer programs, and a fish-cleaning station.

**TRAFFIC**—Little or below average, heaviest in July.

**LOCATION AND DIRECTIONS**—In Greenwood County. From Wichita, head east on U.S. Highway 400 toward the town of Fall River. Turn north away from town on a gravel road to reach the state park. Watch for small hand-painted signs that point the way.

**ENTRY**—State park entrance fees apply at Fredonia and Quarry bays. The park season generally runs April 15 through October 15, when all facilities are available and a naturalist is on staff. Visitors are welcome in the off-season, but should note that not all facilities are available and some parks will be closed.

**ON THE WEB**—www.kdwp.state.ks.us, search "Fall River." Tulsa District COE, www.swt.usace.army.mil, select "recreation" and then "Fall River Lake."

**CONTACT**—Fall River/Cross Timbers KDWP office, (620) 637-2213; COE office at Fall River, (620) 658-4445. Address of KDWP office: 144 Highway 105, Toronto, KS 66777.

**NEARBY—HAWTHORNE RANCH** offers an adventure on horseback. If you're not afraid to ride, they'll have you jumping logs, ducking under branches, and riding through streambeds on private Flint Hills ranchland north of Eureka. This is not your ordinary trail ride. You can even camp on the property with prior permission. Call Sally Hawthorne at (620) 583-5887.

# Elk City Lake and State Park
## and Big Hill Lake

SITUATED IN THE CHAUTAUQUA HILLS REGION, Elk City State Park is nearly on the Oklahoma border. History runs deep along the banks of the Elk River, once home to the Osage Indians and Civil War veterans. The area was even frequented by outlaws such as the Bender and Dalton gangs. Today, Elk City Lake trails offer some of the best hiking in Kansas, characterized by scenery that is often compared to the famous Ozarks. In fact, three trails in the park have qualified as National Recreation Trails. The Kansas Trails Council has been very active in designing and maintaining these inspiring trails, most are rated moderately strenuous—somewhat of a rarity in Kansas.

**WILDLIFE**—White-tailed deer, wild turkeys, bobwhite quail, cottontails, foxes, and gray squirrels abound in the forested hills and river valley. Cedar waxwings might be spotted from trails where cedar trees thrive and the elusive pileated woodpeckers may be heard or spotted among mature trees near Elk River. Local furbearers include raccoons, bobcats, coyotes, gray foxes,

Overlook from the Table Mound National Recreation Trail at Elk City Lake.

and opossums. Beavers, mink, and muskrats haunt the river valleys. Even neotropical birds are known to nest here, such as indigo buntings or summer tanagers. Snow geese and white pelicans may pass through during migration seasons. Great egrets and great blue herons may be seen wading in shallow pools at dusk or dawn. U.S. Highway 160 runs parallel to a waterfowl refuge, allowing convenient viewing opportunities on spring and fall drives. Don't forget to look for collared lizards sunning on rocks and turtles crossing the hiking paths.

**HIKING**—**ELK RIVER NATIONAL RECREATION TRAIL** is a strenuous trail, which begins with switchbacks that climb to scenic overlooks of the reservoir. Rocks are the main attraction along this trail, which begins at the western edge of the dam (across the road from the Corps of Engineers office) and ends 15 miles later at Highway 160. Shorten the route by starting or ending at the Oak Ridge Public Use Area, found 9.5 miles from the eastern trailhead. From the Oak Ridge trailhead to the western trailhead, 5.5 miles of trail wind through woodlands, with overviews of the Elk River and secondary streams. A waterfall provides a scenic landmark on the western half of the trail. While foliage may not be the trail's primary allure, it offers some distraction from the rock formations, boulders, bluffs, and miniature caves. Western buckeye, hawthorn, dogwood, and redbud all flower in the spring. Various wildflowers color the understory in early summer. Hardwoods help make fall the most colorful season of all.

Three trails can be combined for one fantastic day of hiking. Just west of the Elk City State Park office, warm up with the **GREEN THUMB NATURE TRAIL,** which is just under a mile. Beardtongue is an ugly name given to a beautiful wildflower that lines the walkway near the entrance of the trail; look for white bells with purple-striped centers. Red and post oak, hickory, and red cedar grow tall enough to block out the sun on this moderately strenuous loop, which is blazed in white with interpretive signs. With little or no understory, the hike is a pleasure even in the summer and the trail is easy to follow. The path descends to clear, flowing streams and then climbs to rock outcrops dripping with columbine and fern. Enormous rocks cap the rather strenuous hill, but the outcrops and views of the lake make the climb worthwhile.

Sharing a trailhead with the Green Thumb Nature Trail, the **TABLE MOUND NATIONAL RECREATION TRAIL** is a one-way, 3-mile route that skirts a bluff making a gentle climb for the first 2 miles. Blue waters peek through the trees on most of the rugged path, which is blazed in blue. Lichen-covered rock slabs provide nice picnic areas. After crossing the park road in the last mile, the trail becomes steep and challenging, squeezing between stone slabs and rock walls, crossing boulder fields, and passing cave like formations. Some scrambling is required for the northernmost section. The final push is challenging for short legs, but the payoff is a stunning view of a valley below from a rock ledge far above the dam. Wildflowers grow from the rock formations and greenery creates a frame for your photos. Although moderately difficult, this trail is the perfect alternative if you don't have time or a second vehicle for the **ELK RIVER TRAIL.** Be prepared for several stream crossings and fallen log obstacles. The trail ends at the Memorial Overlook, where water and restrooms are available in season and the Post Oak Nature Trail begins.

**POST OAK NATURE TRAIL** is a short loop just east of the Memorial Overlook. Blazed in orange, it wanders along a wooded ledge over the lake and dam for an easy half mile. Careful observation will allow you to hook up with the blue blazes of the Table Mound Trail, thus eliminating the most strenuous (but also most scenic) section on the return trail. When using this shortcut, the downhill return on the Table Mound Trail is much quicker, taking nearly half the time of the ascent.

**SQUAW CREEK MULTI-USE TRAIL** connects the north and south sections of the state park with a half mile of linear, paved trail great for both hiking and biking. In addition, there is a three-quarter-mile exercise loop in the day-use area.

**TIMBER RIDGE HIKING TRAIL** is in the Card Creek public-use area. The trail forms a 2.3-mile loop between Card Creek and the park road. The section nearest the creek is strenuous, but offers views of the river valley; the section that parallels the park road is easy, but is mostly wooded and not as scenic. The Card Creek Area doesn't get the same kind of rave reviews as the state park, but is lovely, less traveled, and more secluded.

**BIKING—EAGLE ROCK MOUNTAIN BIKE TRAIL** begins at the top of the spillway on the north side of the lake, where a sign and map mark the trailhead. Expertly crafted for all levels of ability, the trail is designed to be ridden in a clockwise direction. The trail map indicates sections designed for beginning, intermediate, and advanced skill riders. Roller-coaster dips, head-on climbs, and winding ascents provide a variety of experience for the rider. Double-backs, steep downhills, and log jumps (with ride-around for beginners) allow the same stunning scenery visitors expect throughout the park— riverside views and boulders, old-growth forest, and native grasses. Markers help riders anticipate the course, which is 4.5 miles long. A trailside shelter and bench are an added treat. The trail may be closed in wet periods, when it occasionally suffers from slick, muddy conditions and erosion.

**TRAIL BUILDING**—The Kansas Trails Council coordinates and manages trail work for Eagle Rock Mountain Bike Trail, as well as the Table Mound and Elk River trails. Visit their Web site for contact information if you would like to help: www.kansastrailscouncil.org.

**FISHING AND HUNTING**—Fishing the refuge is permitted from April 1 to August 31. Channel cat, white bass, crappie, flathead, catfish, largemouth bass, and saugeye may be caught in the reservoir. A handicapped-accessible fishing dock is located in the state park and a kids' fishing pond can be found by the Prairie Meadow Campground. Hunting is not permitted in the state park or the refuge at any time, but is allowed in the public lands outside.

**PADDLING**—Paddle the Elk River for just under 10 miles. Put in below the bridge at Elk City just west of Highway 160. Float the winding Elk River through the wildlife area to the reservoir. Paddlers should scout the river, which is classified as levels I and II and also has some fast-moving areas. Boat ramps at Card Creek Area Campground offer a take-out where you can camp on the river.

**CAMPING AND FACILITIES**—Both utility sites for improved camping and primitive sites are offered among four park areas: Elk City State Park, Card Creek, Oak Ridge, and Outlet Channel. Primitive camping is also allowed in designated areas at the wildlife area. Backpackers may camp along the Table Mound and Elk River Trails. Picnic tables, bathhouses, a swimming beach, fishing piers and boat ramps, dump stations, shelters, and basketball courts can all be found throughout the state park. A half-mile exercise apparatus trail and a disc golf trail are available in the state park's day-use area.

**TRAFFIC**—Little or below average, heaviest in June.

**LOCATION AND DIRECTIONS**—In Montgomery County. U.S. Highways 160 and 75 intersect in Independence. Take Highway 160 west for 1 mile and turn north on County Road 3350. The park entrance is marked with a small sign on the north side of the highway. Follow signs to the state park office. Continue northwest past the dam to reach the COE office.

**ENTRY**—Entrance fees apply only in Elk City State Park. Some camp-grounds will be closed in the off-season. Restrooms and water are available only in high season.

**ON THE WEB**—www.kdwp.state.ks.us, search "Elk City." Trail maps for the Eagle Rock and Elk River trails can be found at www.kansastrails council.org.

**CONTACT**—KDWP office in Independence, (620) 331-6295; Tulsa District COE, (620) 336-2741. Call to request the COE's park map, which is not available online. Address of KDWP office: 4825 Squaw Creek Road, Independence, KS 67301.

**NEARBY**—Operated by the Corps of Engineers Tulsa District, **BIG HILL LAKE** offers boating, swimming, camping, hunting, and fishing. Big Hill maintains a 17-mile horse trail, which surrounds three-quarters of the lake and hugs the shoreline, offering varied terrain for riders of all ages. Parking lots can be found in Timber Hill Park and Cherryvale Park and also on the south side of Highway 160. Trail riders can even camp overnight with horses. There is also a 1-mile linear hiking trail that follows the shoreline in the Cherryvale Area, connecting the many features and amenities there. User fees apply. For information, call the COE in Cherryvale, KS, at (620) 336-2741.

# Geology of the Cherokee Lowlands Region

SNEAKING INTO THE SOUTHEAST CORNER OF KANSAS, the Cherokee Lowlands are characterized by deep and fertile, well-drained soil in a rel-atively flat area. Swamps with lush plant life covered the lowlands during the Pennsylvanian Period; after the water receded, layers of mud and sand com-pacted thick layers of decayed plant material. Millions of years later, the result was rich coal deposits. So while some areas of the lowlands were per-fect for fertile farming, mining was also prevalent in the area.

Today, visitors can see remnants of the historic coal mining industry firsthand in Mined Land Wildlife Area, which is detailed in a subsequent chapter.

# Crawford State Park

INITIALLY PART OF THE LOUISIANA PURCHASE, the land of Crawford County later became the source of much contention for the U.S. government, the Cherokee Nation, settlers, and even the railroad industry. Inside the park, an interpretive trail with remnants of a 19th-century military outpost is a reminder of the area's deep-seated history.

In the 1930s, the Civilian Conservation Corps (CCC) constructed a dam and a fish hatchery here. The hatchery still remains, one of only four fish hatcheries currently operated by KDWP for stocking lakes throughout the state. Crawford State Park was established and designated more than 30 years later.

Located in the Cherokee Lowlands Region, this 500-acre park surrounds on a 150-acre lake. Redbud blooms boost scenery in the spring. Oak and hickory hardwood forests reward visitors in the fall. Recent trail improvements and the addition of modern cabins are sure to boost use of this southeastern playground nestled along Drywood Creek.

One of the smallest lakes in the state park system, Crawford Lake has a very casual community of private homes on its west shore. You can familiarize yourself quickly by driving the 5-mile paved loop around the lake. Although small, the lake is big enough for boating and water sports in the main channel, but its long, narrow fingers also allow wildlife watchers to paddle the quiet shoreline on calm days. Day users and tent campers will find a scenic backdrop for picnicking at Cherokee Landing and Lonesome Point, while the South Shelter Group Use Area offers nice facilities with a beautiful view reserved for larger groups.

**WILDLIFE**—A combination of riparian woods, grassland, and cropland lures a variety of wildlife. In addition to common Kansas birds, you might see indigo buntings, Bell's vireos, and yellow-breasted chats. Reptiles such as the endangered broad-headed skink (khaki colored with a red-orange head) and collared lizards seem out of place and far from home. Wildflowers grow quite tall, even by late spring. Patches of cactus are an unexpected sight in southeast Kansas.

**HIKING**—Three self-guided nature trails, on wide, crushed-gravel surface, travel through woods behind the dam, frequently alongside and over Drywood Creek.

**SPIDERLEG BRIDGE TRAIL** is a half-mile loop that features remnants of a military outpost and explains the area's military history. Don't expect to see the former Spiderleg Bridge, replaced long ago with a more sturdy concrete structure. To locate the trailhead, turn left from the park entrance.

**DEER RUN NATURE TRAIL** is a half-mile path with interpretive signs that point out trees and natural features along the way, one of which is poison ivy. A small parking lot can be found at the trailhead just east of the dam. This trail connects with the Spiderleg Bridge Trail.

**CCC MEMORIAL TRAIL** is a quarter-mile loop that features historic remnants of the CCC camp, just west of the dam. Turn right after passing through the park entrance. The trailhead appears quickly on your left.

**BIKING AND HIKING**—DRYWOOD CREEK HIKING AND BIKING TRAIL is about 7 miles long, including 1 mile running behind the dam. Rated moderate with a few technical sections, the singletrack is often level, with a few steep inclines. The surface is natural; while it primarily alternates between mowed grass and dirt, it's quite rocky on the eastern and southern ends of the loop. You will encounter stream crossings, though none are likely to be treacherous unless flooding has occurred. Well-placed rocks help make crossings safe, but they can be slick with moss and algae. The circuit trail wraps around the lake inside the park road, but sometimes travels on the road itself. Look for metal signposts pointing the way back into wooded areas.

One might suspect that views from the west side would be more scenic, as the trail follows the shoreline more closely according to the map. The opposite is true, however, as the trail frequently travels through the yards of houses on the west side. Downy woodpeckers and herons should be easy to spot from the trail on the east side as it traverses a rocky, wooded bluff overlooking the lake. If you're not careful, you might step right over turtles and frogs without seeing them. Be mindful that snakes like the woodlands and damp inlets and that poison ivy, deer ticks, and mosquitoes thrive here as well. You can find a trail map for Crawford Lake in the color booklet for all the state parks. The map is not very detailed, but landmarks will help pinpoint your place on the trail. Hikers can expect to spend about three hours on the trail.

**ROAD BIKING AND AUTO TOUR**—The park road circling the lake offers scenic views along 5 miles of road biking or auto touring. There are no shoulders and the route is steep and curvaceous at the south end.

Look for turtles sunning on driftwood as you drive over the spillway. Limestone outcrops and cliffs can be seen from the road on the south end of the drive. You may be able to spot herons fishing the shallow inlets and lake arms if you pass by early in the morning.

**FISHING AND HUNTING**—Channel cat, crappie, and striped bass are the most predominant species. Lucky anglers may also catch redear sunfish, walleye, or saugeye. Fish attractors are mapped on the state park brochure. Boat ramps, courtesy docks, and a marina help to ensure a successful fishing trip. Hunting is not permitted.

**CAMPING AND FACILITIES**—Camping is a popular activity at Crawford State Park, most likely because so many of its campsites offer lake views. The limited number of sites on the south end offer privacy with a view. Improved campsites with utilities can be reserved, but not primitive sites. The South Shelter Group Use Area has a fire pit and a stunning view. Modern restrooms and bathhouses are also available. On the west shore a modern cabin for six can be reserved. A full-service marina offers food, fuel, and convenience items as well as a restaurant, where breakfast is hearty and inexpensive. Fishing piers, horseshoe pits, children's playgrounds, sand volleyball, picnic areas with grills, and a swimming beach all add up to family fun. Other facilities include an amphitheater used for summer programs.

**TRAFFIC**—Below average, heaviest in June and July.

**LOCATION AND DIRECTIONS**—In Crawford County. Take U.S. Highway 69 south past U.S. Highway 54 and exit onto State Highway 39/7. Follow Highway 7 as it turns south. Turn left at U.S. Highway 277 (West 710th Avenue) to find the park entrance.

**ENTRY**—State park entrance fees apply. The office/visitor center is open April through October. Water is available only from April 1 to November 1.

**ON THE WEB**—A trail map and more information is provided at www.kdwp.state.ks.us, search "Crawford."

**CONTACT**—KDWP office in Farlington, (620) 362-3671; 1 Lake Road, Farlington, KS 66734.

# Frontier Military Scenic Byway

FROM FORT LEAVENWORTH NEAR KANSAS CITY, running the length of the eastern border to the Oklahoma state line, a military trail was mapped to quickly move soldiers and supplies between military bases and forts. Today, many national and state historical sites are strung together like pearls along this scenic route. Beginning on State Highway 5 out of Leavenworth to I-435 around the Kansas City metro area, then along U.S. Highway 69 to the state line, this pleasant stretch of road covers roughly 168 miles. Designated a state byway by the Kansas Legislature on June 15, 1990, the Frontier Military Scenic Byway boasts hiking trails, wildlife viewing, and plenty of interesting sites, often with a historical significance. The byway showcases rural America, including farmland and pasture dotted with cattle, watering holes, and streams. Picturesque barns, ranches, and country homesteads smatter the land. Sandstone and limestone outcrops decorate the roadside. Picture-perfect views of rural America are framed like artwork in your rearview mirror. Major sites of interest are listed below from north to south.

**LEAVENWORTH:** The first city of Kansas is tucked away within the Missouri River valley. Leavenworth Landing Park offers displays that focus on transportation of the time period. Steam locomotives, Conestoga wagons, and steamships all contributed to the town's longevity. A short walking trail provides a scenic view of the Missouri River. An interactive wayside walking and auto tour also begins here, during which 13 sites of significance are illustrated by narrative prompted with the touch of a button. Eight more sites can be experienced from your car. For a map of the tour, go to www.lvks.org and search for "Historic Wayside Tour."

On the north side of town, Fort Leavenworth is still an active military post. Tours are allowed, but vehicles are subject to search and every visitor must show photo identification. The fort was established in 1827 to protect the western frontier, keep peace among Indian tribes, and provide escort along the newly built Santa Fe Trail.

**HIGHWAY 5 AND WYANDOTTE COUNTY LAKE:** From Fort Leavenworth, follow Highway 5 (also called the Kansas Scenic Byway) south for 10.5 miles to I-435. As your map indicates, the road becomes very curvaceous with rolling hills, representing one of the most scenic portions of the

Glaciated Region. You'll be hard-pressed to drive over 40 mph. The lovely Wyandotte County Lake lies at the southeast end of Highway 5. If you have scheduled enough time for a visit here, your options include hiking, a 7-mile scenic drive, boating, or fishing.

To continue, take I-435 south. After a little more than 20 miles on the Interstate, take Exit 81 onto U.S. Highway 69.

**LA CYGNE LAKE AND LINN COUNTY PARK:** It's a bit of a shock to see a factory sitting right on the edge of a scenic lake. True, a power plant doesn't project the image of a natural area, but it is this plant that warms the water and makes fishing and wildlife viewing first-rate, particularly in winter. Other amenities—such as RV, primitive, and cabin camping, a full-service marina, a swimming pool, and picnic shelters—round out this attraction along the scenic byway. For those who want to spend a little more time here, La Cygne offers 20 miles of equestrian trails. Then, it's only about a 10-minute drive to the Marais des Cygnes National Wildlife Refuge for some fantastic bird-watching. Entrance and use fees apply. For more info about La Cygne, call (913) 757-6633 or visit www. linncountyks.com.

**MARAIS DES CYGNES NATIONAL WILDLIFE REFUGE AND WILDLIFE AREA:** Technically, these are two separate parks. The wildlife area is operated by the KDWP for waterfowl management and hunting; the wildlife refuge is maintained by the U.S Fish and Wildlife Service to protect and restore bottomland hardwood forests. Both agencies work to protect the area and manipulate water levels to maintain the desired habitat. Prairie and croplands are maintained and preserved to provide food for migrating waterfowl and upland wildlife. Areas are often closed to provide refuge and minimize human disturbance. About 5,000 of the 7,500 acres of the refuge are available for recreational activities like hunting, fishing, and birding. The wildlife sanctuary comprises the remaining 2,500 acres of the refuge and is not available for public use. The area is named after the Marais des Cygnes River, which runs through the middle of the refuge and is the dominant natural feature of the region. Download a park map from the KDWP Web site.

The town of Trading Post indicates that you have arrived at Unit A. Park at the pullout and walk the gravel service and levee roads alongside the river—and don't forget your binoculars. Ducks and geese float along the Marais des Cygnes River, tiny shorebirds scour the banks, and egrets and herons rest on grasslands and marsh. In spring, warblers sing from the woods that line the gravel road. Follow the signs to Boicourt to reach Unit

G, a larger pond that can be circled on foot. Fishing and hunting (but no trapping) are allowed here with proper license and access permits. Primitive camping is permitted in designated sites. There are no amenities or facilities except parking lots. The park office, located on the west side of Highway 69 just north of Trading Post, offers further information. Call KDWP at (913) 352-8941 to determine what units or viewing hot spots are open to the public. (Note: Construction on Highway 69 has disturbed some units and significant flooding occurred in 2007.)

**MINE CREEK BATTLEFIELD STATE HISTORIC SITE:** The visitor center marks the location of the only Civil War battle fought in Kansas. A wall of glass allows visitors to look out onto the prairie and battlefield where the cavalry engaged along Mine Creek. The dramatic story is told in the form of written accounts and testimonials, as well as displays of uniforms, weapons, and photos from the Civil War era. A booklet for a 1-mile interpretive loop can be purchased or borrowed from the center attendant. Numbered stations along the trail indicate where skirmish lines formed and how the battle unfolded. The brochure relays terrifying accounts of residents watching the battle from their yards and of cabins converted into hospitals. From the trail, visitors can see the one and only Kansas monument established for fallen Confederates who perished in the Battle of Mine Creek. Hikers walk a mowed grass trail (which can get pretty soggy after periods of rain) and cross a wooden footbridge to views of Mine Creek. Opportunities abound for bird and wildlife watching from the riparian woods and open prairie. The site is located 2 miles south of Pleasanton and a half mile west on State Highway 52. Phone (913) 352-8890. The site is open March-November, 9:00 A.M.-5:00 P.M., Wednesday–Saturday, and 1:00 P.M.-5:00 P.M., Sunday (December-February, Friday–Sunday only).

**FORT SCOTT NATIONAL HISTORIC SITE:** The story of Fort Scott is one of America coming of age. The fort walls have seen generations of American history unfold, from early Native American diplomacy through westward expansion and the Civil War to peacekeeping missions during the railroad era. National Park Service Rangers at Fort Scott (and even the citizens of the town) have captivating stories to tell of military life and the frontier army. The fort is on the northern edge of town. Reserve a ranger-guided tour to learn more; stay for reenactments and special events. See www.nps.gov/fosc or call (620) 223-0310. Stay the night and prompt the friendly owners to share their knowledge of the historic Courtland Hotel

Fort Scott National Historic Site on the Frontier Military Scenic Byway.

(courtlandhotel.com). On the west side of town, Gunn Park offers two stocked ponds and the Marmaton River within its boundaries and rents out canoes and paddleboats. Gunn Park is just one of six area parks around Fort Scott. Find out more at www.fortscott.com.

**CRAWFORD STATE PARK:** As described in a previous chapter, Crawford State Park is a small, but charming lake community and public park easy to navigate. You can drive or bike the 5-mile paved loop around the scenic lake. A rugged, 7-miles of trail is maintained for hikers and mountain bikers. Just big enough for boating and water sports in the main channel, the lake also features long, narrow fingers that allow wildlife watchers to paddle the shoreline on calm days. Facilities for day use, as well as primitive and improved camping are convenient to the Military Scenic Byway. (See previous chapter for directions, details, and contact information.)

**MINED LAND WILDLIFE AREA:** It may be difficult to imagine mine-stripped land as a natural area, but the water-filled pits are actually quite scenic now. Land from a vacated coal mine was donated to KDWP by the Pittsburg and Midway Mining Company. Today hundreds of lakes—some quite deep and large—sparkle against a backdrop of wooded lowlands that reflect in Deer Creek. Game trails and old gravel roads offer opportunities for exploration on foot at most units. Unit 21 is recommended for its 2-mile paddle on the Deer Trace Canoe Trail, as well as a fishing trail that runs parallel to a narrow finger of land between two lakes. Unit 6 is also a good choice, as the wildlife area office is located here, along with short hiking trails and plenty of parking. A cabin was recently added for overnight guests. The wildlife area office and Unit 6 are easily reached from Pittsburg. Take East 560th Avenue west to the wildlife area office at 507 East 560th Avenue to obtain maps, or call (620) 231-3173 to request a map of the units in advance.

**ON THE WEB**—Frontier Military Scenic Byway maps and more can be found at www.ksbyways.org.

**CONTACT**—For maps and information, call the Kansas Scenic Byways Program Manager at (800) 684-6966. (The program is a joint initiative between the Kansas Department of Transportation and the Federal Highway Administration.) Visitors can also pick up packets at KDWP regional offices.

# Santa Fe National Historic Trail

ALTHOUGH THE RENOWNED SANTA FE TRAIL lives forever in history, did you know it was only used for a mere 60 years before railroads replaced the wagon route? Despite the trail's short lifespan, it bears much historical significance. For example, the Plains Indians were often displaced along the Trail, causing much contention; and soldiers used the trail to fight during the Mexican–American and Civil Wars. To this day, there is great interest in this short-lived phenomenon. Perhaps talk of the trail ignites our passion for exploration because it was a true test of endurance. Travelers suffered mud, gnats, mosquitoes, dust, heat, storms and blizzards, disease, ambush, wildfires, flooding, and bison stampedes. Perhaps it is the image of great adventurers that commands our attention:

gold diggers, emigrants, mountain men, hunters, guides and translators, and ambitious trailblazers.

Today, the National Park Service and the Santa Fe Trail Association coordinate efforts along with state and local agencies to help preserve buildings, historic sites, landmarks, and original wagon-wheel ruts. The trail originates in Franklin, Missouri, and runs 900 miles across the Great Plains to Santa Fe, New Mexico. Within Kansas, U.S. Highway 56 closely follows the original route of the Santa Fe, with numerous historical points of interest along the way. From east to west, these are some of the natural areas along U.S. 56.

**GARDNER/EDGERTON:** The Lanesfield School and Historical Prairie once served as a mail stop on the Santa Fe Trail. The restored schoolhouse is now the only surviving remnant of Lanesfield. A 1.5-mile loop circles through a 78-acre restored prairie and around one of the largest hackberry trees in Kansas as it crosses Bull Creek. An interpretive brochure is available for the hike and a school-themed history museum is open Tuesday–Sunday, 1:00 P.M.-5:00 P.M. From Highway 56 in Gardner, travel 3 miles west on 175th Street to Dillie Road and then 1.5 miles south. Phone (913) 893-6645 or see www.jocomuseum.org.

**COUNCIL GROVE:** The small town of Council Grove still makes a great stop on your westward journey with historic structures that house restaurants and hotels. Take a self-guided walking tour in town or visit the original Kaw Mission, now a state historic site. At nearby Council Grove Reservoir, you can swim, boat, fish, picnic, or camp out. Walk in the footsteps of the Kanza Tribe at Allegawaho Memorial Heritage Park. (See Council Grove or Flint Hills Scenic Byway for details.)

**MARION:** Marion Reservoir is on the road less traveled, but that road leads to camping, hunting, fishing, and picnicking. The Willow Walk Trail includes two adjoining loops of gravel-surface nature trail at Cottonwood Point Campground. The level trail of either a half or 1 mile allows birdwatching along the shoreline in a small cove with mudflats. The trail then curves away from the lake into fields of prairie grass and wildflowers. An interpretive brochure is available at the trailhead. In town, Central Park features a natural spring that passing pioneers frequented. A walking path meanders through the woods next to Luta Creek.

**CANTON:** Maxwell Wildlife Refuge now sits near the former Santa Fe Trail with a herd of 200 bison and 50 elk. Hike along Gypsum Creek or arrange for a tram tour through the herd on Saturday mornings. (See Maxwell Wildlife Refuge section for more information.)

**PAWNEE ROCK STATE HISTORIC SITE:** At Pawnee Rock, go north on Centre Street a half mile to locate interpretive signs for a natural Dakota sandstone lookout that pioneers used to spot wagon trains from miles away. Jaw-dropping, 360-degree views of the prairie lie far below. See www.kshs.org/places/pawneerock/.

Just west of Pawnee Rock, Fort Larned was established to protect wagon trains on the Santa Fe Trail. **FORT LARNED NATIONAL HISTORIC SITE** provides a glimpse of life in the 1850s through tours, video, displays, and a visitor center open daily, 8:30 A.M. to 5:00 P.M. See www.nps.gov/fols. Two miles west of Larned on State Highway 156, **SANTA FE TRAIL CENTER** interprets the famous trail with exhibits about Native Americans, fur traders, the impact of the railroad, and more. The center is open daily, 9:00 A.M. to 5:00 P.M., except Mondays and holidays. See www.awav. net/trailctr.

**CIMARRON NATIONAL GRASSLAND:** The largest tract of public land in Kansas protects the longest publicly owned stretch of the Santa Fe Trail. At an elevation of 3,540 feet, Point of Rocks is a landmark offering views into Colorado and Oklahoma. Nearly 30 miles of trail and an auto tour make this stop a must. Visit www.fs.fed.us/r2/psicc/cim.

**ON THE WEB**—For information about the Santa Fe Trail, visit www.nps.gov/safe, www.santafetrail.org, or www.awav.net/trailctr.

**CONTACT**—National Park Service, National Trails System office in Santa Fe, NM, (505) 988-6888. For activities and membership information, contact the Santa Fe Trail Association and Trail Center in Larned, (620) 285-2054.

# Kansas State Symbols and Statistics

STATE FLOWER: sunflower

STATE TREE: cottonwood

STATE SONG: "Home on the Range"

STATE BIRD: western meadowlark

STATE ANIMAL: bison

HIGH POINT: Mount Sunflower at 4,039 feet

LOW POINT: Verdigris River at 680 feet

NUMBER OF STATE PARKS: 25 (including 3 day-use areas)

NATIONAL WILDLIFE REFUGES: 4

NATIONAL RECREATION TRAILS: 12

SCENIC BYWAYS: 9

NATURE CENTERS: 6

NATIONAL PRESERVES: 1

NATIONAL GRASSLANDS: 1

NATIONAL NATURAL LANDMARKS: 5

# Bibliography

## BROCHURES

*Arikaree Breaks Cheyenne County Kansas: A Self-Guided Driving Tour of the Arikaree Breaks.*

*Birds of the Cheyenne Bottoms Wildlife Area,* provided by KDWP.

*Cheyenne Bottoms Driving Tour,* funded by Kansas Audubon.

*Cheyenne Bottoms Wildlife Area,* general information brochure provided by KDWP.

*Kansas Fishing Forecast 2007:* Kansas Department of Wildlife and Parks.

*Santa Fe Trail Official Map and Guide,* National Park Service, U.S. Department of the Interior.

## WEB SITES

Kansas Scenic Byways, www.ksbyways.org

Kansas Geological Survey, www.kgs.ku.edu

Kansas Trails Council, www.kansastrailscouncil.org

Natural Kansas, www.naturalkansas.org

St. Francis Area Chamber of Commerce, www.stfranciskansas.com

## BOOKS

Eddy, William B., and Richard O. Ballentine. *Hiking Kansas City.* Pebble Publishing, Inc., fourth edition, 2001.

Gress, Bob, and George Potts. *Watching Kansas Wildlife: A Guide to 101 Sites.* Funded by the Kansas Department of Parks and Wildlife. University Press of Kansas, 1993.

Hauber, Catherine M., and John W. Young. *Hiking Guide to Kansas.* University Press of Kansas, 1999.

Penner, Marci. *The Kansas Guidebook for Explorers.* Kansas Sampler Foundation, 2005.

DeLorme. *The Kansas Atlas and Gazetteer.* Rand McNally & Company, third edition, 2006.

# Index